William and Maxine
Hedback
Memorial Fund

Other books by the authors

Sweet Seduction: Chocolate Truffles (Adrienne Welch)
Pretty Cakes (both authors)
Glorious Chocolate: The Ultimate Chocolate Cookbook (both authors)

UNBELIEVABLE MICROWAVE DESSERTS

Adrienne Welch

and

Mary Goodbody

SIMON & SCHUSTER

New York   York   London   Toronto   Sydney   Tokyo   Singapore

SIMON & SCHUSTER
Simon & Schuster Building
Rockefeller Center
1230 Avenue of the Americas
New York, New York 10020

DESIGNED BY CAROLINE CUNNINGHAM

ILLUSTRATIONS BY LAURIE DAVIS

Manufactured in the United States of America

1 2 3 4 5 6 7 8 9 10

Library of Congress Cataloging-in-Publication Data

Welch, Adrienne, 1955–
Unbelievable microwave desserts / Adrienne Welch and Mary Goodbody.
p.   cm.
Includes index.
1. Microwave cookery.   2. Desserts.   3. Baking.   I. Goodbody,
Mary.   II. Title.
TX832.W45 1992
641.5'882—dc20   91-37407
CIP
ISBN: 0-671-69326-3

Acknowledgments

Most books are a collaboration, and this one was no exception. Primarily, it was a collaboration between the two of us, and we each greatly appreciate the support, expertise, and good fellowship of the other.

But there is more. No doubt about it, the book would not have been written without the help of our friends, families, and colleagues, who, believing in us, lent a hand or an ear or, when appropriate, told us to get off the telephone and get back to work!

We acknowledge the following people in particular: Mary Dauman, for editorial assistance, recipe-testing help, and unflagging cheerfulness regardless of the disarray of the manuscript in progress; Isabelle Vita, Cathy Garvey, Leticia Alexander, and Elizabeth Wheeler for invaluable help testing recipes; both our families (too numerous to identify by name, and besides, they know who they are), Jean Housepian, Robert Jaffey, Marie Chen, Lawrence Bass, Barbara Albright, and Michael Schneider for support and lots of encouragement; Susan Lescher for wise counsel; Mark Bittman for a sharp editorial eye; John Carafoli and Brian Hagawara for food styling and photography; and our editors at Simon & Schuster, Carole Lalli, Kerri Conan, and Toula Polygalaktos, for seeing the project through with good advice, good humor, and great enthusiasm.

In addition, we thank the members of the Radiology Department of Columbia-Presbyterian Hospital in New York for their willingness to taste our creations—particularly those containing chocolate—and the staff of Jacoby Medical Center in the Bronx and the members of the informally organized but gastronomically dedicated Wine Tasting Supper Club for being good sports in their roles as guinea pigs. We also thank the Nestlé Food Corporation for donating chocolate for recipe development and Nordic Ware for donating microwave-safe cookware.

The book is dedicated to the desserts we have always treasured—desserts that inspired us to reform them for success in the microwave. It is also dedicated to our readers, who are willing to attempt cooking and baking in the microwave even if before now they have only heated a mug of coffee in it. And finally, it is dedicated, with love, to David and Laura.

Contents

Introduction

We'll never forget how hot it was that day. Adrienne and I were sitting hunched over the computer, brainstorming possible recipe titles for a book on microwave baking and desserts. We had arranged to meet at my family's house in the country where I was staying for several weeks on one of those "working vacations" freelance writers like to take. There was no air conditioning, and we greedily welcomed soft whispers of relief as the revolving fan worked its way around the tiny room. We would have preferred to be outside or on the screened porch with tall glasses of iced tea. But no. We were determined to complete the job before us, which was becoming more and more exciting as the day wore on.

The idea had arisen following Adrienne's success with the Walnut Brownie Cake (see page 104) she developed for *Chocolatier* magazine, where she is food editor. Until then she had viewed the microwave as a handy appliance, great for softening butter and cream cheese and the very best place to melt chocolate. She almost always cooked vegetables and rice in the microwave (still does), and with every new experiment was convinced she could translate her baking and dessert-making skills to it. I was involved with microwave cooking, too, having edited a couple of short books on the subject. And as the mother of a young child, I used the microwave with some regularity—it's great for reheating spaghetti!

Adrienne loves a challenge in the kitchen, and after her success with the Walnut Brownie Cake, she was more than ready to try lots of other desserts and baked goods. The recipes on the following pages represent a challenge met with fantastic success, although not without its share of frustrations and out-and-out failures along the way.

We learned an incredible amount about the microwave as we went along, while researching the *idea* for the book and then during recipe development and testing. We pass along our findings so that, with book in hand, you can create desserts and baked goods in the microwave that are every bit as good (or better) than those prepared more conventionally. We have all heard the numerous myths about what the microwave can and cannot do, and we debunk many of them here. We found the appliance to be a welcome friend in the kitchen that, once understood, rarely let us down.

The recipe notes guide you as you make each recipe. The chapter introductions, with their long lists of general microwave tips, provide an overview of particular types of recipes: cakes, puddings, pies, and so forth. As we worked on the book we found these tips wildly helpful and were constantly adding to them with every new discovery. Chapter 1 contains useful information about how the microwave works, how different ingredients react to it, the sort of equipment needed, and general microwave cooking procedures.

There is a lot more to learn, and as microwave manufacturers continue to improve, upgrade, and otherwise change the appliances, we will continue to experiment and expand our knowledge. Writing this book confirmed what we suspected when we began: Microwave cooking is as variable and challenging as conventional cooking and equally, if not more, exciting.

We hope you enjoy exploring your microwave oven's potential as you create the many soul-satisfying, tantalizing baked goods and other desserts on the following pages. Your kitchen will fill with tempting aromas, your family will eagerly await dessert, and your recipe repertoire will increase with fabulous cakes, muffins, puddings, mousses, sauces, ice creams, and pies.

CHAPTER ONE

General Microwaving Information, Helpful Hints, and Tips

The Microwave Ovens We Used

We used two 700-watt microwave ovens and one 600-watt microwave oven for our recipe development and testing: Sharp Carousel II Microwave Convection, General Electric Dual Wave II, and Panasonic "The Genius" model NN5809. The first two are top-of-the-line 700-watt ovens; the Panasonic is a top-of-the-line 600-watt, or midsize, oven. The Sharp and Panasonic ovens were equipped with turntables. The GE was not, but its dual-wave construction is designed to cook foods evenly; however, as the manufacturer suggested, we rotated dishes cooked in it.

These represent the ovens most likely to be found in home kitchens. Brand names vary, of course, as do wattages, cavity sizes, and special features, but we have covered most contingencies to make our recipes accessible to the majority of microwave users. As a double check and "security blanket," we asked a number of colleagues and friends to test a few recipes in their homes. The results were excellent.

When a recipe was developed in a 700-watt oven, we tested it in the 600-watt oven; if it was developed without the benefit of a turntable, we made an effort to test it in an oven with a turntable. We cooked most of the recipes in all three ovens. This accounts for the relatively wide time ranges in the recipes. It also explains why we are so insistent that you check the food with our visual doneness tests rather than rely only on time.

All microwave ovens perform differently, depending on the type of oven and the type of food being cooked. Some of the variables are the brand and model of microwave, its wattage, its efficiency in distributing microwaves, and whether it is affected by power surges. The temperature of the kitchen and the size of the microwave cavity make a difference, too, as does the temperature of the food, its size and shape, how tightly it is covered, how it is arranged, and how often it is taken from the microwave to be stirred, rotated, and so on.

Even the time of day makes a difference. When we cooked during a peak energy-use time, such as midday, the ovens were less effective than when we cooked late in the evening or early in the day when the rest of the world was not demanding lots of electricity. The demand caused power surges and slight cutbacks (neither of which you would notice in appliances such as lamps and televisions), affecting cooking times. This problem was most pronounced during the summer when air conditioners were chugging away all over town and was more evident for Adrienne, who lives in an apartment building in Manhattan, than for Mary, who lives in a single-family suburban house.

Many of these variables, however, apply equally to conventional ovens, which also perform differently according to brand, size, and type. Just as every cook must get to know his or her stove, every cook must get to know his or her microwave oven.

How the Microwave Oven Works

Regardless of the method, food cooks by being heated. Conventional cooking methods produce heat that is transferred to the food; microwave cooking causes the food itself to heat up and thus cook. This is accomplished when tiny, invisible electromagnetic waves of energy—microwaves—are sent into the oven cavity. Water, fat, and sugar molecules absorb the microwaves, and this causes them to spin rapidly. The molecular movement causes friction, which in turn produces heat.

Although some people worry that microwaves can be dangerous, they are as safe as television or radio waves. Microwaves are *nonionizing radiant energy,* similar to radio waves and visible light. On the other hand, *ionizing radiant energy,* which includes ultraviolet, gamma, cosmic, and X rays, does not produce heat. Radiant energy travels in a wavelike motion at the speed of light and stops instantly when the source of production stops. With microwaves, production stops when the timer switches the oven off or when the door is opened. No microwaves linger in the food, and none pop out when you open the door.

Microwaves can be reflected, transmitted, or absorbed. Metal reflects microwaves and therefore does not get hot. This is why microwave ovens are lined with metal and also why metal containers cannot be used in the microwaves: The energy waves would never reach the food. With most metal the deflection of the microwaves causes arcing, which produces sparks that can damage the oven and perhaps start a fire.

Microwaves pass through glass, china, ceramics, paper, and plastic. These materials do not heat up when the microwaves pass through them and are therefore used to hold and cover food. In most cases the hot food transfers heat to these materials so you should take care to use pot holders and other commonsense precautions when removing them from the oven.

When the water, fat, and sugar molecules present in all foods attract and absorb microwaves, these microwaves penetrate usually to a depth of one to one and a half inches. Once the outer layers of the food are heated, heat is transferred deeper into the food by thermal conduction, just as in conventional cooking. This is why thin piecesof food cook more quickly than thicker ones and why pieces of uniform size and shape cook most efficiently in the microwave oven. (This also means that food does not cook from the inside out, as some people believe!)

The cavity of the microwave oven stays relatively cool during cooking; it becomes warm when heated by the food itself. The cool oven temperature keeps the surface of the food cooler than its interior. This explains the need for "standing time." Not only does food continue to cook inside, but the interior of some foods—a jelly doughnut, for example—may be too hot to eat, despite its seemingly cool exterior.

Energy Efficiency

Microwaves are more energy efficient than conventional stoves and ovens. Because they operate with 115 or 120 volts of power, they use less energy than electric ranges, which need 240 volts. Also, they cook many foods in a quarter to a third of the time a conventional oven does and do not require preheating, which can take from 5 to 20 minutes.

When food is taken in and out of the microwave oven for stirring, turning, or checking, no heat is lost. When a conventional oven door is opened, heat escapes and must be regained, which increases both energy use and cooking time.

Microwaves do not heat up the kitchen as they operate, while conventional ovens and stoves can cause the room temperature to rise by as much as 10 or 15 degrees. Not only is this more pleasant for the cook—particularly in the summer— but it does not strain an air-conditioning system as a conventional oven might.

Cleanup

We found that industry claims about easy cleanup are mostly true. Food cooked in the microwave oven does not "bake" on dishes or pans, making them far easier to wash. By the same token, food does not bake onto the walls of the oven, making it easy to clean with mild cleanser or plain soap and water. And because you cannot cook large amounts of food in the microwave oven, you never have to deal with giant pots or roasting pans, either.

With the microwave oven, mixing and cooking are often done in the same container, which saves cleaning up, too. For instance, puddings and sauces may be mixed in a large microwave-safe Pyrex measuring cup and then cooked in the same cup. Poaching syrup can be reduced in the same casserole in which the fruit is to be poached.

Although microwave oven manufacturers tout the benefits of using disposable containers, we emphatically do not. They may be efficient and easy for the cook, but because they add to our enormous garbage disposal problem, we cannot condone them.

Which Foods Cook Best

This may appear to be a useless subject to cover here since all our recipes work beautifully. We are not gong to tell you to cook something that will not work well in the microwave oven, but we found some foods cooked better than others, and understanding the differences will aid you as you try the recipes.

Since water, fat, and sugar molecules attract and absorb microwaves, it stands to reason that foods containing a large proportion of these molecules would work best. This is true to an extent.

Fruit, with its high concentration of water, does very well in the microwave oven, cooking quickly and evenly with little loss of color, texture, and nutrients. Poached and baked whole fruits are wonderful, as are fruit-based sauces. Adding fruit and berries to cake and muffin batters helps them cook evenly and provides needed moisture. Vegetables such as pumpkin and squash accomplish the same thing.

Stirred custards work beautifully in the microwave oven, but when we first tried to make baked custards, we ran into some tricky problems. Because of their particular chemistry of eggs, fat, and sugar, it was hard to keep them from boiling before cooking. We explain in Chapter 2 how we solved this problem and came up with terrific custard recipes. Fat content is also tricky: In cakes and muffins too little or too much results in a tough or dry, crumbly texture. Precision, therefore, is important.

A little sugar helps the food cook well; a lot can cause problems. For instance, the Cinnamon Swirl Coffee Cake (page 236), which has a filling made from brown sugar and nuts (both high in fat), must be watched carefully. The sugar heats up rapidly and can overcook the crumb of the cake in, literally, seconds.

How food is arranged in the microwave oven also makes a big difference in how it cooks. Most experts seem to agree that the "doughnut" shape is best. Therefore, we usually use round containers and when possible arrange the food in a circle (individual custard cups, for example). We use a six-cup Bundt pan for many of our cakes to promote even cooking.

Finally, some preparations simply do not work in the microwave oven or do so poorly that we cannot recommend them. Cakes that depend on the incorporation of air for leavening, such as angel food cakes and genoises, do not do well. Cookies are not worth the trouble because you can cook only a few at a time, and even then their texture is not good. Items made from *pâte à choux,* such as cream puffs and eclairs, do not dry out in the relatively moist environment of the microwave. The same is true of crisp meringues and dacquoise. Popovers and yeast breads with thick crusts (which we particularly like) do not cook well in the microwave oven, and we do not recommend deep-frying doughnuts or anything else because the oil can get dangerously hot.

Equipment

Not all glass, plastic, ceramic, and paper are created equal when it comes to microwaving. We repeat the words "microwave-safe" in every recipe. At the end of this section we list recommended equipment. This list may look long and cause you to throw up your hands in dismay and say, "There is no way I am going to spend a lot of money and time searching for special pans, and bowls, and plates."

Please don't despair. You probably already have many of the items we list: Pyrex measuring cups, glass pie plates, a square cake (brownie) dish, mixing bowls, casseroles, and custard cups. You may not have the cake dishes or molds we suggest, but they are easily found at most discount stores selling cookware, such as K-Mart, TruValue, and Caldors. (We also list mail-order sources at the end of the book and provide instructions, when possible, for alternative equipment.) Unlike for conventional cooking—which requires heavy saucepans, double boilers, long-handled skillets, and sheet pans—most equipment suitable for microwave cooking is inexpensive.

Manufacturers' labels reading "microwave-safe" or "microwavable" are usually reliable. Products under the brand names Corning, Pyrex, and Vision are good for microwave cooking. Nordic, Anchor Hocking, and Wilton all produce microwave cake pans in various shapes and sizes, and glass ceramic casseroles and containers are excellent for the microwave oven. Thin plastic containers, such as those that hold food from the delicatessen do not stand up well to microwaving, although they often suffice for briefer heating. Check everything for cracks—they could break in the microwave oven—and for metal trim or designs, which will cause arcing.

You might occasionally wonder if a product you already own is acceptable for microwaving. You can perform a few simple tests to determine this. All follow the same principle. We like the one suggested in *Microwave Cooking Handbook* by the International Microwave Power Institute of Clifton, Virginia:

> *Place a [microwave-safe] glass measure [measuring cup] with ½ cup water in the microwave oven. Set the dish to be tested near the measure but not touching. Microwave on HIGH (100 percent) power for one minute. If the dish is cool or*

slightly warm to the touch, the dish is acceptable for microwave cooking. The water should be quite warm or hot. If the dish is hot, do not use it in a microwave oven. (page 10)

Size and shape of the dish: The size and shape of the dish or measure used make a difference in the outcome of the recipe. Round pans and casseroles promote even cooking. Food in corners will cook faster than the food in the rest of the dish, which is why we often shield corners with strips of foil to inhibit cooking. The foil is turned shiny side up to reflect the microwaves most effectively. Ring pans permit the microwaves to enter the food from the center of the pan, too. Microwaves can more easily reach the bottom of dishes elevated on inverted pie plates.

Cakes, muffins, and cupcakes rise higher in microwave ovens than in conventional ovens because no protective crust forms to "weight" them down. Therefore, batter in a pan that is too small or is overfilled may overflow. As a general rule, fill cake dishes half full of batter; fill cupcake and muffin pans half to three-quarters full.

If individual pieces of food, such as whole fruits, are arranged too snugly, the microwaves will not be able to reach them easily on all sides, and cooking will be uneven. There should be a little space between each piece.

In some instances if a deep dish is used when a shallow one is called for, it will take more time for the food in the center of the dish to heat by thermal conduction. The surface of the food, penetrated by microwaves, may overcook before this happens. As a general rule try to use the dish specified in each recipe.

Thermometers: We call for a microwave-safe candy thermometer in a number of the recipes. This is important because conventional candy thermometers are not safe to use in the microwave oven and will not read the temperature quickly enough for accuracy when used outside the microwave oven. If you own an instant-read candy thermometer, you can use it but not inside the oven cavity. You can order a microwave-safe candy thermometer from Maid of Scandinavia (see the equipment list on page 21 for mail-order sources) or buy one where microwave-safe cookware is sold. (Adrienne saw one in a local supermarket.)

Chapter 9, Candies and Chocolates, calls for a chocolate thermometer. Candy thermometers do not have a broad enough range to be used for chocolate. For accurate, easy-to-read chocolate thermometers, we suggest one of two brands: Digital Dial Thermometer and Bi-Therm Dial Instant Read thermometer (see the equipment list on pages 20–21 for mail-order source).

Plastic wrap, waxed paper, and paper towels: Because a lot of moisture escapes during microwave cooking, we frequently ask that you cover food with plastic wrap, waxed paper, or paper towels. Plastic wrap forms the tightest seal and for some recipes is absolutely necessary. Where it is not, we use waxed paper. This means that some of our recipes may take a minute or so longer than if we used plastic, but we hate using nonbiodegradable materials when there is no good reason. If used correctly and as specified in our recipes, there is no danger of the paraffin on the waxed paper melting in the microwave. We also occasionally call for baking parchment, which is sturdier than waxed paper.

Not all plastic wrap is ideal for use in the microwave. Saran Wrap, which is composed primarily of polyvinylidene chloride (PVDC), is a little less permeable than Reynolds Plastic Wrap, which is made of polyvinyl chloride film (PVC). The PVDC makeup provides an impenetrable shield, while a small amount of air can pass through PVC wrap. Glad plastic wrap and Handi-Wrap, composed of simple polyethylene film, are the least sturdy of all and are advisable only for covering food for reheating. We recommend Saran Wrap or Reynolds Wrap, and we advise you to turn back a bit of the plastic to vent the dish in order to avoid scalding.

We frequently use microwave-safe paper towels to form a loose shield over cake batters. The towel holds in just enough moisture to promote even cooking and prevents the cake batter from drying out. At the same time it allows excess moisture to escape. Once the cake is removed from the microwave, we leave the paper towel in place to hold in the heat so that the cake batter on the bottom of the pan can finish cooking. The towel also prevents the surface from drying out during cooling, performing much the same function as the protective brown crust on a conventionally baked cake.

Paper towels are a benign material for microwaving, provided you follow a few simple guidelines. First, use only white paper towels that say "microwave-safe" on the package. The dye in "decorator" towels can leach into the food. Second, do not use paper towels made from recycled paper. Unfortunately, these may contain impurities such as newsprint and metal shavings. A metal shaving caught at the wrong angle could cause arcing. Finally be sure the paper towels you select are free of nylon or other synthetic materials because these could ignite.

Equipment List

Following is a list of suggested microwave cookware for baking and dessert making. Not everything is necessary for every recipe, of course, but we found that these items were convenient and reliable to use, clean, and store. Keep in mind that the size of the bowl, dish, or pan recommended in each recipe is crucial to the outcome.

For measuring:
Set of measuring spoons (Foley)
Set of metal dry measuring cups (Foley)
1-cup glass measuring cup (Pyrex)

GENERAL MICROWAVING INFORMATION, HELPFUL HINTS, and TIPS   19

2-CUP GLASS MEASURING CUP (PYREX)
1-QUART GLASS MEASURING CUP (PYREX)
2-QUART GLASS MEASURING CUP (PYREX)

Cake pans, loaf pans, and cake dishes:
8¼-INCH ROUND CAKE DISH (PYREX ORIGINALS)
STRAIGHT HIGH-SIDED 2-QUART ROUND GLASS CASSEROLE (ANCHOR HOCKING)
2-QUART KNOB-COVERED ROUND GLASS CASSEROLE (PYREX ORIGINALS)
2-QUART SQUARE CAKE DISH (PYREX ORIGINALS) WITH ROUNDED CORNERS (8 BY 8 BY
     2 INCHES)
2-QUART OBLONG BAKING DISH (PYREX ORIGINALS) WITH ROUNDED CORNERS (11 BY 7
     BY 1½ INCHES)
8½ BY 4½ BY 2½ INCHES, 1½ QUART LOAF DISH (PYREX ORIGINALS)
12-CUP MICROWAVE-SAFE BUNDT PAN (NORDIC WARE)
6-CUP MICROWAVE-SAFE BUNDT PAN (NORDIC WARE)

Custard cups, ramekins, and casseroles:
6-OUNCE CUSTARD CUPS (PYREX)
6-OUNCE WHITE CERAMIC RAMEKINS
10-OUNCE PIE DISHES (PYREX)
HIGH-SIDED 2-QUART ROUND GLASS CASSEROLE (ANCHOR HOCKING)
HIGH-SIDED 1½-QUART GLASS CERAMIC CASSEROLE (CORNINGWARE FRENCH WHITE)
3-QUART GLASS CERAMIC CASSEROLE (CORNINGWARE FRENCH WHITE)

Pie plates, tart pans:
9-INCH PIE PLATE (PYREX)
10-INCH PIE PLATE (PYREX)
9-INCH CERAMIC FLUTED TART PAN

Bowls:
SET OF 3 MIXING BOWLS (PYREX ORIGINALS): 1 QUART, 1½ QUARTS, 2½ QUARTS
4-QUART MIXING BOWL (PYREX ORIGINALS)
METAL MIXING BOWLS: 1 QUART, 1½ QUARTS, 2½ QUARTS, 3 QUARTS, 4 QUARTS

Microwave thermometers:
MICROWAVE CANDY THERMOMETER (ACU-RITE, AVAILABLE BY MAIL FROM MAID OF
     SCANDINAVIA, 3244 RALEIGH AVENUE, MINNEAPOLIS, MN 55416; TELEPHONE
     800-328-6722 OR MICROWAVE AND MORE, 779 MT. READ BOULEVARD,
     ROCHESTER, NY 14606; TELEPHONE 716-254-6520)

Chocolate thermometer (Bi-Therm Dial Instant Read thermometer, Model #6075-1 made by Taylor and available by mail from Maid of Scandinavia, see address and telephone number above)

Sieve, food mill, grater:
7-inch-diameter fine-meshed sieve (used for sifting flour)
Food mill
Hand-held grater (for zesting)

Muffin and cupcake pan:
9¾-inch muffin pan (Anchor Hocking)
Paper baking cups

Tools:
4½- and 7¾-inch Offset (crooked) metal cake spatulas
8- and 10-inch flat metal cake spatulas
Rubber spatula
Wire whisk
Paring knife
Large, sharp knife for chopping
Swivel vegetable peeler
Melon-baller
Polyester pastry bags
Pastry tips
Wooden toothpicks

Electric appliances:
Food processor with metal chopping blade and shredding attachment
Hand-held electric mixer

The Recipes

We will now touch upon some of the more important points made throughout the book. At the beginning of each chapter is a list of general tips to help you achieve splendid results. You will also find a note preceding each recipe, giving specific tips and reinforcing certain procedures. We also include preparation and microwave times. Since everyone chops, measures, and sifts at different rates, the preparation time is a guide only, to give you an idea of how long and involved the recipe is. The microwave time is cooking time.

The recipes are precise and exacting, and we have taken great care to ensure that you will not make mistakes if you carefully follow our instructions. You may notice that we repeat directions from recipe to recipe, and sometimes even within individual recipes. As much as we hope you will make many of the desserts and baked goods found on the following pages, we cannot be sure of it. Therefore, each recipe has to stand on its own.

Measuring: Careful measuring is crucial to microwaving success. Because the quantities are so small and the cooking times so brief, a small error in measurement can mean failure. Use the metal measuring cup designed for dry ingredients: Lightly spoon flour, cornstarch, or confectioners' sugar into the measuring cup until the cup overflows and then sweep the top with the straight edge of a knife to level the dry ingredient.

We also always instruct you to measure *sifted* flour. Sift the flour onto a piece of waxed paper or a plate and then spoon it into the cup measure. This exercise ensures that you will not overmeasure the flour. We repeat again and again to spoon cornstarch lightly into the measuring cup and then to sweep the top with a knife. This is important. Too much cornstarch will make a pudding or pie filling too stiff.

In the recipe ingredient list we alert you to the fact that some ingredients will be used in two different measurements at different stages of cooking. We indicate this with the words "used in two measurements" or "each measurement used separately." This way you will not add all the sugar, milk, lemon zest, or whatever, to the recipe at once.

Mixing: It is important to mix all ingredients in order and to the degree we specify. For example, we will instruct you to use a wire whisk and complete twelve to fifteen strokes to ensure that *dry* ingredients are thoroughly blended. This mixes them more effectively than sifting or simply stirring them with the liquid ingredients without premixing. This is especially important when a leavener such as baking powder or soda is combined with the flour.

When we warn against overmixing or overfolding, we do so to prevent the result from being grainy (as in a mousse) or tough (as in a cake). Use a light hand.

We recommend that you use a hand-held electric mixer. Most cooks have these handy appliances, but their popularity is not our only concern. Most of our batters are such small quantities that it seems silly to use a big, powerful standing mixer for them. However, there are times that you may want to use a large machine—when making some mousses, for example. But always remember not to overmix the ingredients and to use the visual tests. For instance, the recipe may tell you to cream butter and sugar "for 1 to 2 minutes, until it is nearly white and its texture is light." Rely on the visual description, not the time range, which is merely a guide.

Microwave time and standing time: We always provide a time range for final microwave cooking. This is to take into account the many variables of microwave ovens. Again, use the visual tests for doneness rather than time alone. The microwave oven is not a magical appliance that with the push of a button removes all judgment, trial and error, and experimentation from cooking. As with conventional cooking, success depends on good recipes, good ingredients, and careful cooks. The rewards—from the heavenly aromas wafting through the kitchen to the appealing and tasty final dish—are just as great, too.

Standing times are also important; do not cavalierly dismiss them. Cooking continues as the food stands *outside* the microwave oven. This is particularly crucial with cakes because the batter on the bottom of the cake may not be thoroughly cooked when it is time to take the cake dish from the oven.

Specific ingredients: For the most part we use ingredients found in every supermarket: all-purpose, cake and whole wheat flour, sugar, butter, milk, cream, sour cream, yogurt, lemons, oranges, apples, pears, unsweetened cocoa, chocolate, and so on. For convenience we use frozen berries when they work as well as fresh. We use whole milk, and Grade A large eggs, unless otherwise specified. In some recipes we prefer a vanilla bean but also supply instructions for using vanilla extract.

We developed and tested recipes with Baker's and Nestlé's chocolate, although we often tried them with European chocolate, too, such as Lindt. We call for both alkalized and nonalkalized unsweetened cocoas. Alkalized cocoa is also known as Dutch-processed or European-style cocoa and is treated with an alkali to neutralize some of the natural acidity in the cocoa. Generally it tastes less harsh and is darker (often redder) than nonalkalized cocoa. Nonalkalized (natural) cocoa, such as regular Hershey's cocoa in the familiar brown canister, is naturally acidic and generally has a fruitier flavor than alkalized.

We found that Jack Frost or Town House fine granulated sugars are the best for microwaving (and most baking needs) because their particles are small and dissolve quickly and easily. You can use other sugar, of course, but we recommend sifting it through a fine sieve before measuring it. Do not use superfine granulated sugar.

A good number of our recipes call for liquor and liqueurs. In many of them you can safely omit the alcohol if you wish. Others really need it for overall flavor and balance. We try not to use esoteric spirits, relying for the most part on dark rum, orange-flavored liqueur such as Grand Marnier, Cointreau, and Triple Sec, and coffee-flavored liqueur such as Kahlua and Tía Maria.

It is a good idea to use the ingredients specified and not to substitute ingredients. We offer substitutions when appropriate and try to make each recipe as trouble-free as possible.

Microwave Cooking Tips

We offer here a few ways to accomplish ordinary and simple kitchen tasks in the microwave oven. Throughout the book we will refer to these methods when appropriate for a specific recipe. You will also find them handy for other culinary needs.

Softening butter: For 1 to 16 tablespoons of unsalted butter, put it in a microwave-safe glass bowl and cover with waxed paper. Microwave on HIGH (100 percent) power for 15 to 60 seconds, until the butter is slightly softened but not melted. Note: Amounts of butter 4 tablespoons or less can be softened in a 6-ounce custard cup.

Melting butter: For 1 to 8 tablespoons of unsalted butter, put it in a 1-cup microwave-safe glass measuring cup. Cover with waxed paper and microwave on MEDIUM-HIGH (70 percent) power for 45 seconds to 2½ minutes, just until melted.

Softening cream cheese: For 3 to 8 ounces of cream cheese, put on a microwave-safe plate or in a 1-quart microwave-safe glass bowl. Cover with waxed paper and microwave on HIGH (100 percent) power for 15 to 60 seconds, until the cream cheese is slightly softened.

Softening brown sugar: For 1 pound of light or dark brown sugar, put it in a 1½-quart microwave-safe glass bowl with half an apple. Cover with plastic wrap and vent by folding back a bit of the wrap. Microwave on MEDIUM-HIGH (70 percent) power for 30 seconds to 1½ minutes, until softened.

Take the amount of sugar needed for the recipe. Leave the remaining sugar in the bowl with the apple. Recover tightly with plastic wrap and let the sugar stand for 1 to 2 hours. Discard the apple and store the softened brown sugar in an airtight container. This will keep it soft.

Softening ice cream: For 1 pint of ice cream, remove the lid and foil, if any, from the container. Microwave on MEDIUM (50 percent) power for 10-second intervals, until the ice cream starts to soften

Bringing milk and buttermilk to room temperature: For ¼ to 1 cup of cold milk, put in a 1-cup microwave-safe measuring cup. Microwave on MEDIUM-LOW (30 percent) power for 20 seconds to 2 minutes, stirring every 20 seconds, until the chill is off.

Bringing sour cream and yogurt to room temperature: For ¼ to 1 cup of cold sour cream or yogurt, put it in a 1-cup microwave-safe measuring cup. Microwave on MEDIUM-LOW (30 percent) power for 10 to 60 seconds, stirring every 10 seconds, until the chill is off.

Bringing egg whites to room temperature: For 1 to 4 large egg whites, put them in a 1-cup microwave-safe glass measuring cup. Microwave, uncovered, on LOW (10 percent) power for 15 to 30 seconds per egg white, stirring every 15 seconds, until the chill is off. Room-temperature egg whites beat to a higher volume than cold ones.

Melting chocolate: For 1 to 8 ounces of semisweet, milk, or white chocolate chips, or the same amount of chopped chocolate squares or bars, put the chocolate in a 1-quart microwave-safe glass bowl. Microwave, uncovered, on MEDIUM (50 percent) power for 2 to 5 minutes, stirring after 2 minutes, until the chocolate is shiny. Stir until the chocolate is completely smooth and melted. Note: Amounts of chocolate 3 ounces or less can be melted in a 6-ounce custard cup. (Chocolate squares or bars melt best when chopped first; this is easily done with a sharp knife.)

For juicy citrus fruit: For 1 grapefruit, lemon, lime, or orange, microwave the whole fruit on HIGH (100 percent) power for 15 to 45 seconds, turning the fruit every 15 seconds. Warmed fruit yields the maximum amount of juice.

Peeling a peach: For 1 firm, ripe peach, wrap it in microwave-safe plastic wrap. Microwave on HIGH (100 percent) power for 1 to 2 minutes, turning the peach every 30 seconds, until it feels hot to the touch. Let the peach stand, still wrapped, for 1 minute. Using a small knife, peel the skin, being careful not to nick the flesh. This method will not work with soft, mealy peaches.

Toasting sliced almonds: For 2 tablespoons to 1 cup of sliced natural or blanched almonds, put them in a 9-inch microwave-safe glass pie plate and spread them in a single layer. Microwave, uncovered, on HIGH (100 percent) power for 2 minutes. Stir the almonds with a wooden spoon. Continue to microwave, uncovered, on HIGH (100 percent) power for 3 to 7 minutes, stirring every 60 seconds, until the color of the nuts turns from white to tan.

Let the almonds cool in the pie plate set on a flat heatproof surface for 10 minutes. They will continue to toast slightly after they have been removed from the microwave oven. Let them cool completely. Store in an airtight container for up to five days. Note: 2 tablespoons of almonds may be toasted in a 6-ounce custard cup.

Toasting hazelnuts: For 2 tablespoons to 1 cup of hazelnuts, put them in a 9-inch microwave-safe glass pie plate and spread them in a single layer. Microwave, uncovered, on HIGH (100 percent) power for 2 minutes. Stir the hazelnuts with a wooden spoon. Continue to microwave, uncovered, on HIGH (100 percent) power for 4 to 7 minutes, stirring every 60 seconds, just until the skins crack and the nuts are lightly browned. To test for doneness, cut several nuts in half; they should be lightly browned on the inside. Overtoasted hazelnuts char inside and taste bitter.

Wrap the hot nuts in a clean kitchen towel and cool completely. Transfer them to a large sieve and rub them back and forth against the screening with your fingers to remove the loose skins. Store in an airtight container for up to five days. Note: 2 tablespoons of hazelnuts may be toasted in a 6-ounce custard cup.

Toasting coconut: For 2 tablespoons to 1 cup of sweetened flaked coconut, spread it in a 9-inch microwave-safe glass pie plate. Microwave, uncovered, on HIGH (100 percent) power for 1 minute. Stir with a wooden spoon. Continue to microwave, uncovered, on HIGH (100 percent) power for 4 to 7 minutes, stirring every 30 seconds, until the coconut is golden. Let the coconut cool slightly or completely before using. Note: 2 tablespoons of coconut may be toasted in a 6-ounce custard cup.

Making chocolate curls or shavings: For two 1-ounce squares of semisweet, milk, or white chocolate, put one 1-ounce square of chocolate on a piece of waxed paper. Microwave on MEDIUM (50 percent) power for 15-second intervals, until the chocolate starts to soften.

Line a baking sheet with waxed paper. Grip the chunk of chocolate with a folded paper towel so that your hand does not melt it further. Using a vegetable peeler, scrape the long edge of the chocolate chunk in a downward motion, forming curls or flat shavings. As you form the curls or shavings, let them fall onto the paper-lined baking sheet. Follow the same procedure with the remaining square of chocolate.

Refrigerate the curls or shavings until you are ready to use them. Store any leftovers in an airtight container at cool room temperature or in the refrigerator for up to two weeks. This makes about 1 cup.

Note: You can use chunks of chocolate larger than the 1-ounce pieces we suggest. Larger pieces take a little longer to soften in the microwave. The width and degree of softness of the chocolate square, chunk, or bar will determine the size and shape of the curls or shavings. Chocolate that is only slightly softened will produce tight curls. Chocolate softened more will curl very little, forming flat shavings.

Warming a muffin, doughnut, or slice of coffee cake: Wrap the muffin, doughnut, or slice of cake in a microwave-safe paper towel. Microwave on MEDIUM (50 percent) power for 10-second intervals, until warm. The paper towel keeps the muffin, doughnut, or cake moist. If warming a jelly doughnut, let it cool a little before biting into it.

CHAPTER TWO

Puddings and Custards

Vanilla Bean Pudding

Butterscotch Velvet Pudding

Chocolate Pudding

Diner-Style Rice Pudding

Lemon Lover's Pudding

Caribbean Banana Rum Pudding

Danish Rum Pudding with Melba Sauce

Lemon Pudding Cake

Brownie Pudding Cake

Cinnamon Raisin Bread Pudding with Hot Cider
    Sauce

Cappuccino Trifle

Crème Brulée

Mocha Pots de Crème

Pumpkin Caramel Custard

Upside-Down Lemon Caramel Custard

Since both puddings and custards do very well in the microwave oven, we had to restrain ourselves from developing one after another and get on with the business of the more challenging cakes and candies. But first we offer wonderful recipes for all sorts of puddings: simple, straightforward chocolate, vanilla, and rice puddings, a luscious banana pudding, and a terrifically "lemony" lemon pudding. We have a rum pudding sure to please most adults and a butterscotch pudding that tastes intensely of real, honest-to-goodness butterscotch without being overly sweet. We also have a sophisticated cappuccino trifle layered with pound cake and a rich, custard-based cinnamon bread pudding. Finally, our lovely lemon pudding cake is sure to bring back childhood memories for many of you.

In many recipes we rely on cornstarch and egg yolks for thickening; in others we also use a little gelatin. You will notice a similarity in method for many of the stirred puddings so that once you master one or two, you can easily make the rest. Whatever your pleasure, we hope you will come to like these puddings as much as we do and discover that the microwave oven is a grand place for them. You will rarely be tempted to use packaged pudding mixes again. We promise.

It has been our experience that most people like baked custards as much as puddings. Adrienne tried again and again to make a light lemony custard and a rich vanilla custard. They *almost* worked, but their textures were not up to her exacting standards. Try as she would, a quarter inch of the bottom would not complete cooking before the rest of the custard turned unpleasantly watery and full of small holes.

The solution came when she tried caramelized custards. Bingo! Because sugar attracts microwaves, lining the bottom of the custard cups with caramel transfers heat to the area that did not cook correctly. The final product was wonderfully smooth and satiny. We *love* our caramel custards as well as our versions of crème brulée and pots de crème—two classics made without fuss in the microwave.

Pudding- and Custard-Making Tips

*Measure cornstarch by spooning it lightly into the measure and then leveling it with the straight edge of a knife. This ensures that you do not overmeasure the cornstarch.

*Be sure the puddings that are a combination of cornstarch and egg yolks come to a full boil. Otherwise the starch will not cook fully, and the pudding will taste pasty.

*Watch the pudding carefully in the microwave as you heat it to a boil. Once it comes to a full boil, stop the cooking process. If it boils too much, the cornstarch will lose its thickening properties, and the pudding will not set. This explains why puddings thin a little after they boil but thicken again as the pudding cools.

*For a silky texture we recommend straining the pudding. You may skip this step, but the pudding will not be velvety and smooth.

*In many of the following recipes we instruct you to whip cream in a chilled metal bowl. To save time use the same bowl that contained the ice and ice water used to chill the pudding. After emptying it of the ice and ice water, completely dry the bowl and use it to whip the cream.

*We like the light, creamy texture that whipped cream lends to classic puddings, such as Vanilla Bean Pudding and Lemon Lover's Pudding. But if you object to the cream for reasons of diet or because you feel it threatens the integrity of the classics, please leave it out. The yields will be smaller and the consistency of the puddings heavier.

*We cool the puddings over a bowl of ice water to reduce chilling time and eliminate the formation of skin. Some folks prefer skin on their puddings, however; if you do, do not chill the pudding over ice water but let it cool in the refrigerator.

*Puddings that call for refrigerator chilling may be "quick chilled" in the freezer. Do not leave them in the freezer for longer than 30 to 45 minutes, and take them out before they freeze.

*For a smooth-textured custard, take care not to overmix the eggs. Too many air bubbles in the mixture will make the texture of the custards unpleasantly porous. Dissolving the sugar in the hot milk before mixing with the eggs also contributes to a silky texture.

*As in a conventional oven, microwave-baked custards are cooked in a hot water bath. It is important to use the recommended 9-inch pie plate because the custard will cook unevenly in a larger dish.

*If you notice the custard starting to bubble around the edges at any time, immediately lower the microwave cooking power by 10 to 20 percent. The custard must cook gently to achieve a silky texture.

*During baking be sure to turn the custard cups every 3 minutes so that they cook evenly. Start the cooking process on MEDIUM (50 percent) power, and after the time specified in the recipe (usually about 6 minutes), lower it to MEDIUM-LOW (30 percent) power. Gentle cooking prevents the custard from boiling, which is a sure way to spoil the texture.

*Caramel, easily made in the microwave, must be watched carefully during the last minute of cooking to make sure it does not burn. Burned caramel tastes bitter.

*When making caramel be sure to use a high-sided 1½-quart microwave-safe glass ceramic casserole. A plain glass casserole, even one that is microwave-safe, or a measuring cup may crack with the heat of the caramel.

Vanilla Bean Pudding

serves 4

preparation time: ABOUT 15 MINUTES PLUS 10 MINUTES STANDING (ONLY IF USING A VANILLA BEAN), 5 TO 10 MINUTES COOLING, AND ABOUT 1 HOUR CHILLING

microwave time: 7 TO 13 MINUTES (IF USING A VANILLA BEAN); 6½ TO 11½ (IF USING VANILLA EXTRACT)

The words ''vanilla bean'' conjure up a rich, full-flavored vanilla pudding, which is precisely correct in this instance. But you don't need a vanilla bean to make the pudding; substitute pure vanilla extract if you like. If you do have a vanilla bean, use it; the flavor will be a little fuller than with extract. Either way, this dessert is satisfying and delicious—with or without the strawberries and whipped cream, which turn it into a very special treat.

¼ CUP CORNSTARCH (LIGHTLY SPOONED INTO A MEASURING CUP AND LEVELED WITH THE EDGE OF A KNIFE)

2⅓ CUPS MILK (USED IN TWO MEASUREMENTS)

2 LARGE EGG YOLKS

½ CUP GRANULATED SUGAR

PINCH OF SALT

1 VANILLA BEAN OR 2 TEASPOONS VANILLA EXTRACT

⅓ CUP HEAVY CREAM

WHIPPED CREAM FOR GARNISH (OPTIONAL)

STRAWBERRY HALVES FOR GARNISH (OPTIONAL)

Unbelievable Microwave Desserts

1   Put the cornstarch in a 1-quart bowl. Slowly whisk in ⅓ cup of milk until smooth. Whisk in the egg yolks just until blended, then set aside.

2   In a 1-quart microwave-safe glass measuring cup, combine the remaining 2 cups of milk with the sugar and salt. If using a vanilla bean, split it in half lengthwise with a small, sharp knife and add it to the milk and sugar mixture. (If using vanilla extract, do *not* add it now.)

3   Cover the cup with plastic wrap, turning back a fold over the pouring spout. Microwave the pudding on HIGH (100 percent) power for 3 to 5 minutes, stirring once after 2 minutes, until the mixture is steaming hot.

4   If using a vanilla bean, let the mixture stand, covered, for 10 minutes to give it time to infuse with flavor. Reheat the mixture, still covered, in the microwave set on HIGH (100 percent) power for 30 seconds to 1½ minutes, until steaming hot. Remove the vanilla bean.

5   Whisk ½ cup of the hot milk into the egg yolk mixture. Pour this back into the measuring cup holding the rest of the hot milk.

6   Cover the cup again, turning back a fold over the pouring spout, and microwave on HIGH (100 percent) power for 3 to 5 minutes, until the mixture starts to bubble around the edges. Remove the measuring cup from the microwave and whisk until smooth.

7   Cover the cup again, turning back a fold over the pouring spout, and microwave on HIGH (100 percent) power for 30 seconds to 1½ minutes, until the mixture comes to a full boil. Note that the pudding will be very thick at first; after it boils its consistency will thin a little.

8   Strain the pudding through a fine-meshed sieve into a noncorrosive metal 2½-quart bowl. Push the pudding through the sieve with a rubber spatula.

9   Set the bowl over a larger bowl containing ice and ice water for 5 to 10 minutes, stirring frequently, until the pudding is cold and starts to thicken. Remove the bowl from the larger bowl of ice water. If using vanilla extract, whisk it in now.

10   Chill a 2½-quart bowl. Whip the cream in the bowl using a hand-held electric mixer or a wire whisk until soft peaks start to form. Using a rubber spatula, fold the cream into the cooled pudding.

11   Spoon the pudding into four 6-ounce dessert glasses or custard cups. Cover and refrigerate for about 1 hour, until completely chilled and set. Just before serving, garnish the pudding with rosettes or dollops of whipped cream and sliced strawberries, if desired.

> **kitchen note:**
>
> *Take careful note of how we measure cornstarch. If you scoop it or pour it into the measuring cup, you will have more than you need for the recipe. Spoon it into the cup with a light hand and then gently sweep the top with the edge of a knife.*

Butterscotch Velvet Pudding

serves 4

preparation time: ABOUT 15 MINUTES PLUS 5 TO 10 MINUTES COOLING AND ABOUT 1 HOUR CHILLING

microwave time: 9½ TO 11½ MINUTES

*T*he way we see it, if you are going to make butterscotch pudding, it ought to have a rich butterscotch flavor. Fortunately, this is easy to achieve in the microwave oven because it is simple to make a luxuriously creamy, caramelized base with heavy cream and brown sugar. In other words, this pudding does not rely on the combination of melted butter and brown sugar as so many others do. Be sure to use skim milk; otherwise the pudding will be too rich. You will also need a microwave-safe candy thermometer to achieve success (see pages 20–21 of Chapter 1).

¼ CUP CORNSTARCH (LIGHTLY SPOONED INTO A MEASURING CUP AND LEVELED WITH THE EDGE OF A KNIFE)

2 CUPS SKIM MILK (USED IN TWO MEASUREMENTS)

2 LARGE EGG YOLKS

¾ CUP HEAVY CREAM

½ CUP PACKED BROWN SUGAR

PINCH OF SALT

2 TEASPOONS VANILLA EXTRACT

WHIPPED CREAM FOR GARNISH (OPTIONAL)

CHOPPED PECANS OR WALNUTS FOR GARNISH (OPTIONAL)

1   Put the cornstarch in a 1-quart bowl. Slowly whisk in ¼ cup of milk until smooth. Whisk in the egg yolks just until blended, then set aside.

2   In a 1-quart microwave-safe glass measuring cup, combine the heavy cream, brown sugar, and salt. Stir with a wooden spoon until the lumps of brown sugar are broken up. Cover with a piece of waxed paper and microwave on HIGH (100 percent) power for 1 minute. Stir until smooth.

3   Attach a microwave-safe candy thermometer to the right side of the measuring cup, making sure the bulb is submerged. Microwave on HIGH (100 percent) power for 5 to 9 minutes, or until the thermometer registers 250°F., hard-ball stage.

4   Use a long-handled wooden spoon to stir in the remaining 1¾ cups of milk until smooth. Add the egg yolk mixture and whisk well.

5   Cover the cup with plastic wrap, turning back a fold over the pouring

spout. Microwave on HIGH (100 percent) power for 3 minutes. Whisk until smooth.

6   Cover the cup again, turning back a fold over the pouring spout, and microwave on HIGH (100 percent) power for 2 to 5 minutes, whisking every 60 seconds until the mixture thickens and starts to bubble around the edges.

7   Cover the cup again, turning back a fold over the pouring spout, and microwave on HIGH (100 percent) power for 30 seconds to 1½ minutes, until the mixture comes to a full boil. Note that the pudding will be very thick at first; after it boils, its consistency will thin a little. Whisk until smooth.

8   Strain the pudding through a fine-meshed sieve into a noncorrosive metal 2-quart bowl. Push the pudding through the sieve with a rubber spatula.

9   Set the bowl over a larger bowl containing ice and ice water for 5 to 10 minutes, stirring frequently, until the pudding is cold and starts to thicken. Remove the bowl from the larger bowl of ice water. Whisk in the vanilla extract.

10   Spoon the pudding into four 6-ounce dessert glasses or custard cups. Cover and refrigerate for about 1 hour, or until completely chilled. Just before serving, garnish with whipped cream and a sprinkling of chopped nuts, if desired.

Chocolate Pudding

serves 6

preparation time: ABOUT 15 MINUTES PLUS 10 TO 15 MINUTES COOLING AND ABOUT 1 HOUR CHILLING

microwave time: 10½ TO 15 MINUTES

S*ince we share a penchant for chocolate, we included a good, old-fashioned chocolate pudding in this chapter. Wait until you taste it! This one is thick, rich, dark, smooth, chocolaty—everything a chocolate pudding ought to be. Adrienne developed the recipe using easily available brands of chocolate, such as Hershey, Nestlé, or Baker's. If you happen to like the skin that sometimes forms on the top of chocolate pudding, do not cool the pudding over ice and ice water; let it cool more slowly once it is spooned into dessert glasses or custard cups.*

3 TABLESPOONS COLD WATER

1½ TEASPOONS UNFLAVORED GELATIN

¼ CUP CORNSTARCH (LIGHTLY SPOONED INTO A MEASURING CUP AND LEVELED WITH THE EDGE OF A KNIFE)

3 CUPS MILK (USED IN TWO MEASUREMENTS)

3 LARGE EGG YOLKS

½ CUP GRANULATED SUGAR

⅛ TEASPOON SALT

10 OUNCES SEMISWEET OR BITTERSWEET CHOCOLATE, FINELY CHOPPED

2 TABLESPOONS UNSALTED BUTTER, SOFTENED

4 TEASPOONS VANILLA EXTRACT

WHIPPED CREAM FOR GARNISH (OPTIONAL)

CHOCOLATE CURLS FOR GARNISH (OPTIONAL)

kitchen note:

Please use bar semisweet chocolate, not chips. The chips are sweeter, and because they contain less cocoa butter than semisweet or bittersweet chocolate, the pudding will not be as creamy.

1   Put the water in a small cup. Sprinkle the gelatin over the water and let the mixture soften for at least 5 minutes.

2   Put the cornstarch in a 2-quart microwave-safe glass measuring cup. Slowly whisk in ¼ cup of milk until smooth. Add the egg yolks, sugar, and salt, and whisk until well blended.

3   Add the remaining 2¾ cups of milk and whisk until blended. Cover the cup with plastic wrap, turning back a fold over the pouring spout. Microwave the pudding on HIGH (100 percent) power for 5 minutes. Whisk until smooth.

4   Cover the cup again, turning back a fold over the pouring spout, and microwave on HIGH (100 percent) power for 4 to 7 minutes, whisking every 60 seconds, until the pudding thickens and starts to bubble around the edges. Whisk until smooth.

5   Cover the cup again, turning back a fold over the pouring spout, and microwave on HIGH (100 percent) power for 1½ to 3 minutes, until the mixture comes to a full boil. Note that the pudding will be very thick at first; after it boils its consistency will thin a little.

6   Stir in the softened gelatin, making sure it is completely dissolved. Stir in the chopped chocolate and let the mixture stand for 30 seconds. Add the butter and whisk until smooth.

7   Strain the pudding through a fine-meshed sieve into a noncorrosive metal 2½-quart bowl. Push the pudding through the sieve with a rubber spatula.

8   Set the bowl over a larger bowl containing ice and ice water for 10 to 15

minutes, stirring frequently, until the pudding is cold and starts to thicken. Remove the bowl from the larger bowl of ice water. Whisk in the vanilla extract.

9 Spoon the pudding into six 6-ounce dessert glasses or custard cups. Cover and refrigerate for about 1 hour, or until completely chilled and set. Just before serving, garnish the top of each pudding with a rosette or dollop of whipped cream and chocolate curls, if desired.

Diner-Style Rice Pudding

serves 6

preparation time: ABOUT 15 MINUTES PLUS 5 TO 10 MINUTES COOLING AND ABOUT 1 HOUR CHILLING

microwave time: 5½ TO 8½ MINUTES

We have always liked the sort of rice pudding served at good diners—thick and creamy, with the grains of rice very much in evidence—and so are especially pleased with our microwave version. Serve the pudding on the day you make it, if possible, and don't keep it refrigerated too long. We add the raisins for authenticity and great flavor, but we made them optional because a lot of people don't like them. Also, if you do not have them in the house, we don't want to discourage you from trying the dessert. If you want to dress the pudding up a little, add ½ teaspoon of finely grated lemon zest or ¼ teaspoon of finely grated orange zest along with the vanilla extract.

3 TABLESPOONS CORNSTARCH
2⅓ CUPS MILK (USED IN TWO MEASUREMENTS)
2 LARGE EGG YOLKS
½ CUP GRANULATED SUGAR
⅛ TEASPOON SALT

WHOLE NUTMEG, FOR GRATING
2 CUPS COOKED LONG-GRAIN RICE
2 TABLESPOONS RAISINS (OPTIONAL)
1 TABLESPOON VANILLA EXTRACT
GROUND CINNAMON FOR GARNISH

1 Put the cornstarch in a 1-quart microwave-glass measuring cup. Slowly whisk in ⅓ cup of milk until smooth. Add the egg yolks, sugar, and salt, and whisk until well blended. Add the remaining 2 cups of milk and grate a little nutmeg over the top. Whisk until blended.

2 Cover the cup with plastic wrap, turning back a fold over the pouring spout. Microwave the pudding on HIGH (100 percent) power for 3 minutes. Whisk until smooth.

3 Cover the cup again, turning back a fold over the pouring spout, and microwave on HIGH (100 percent) power for 2 to 5 minutes, whisking every 60 seconds until the mixture starts to bubble around the edges. Whisk until smooth.

4 Cover the cup again, turning back a fold over the pouring spout, and microwave on HIGH (100 percent) power for 30 seconds to 1½ minutes, until the mixture comes to a full boil. Note that the pudding will be very thick at first; after it boils its consistency will thin a little.

5 Strain the pudding through a fine-meshed sieve into a noncorrosive metal 2½-quart bowl. Push the pudding through the sieve with a rubber spatula. Stir in the rice and raisins.

6 Set the bowl over a larger bowl containing ice and ice water for 5 to 10 minutes, stirring frequently, until the pudding is cold and starts to thicken. Remove the bowl from the larger bowl of ice water. Stir in the vanilla extract.

7 Spoon the pudding into six 6-ounce dessert glasses or custard cups. Cover and refrigerate for about 1 hour, or until completely chilled and set. Just before serving, garnish the top of each pudding with a light sprinkling of ground cinnamon.

Lemon Lover's Pudding

serves 4

preparation time: ABOUT 15 MINUTES PLUS 5 TO 10 MINUTES COOLING AND ABOUT 1 HOUR CHILLING

microwave time: 5½ TO 9½ MINUTES

*W*hen *Mary tested this recipe, she wrote ''nice, perky lemon flavor'' in her notes. We won't spend time wondering why people use words such as ''perky'' to describe lemons, but this pudding does have wonderfully fresh flavor. Please use fresh lemon juice, not the bottled kind. It is easy to squeeze, and you can use some of the same lemons for the zest.*

¼ CUP CORNSTARCH (LIGHTLY SPOONED INTO A MEASURING CUP AND LEVELED WITH THE EDGE OF A KNIFE)

2 CUPS MILK (USED IN TWO MEASUREMENTS)

2 LARGE EGG YOLKS

⅔ CUP GRANULATED SUGAR

1½ TEASPOONS FINELY GRATED LEMON ZEST (USED IN TWO MEASUREMENTS)

⅛ TEASPOON SALT

⅓ CUP PLUS 1 TABLESPOON FRESH LEMON JUICE

2 TEASPOONS VANILLA EXTRACT

⅓ CUP HEAVY CREAM

LEMON SLICES FOR GARNISH (OPTIONAL)

1   Put the cornstarch in a 1-quart microwave-safe glass measuring cup. Slowly whisk in ¼ cup of milk until smooth. Add the egg yolks, sugar, 1 teaspoon of lemon zest, and salt, and whisk until well blended. Stir in the remaining 1¾ cups of milk.

2   Cover the cup with plastic wrap, turning back a fold over the pouring spout. Microwave the pudding on HIGH (100 percent) power for 3 minutes. Whisk until smooth.

3   Cover the cup again, turning back a fold over the pouring spout, and microwave on HIGH (100 percent) power for 2 to 5 minutes, whisking every 60 seconds, until the mixture thickens and starts to bubble around the sides of the cup. Whisk until smooth.

kitchen note:

This pudding is best eaten on the day it is made. After two days it may become watery due to the reaction of the egg yolks and starch with the acid in the lemon juice.

(CONTINUED)

4   Cover the cup again, turning back a fold over the pouring spout, and microwave on HIGH (100 percent) power for 30 seconds to 1½ minutes, until the mixture comes to a full boil. Note that the pudding will be very thick at first; after it boils its consistency will thin a little.

5   Strain the pudding through a fine-meshed sieve into a noncorrosive metal 2-quart bowl. Stir in the remaining ½ teaspoon of lemon zest and the lemon juice.

6   Set the bowl over a larger bowl containing ice and ice water for 5 to 10 minutes, stirring frequently, until the pudding is cold and starts to thicken. Remove the bowl from the larger bowl of ice water. Whisk in the vanilla extract.

7   Chill a 2-quart bowl. Whip the cream in the bowl using a hand-held electric mixer or a wire whisk until soft peaks start to form. Using a rubber spatula, fold the cream into the cooled pudding.

8   Spoon the pudding into four 6-ounce dessert glasses. Cover and refrigerate for about 1 hour, or until completely chilled and set. Just before serving, garnish the top of each pudding with a thin slice or twist of lemon.

Caribbean Banana Rum Pudding

serves 8

preparation time: ABOUT 20 MINUTES PLUS 5 TO 10 MINUTES COOLING, AND ABOUT 1 HOUR CHILLING

microwave time: 5½ TO 9½ MINUTES

This quickly became one of our all-time favorites. The texture is a sublime blending of smooth pudding and moist cake; the flavor is sweet without being cloying. You do not need to add the rum if your children or anyone else might object; use orange juice instead. On the other hand, it is a fairly small amount and really does contribute to the overall flavor. Adrienne made this several times during a Caribbean vacation using dark Tortuga rum—to rave reviews. The addition of the diced pound cake and bananas to the pudding gives it bulk, which explains why this recipe serves eight (most of our other pudding recipes serve four or six).

3 TABLESPOONS WATER

1 TEASPOON UNFLAVORED GELATIN

1/4 CUP CORNSTARCH (LIGHTLY SPOONED INTO A MEASURING CUP AND LEVELED WITH THE EDGE OF A KNIFE)

2 CUPS MILK (USED IN TWO MEASUREMENTS)

2 LARGE EGG YOLKS

1/2 CUP GRANULATED SUGAR

PINCH OF SALT

2 TEASPOONS VANILLA EXTRACT

3/4 CUP HEAVY CREAM

1 3/4 CUPS 1/2-INCH-DICED POUND CAKE

1/4 CUP DARK RUM OR FRESH ORANGE JUICE

1 3/4 CUPS 1/4-INCH-DICED RIPE BANANA (2 TO 3 MEDIUM BANANAS)

WHIPPED CREAM FOR GARNISH (OPTIONAL)

SLICED BANANAS FOR GARNISH (OPTIONAL)

1 Put the water in a small cup. Sprinkle the gelatin over the water and let the mixture soften for at least 5 minutes.

2 Put the cornstarch in a 1-quart microwave-safe glass measuring cup. Slowly whisk in 1/4 cup of milk until smooth. Add the egg yolks, sugar, and salt, and whisk until well blended. Add the remaining 1 3/4 cups of milk and whisk again until blended.

3 Cover the cup with plastic wrap, turning back a fold over the pouring spout. Microwave the pudding on HIGH (100 percent) power for 3 minutes. Whisk until smooth.

4 Cover the cup again, turning back a fold over the pouring spout, and microwave on HIGH (100 percent) power for 2 to 5 minutes, whisking every 60 seconds, until the mixture thickens and starts to bubble around the edges. Whisk until smooth.

5 Cover the measuring cup again, turning back a fold over the pouring spout. Microwave on HIGH (100 percent) power for 30 seconds to 1 1/2 minutes, until the mixture comes to a full boil. Note that the pudding will be very thick at first; after it boils its consistency will thin a little.

6 Stir the softened gelatin into the hot mixture, making sure it dissolves completely.

7 Strain the pudding through a fine-meshed sieve into a noncorrosive metal 2 1/2-quart bowl. Push the pudding through the sieve with a rubber spatula.

8 Set the bowl over a larger bowl containing ice and ice water for 5 to 10 minutes, stirring frequently, until the pudding is cold and starts to thicken. Remove the bowl from the larger bowl of ice water. Whisk in the vanilla extract.

9 Chill a 2 1/2-quart bowl. Whip the cream in the bowl using a hand-held electric mixer or a wire whisk until soft peaks start to form. Using a rubber spatula, fold the cream into the cooled pudding.

10 Toss the cubed pound cake with the rum or orange juice in a 1-quart bowl. Gently fold the diced banana and moistened pound cake into the pudding.

11   Spoon the pudding into eight 6-ounce dessert glasses or custard cups or into a 1½-quart bowl. Cover and refrigerate for 1 to 2 hours, or until completely chilled and set. Just before serving, garnish the pudding with whipped cream and sliced bananas, if desired.

Danish Rum Pudding with Melba Sauce

serves 8

preparation time: ABOUT 20 MINUTES PLUS 5 TO 10 MINUTES COOLING AND ABOUT 1 HOUR CHILLING

microwave time: 10½ TO 15 MINUTES

Adrienne adapted this recipe for the microwave from one given to her by her husband David's Danish grandmother. We think the results speak for themselves. (Although kids may not like it, you will.) Imagine spooning this from an elegant dessert glass while sitting in a charming little cafe in Tivoli Gardens. We can dream, can't we?

If you wanted to, you could substitute orange juice for the rum for a nice, light pudding. But we think the rum is the best part!

¼ CUP COLD WATER

2¼ TEASPOONS UNFLAVORED GELATIN

¼ CUP PLUS 2 TABLESPOONS CORNSTARCH (LIGHTLY SPOONED INTO A MEASURING CUP AND LEVELED WITH THE EDGE OF A KNIFE)

3 CUPS MILK (USED IN TWO MEASUREMENTS)

3 LARGE EGG YOLKS

1 CUP GRANULATED SUGAR

⅛ TEASPOON SALT

⅓ CUP DARK RUM

4 TEASPOONS VANILLA EXTRACT

1⅓ CUPS HEAVY CREAM

MELBA SAUCE (PAGE 282)

1   Put the water in a small custard cup and sprinkle the gelatin over it. Let the mixture stand for 5 minutes to soften.

2   Put the cornstarch in a 2-quart microwave-safe glass measuring cup and gradually add ¼ cup of milk, whisking until completely smooth. Add the egg yolks, sugar, and salt, and continue whisking until blended. Stir in the remaining 2¾ cups of milk.

3   Cover the cup with plastic wrap, turning back a fold over the pouring spout. Microwave the pudding on HIGH (100 percent) power for 5 minutes. Whisk until smooth.

4   Cover the cup again, turning back a fold over the pouring spout, and microwave on HIGH (100 percent) power for 4 to 7 minutes, whisking every 60 seconds, until the mixture thickens and starts to bubble around the edges. Whisk until smooth.

5   Cover the measuring cup again, turning back a fold over the pouring spout. Microwave on HIGH (100 percent) power for 1½ to 3 minutes, until the mixture comes to a full boil. Note that the pudding will be very thick at first; after it boils its consistency will thin a little.

6   Stir the softened gelatin into the pudding, making sure it is completely dissolved.

7   Strain the pudding through a fine-meshed sieve into a noncorrosive metal 2½-quart bowl. Push the pudding through the sieve with a rubber spatula.

8   Set the bowl over a larger bowl containing ice and ice water for 5 to 10 minutes, stirring frequently, until the pudding is cold and starts to thicken. Remove the bowl from the larger bowl of ice water. Whisk in the rum and vanilla extract.

9   Chill a 2½-quart bowl. Whip the cream in the bowl using a hand-held electric mixer or a wire whisk until soft peaks start to form. Using a rubber spatula, fold the cream into the cooled pudding just until it is combined.

10   Spoon the pudding into eight 8-ounce stemmed dessert glasses. Cover and refrigerate for 30 to 60 minutes, or until set. Just before serving, spoon Melba Sauce over each glass of pudding. This pudding may be prepared up to two days ahead of time.

Lemon Pudding Cake

serves 4

preparation time: 8 TO 10 MINUTES

microwave time: 14 TO 17½ MINUTES PLUS 10 MINUTES STANDING

T*his warm, lemony pudding cake is modeled after a similar cake Adrienne recalls loving as a child. As the pudding cake bakes, it makes its own lemony sauce, which pools beneath a top layer of cake. One bite and you will quickly understand why children as well as adults like this soft, soothing dessert.*

2 TABLESPOONS UNSALTED BUTTER

⅓ CUP SIFTED ALL-PURPOSE FLOUR

¼ TEASPOON DOUBLE-ACTING BAKING POWDER

¼ TEASPOON SALT

1 CUP MILK (USED IN TWO MEASUREMENTS)

2 LARGE EGGS, SEPARATED

¾ CUP GRANULATED SUGAR

½ TEASPOON FINELY GRATED LEMON ZEST

1 TEASPOON VANILLA EXTRACT

¼ CUP FRESH LEMON JUICE

1 CUP HOT TAP WATER

WHIPPED CREAM OR PLAIN YOGURT FOR GARNISH

kitchen note:

By setting the casserole in a pie plate filled with hot tap water you are in effect steaming the cake. Take care not to overcook the pudding cake. If you do, the cake layer will absorb the sauce.

1   Put the butter in a 6-ounce microwave-safe custard cup and cover with waxed paper. Microwave on MEDIUM-HIGH (70 percent) power for 1 to 1½ minutes, until the butter is melted. Set aside.

2   Combine the flour, baking powder, and salt in a 2½-quart bowl. Use a wire whisk and complete 10 or 12 strokes to ensure that the ingredients are thoroughly blended.

3   Gradually add ¼ cup of milk, whisking until smooth. Whisk in the melted butter, egg yolks, sugar, lemon zest, and vanilla extract until blended. Stir in the lemon juice. Whisk in the remaining ¾ cup of milk.

4   Put the egg whites in a grease-free 2½-quart bowl. Using a hand-held electric mixer set at high speed, beat the whites until stiff and shiny peaks form when the beaters are lifted.

5   Whisk the beaten egg whites into the milk mixture until smooth. Pour the batter into a shallow 1-quart microwave-safe round casserole. Set the casserole in a 10-inch microwave-safe glass pie plate. Pour the hot water into the pie plate. It should come about halfway up the sides of the casserole.

6   Microwave, uncovered, at MEDIUM (50 percent) power for 8 minutes. If not using a turntable, rotate the pie plate a quarter turn after 4 minutes.

7   Cover the casserole with a microwave-safe paper towel and microwave on HIGH (100 percent) power for 3 to 6 minutes. If not using a turntable, rotate the pie plate a quarter turn every 1½ minutes. Test for doneness after 3 minutes. The cake is done when the pudding layer is bubbling rapidly around the edges and the surface of the cake layer appears dry.

8   Let the pudding cake stand for 10 minutes, uncovered. Serve warm, topped with whipped cream or plain yogurt.

Brownie Pudding Cake

serves 6

preparation time: ABOUT 10 MINUTES

microwave time: 9½ TO 13 MINUTES PLUS 10 MINUTES STANDING

This is the dessert we all ate by the bowlful when we were children and our grannies made rich, chocolaty pudding cakes for us on snowy afternoons. Whether this is true or not, desserts as warm and satisfying as this make special memories. Prepare it for your own children or grandchildren, friends, or simply for yourself. We think you will agree this pudding cake is just wonderful—and so easy to make since we use just one bowl for mixing and cooking. This dessert is also known as Mississippi mud and chocolate sundae cake.

Brownie batter:

1 CUP PLUS 2 TABLESPOONS SIFTED ALL-PURPOSE FLOUR

2/3 CUP GRANULATED SUGAR

1/2 CUP SIFTED UNSWEETENED ALKALIZED COCOA POWDER SUCH AS HERSHEY'S EUROPEAN-STYLE OR DROSTE

2 1/4 TEASPOONS DOUBLE-ACTING BAKING POWDER

1/4 TEASPOON SALT

1/2 CUP MILK

1/2 CUP FINELY CHOPPED WALNUTS (OPTIONAL)

1/4 CUP VEGETABLE OIL

1 TABLESPOON VANILLA EXTRACT

Topping:

2/3 CUP PACKED LIGHT BROWN SUGAR

1/4 CUP UNSWEETENED ALKALIZED COCOA POWDER SUCH AS HERSHEY'S EUROPEAN STYLE OR DROSTE (LIGHTLY SPOONED INTO A MEASURING CUP AND LEVELED WITH THE EDGE OF A KNIFE)

2 TEASPOONS INSTANT COFFEE GRANULES (OPTIONAL)

1 CUP HOT TAP WATER

VANILLA OR COFFEE ICE CREAM

---

kitchen note:

For the lightest texture it is important to sift the flour and cocoa for the batter before measuring. However, use unsifted cocoa for the topping. We give the coffee flavoring as an option but find that the coffee enhances the chocolate flavor and cuts the sweetness of this rich dessert.

1 TO MAKE THE BROWNIE BATTER: Put the flour, sugar, cocoa, baking powder, and salt in a 2-quart high, straight-sided round microwave-safe casserole. Complete 12 to 15 strokes with a wire whisk to ensure that the ingredients are thoroughly blended. Make a well in the center of the flour mixture and add the milk, walnuts, if desired, oil, and vanilla extract. Stir with a wooden spoon just until moistened. Note that the batter will be stiff. Spread it evenly in the bowl with the back of a spoon.

2 TO MAKE THE TOPPING: Sprinkle the brown sugar, cocoa, and instant coffee evenly over the top of the brownie batter. Pour the hot water over the top of the batter.

3 Cover the casserole with a microwave-safe paper towel and set it on an inverted 9-inch glass pie plate. Microwave on MEDIUM (50 percent) power for 8 minutes. If you are not using a turntable, rotate the casserole a half turn after 4 minutes.

4 Without removing the paper towel, microwave on high (100 percent) power for 1 1/2 to 5 minutes more, until the surface of the pudding looks dry. Remove the paper towel and let the pudding stand on a flat heatproof surface for 10 minutes. Spoon the warm pudding into dessert dishes and serve with ice cream.

Cinnamon Raisin Bread Pudding with Hot Cider Sauce

serves 4

preparation time: ABOUT 20 MINUTES

microwave time: 13 TO 18 MINUTES PLUS 10 MINUTES STANDING

We could not consider a pudding chapter complete without a recipe for bread pudding. This one is homey, warm, and comforting, just as bread puddings are meant to be. And it is easy, too.

We made the bread pudding in individual servings because it is more attractive that way. For the best texture try to serve it warm. The accompanying cider sauce is lighter than the traditional custard sauce commonly spooned over bread pudding.

Bread pudding:

- 2 LARGE EGGS PLUS 1 LARGE EGG YOLK
- 2 TABLESPOONS GRANULATED SUGAR
- 1/8 TEASPOON SALT
- 3/4 CUP MILK
- 1/4 CUP HEAVY CREAM

- 2 TEASPOONS DARK RUM (OPTIONAL)
- 1 TEASPOON VANILLA EXTRACT
- 6 SLICES CINNAMON RAISIN BREAD, CRUSTS REMOVED AND CUT INTO 1/2-INCH CUBES
- 2 CUPS HOT TAP WATER

Cider sauce:

- 1 CUP FRESH APPLE CIDER
- 2 TABLESPOONS DARK RAISINS
- 4 TEASPOONS LIGHT BROWN SUGAR
- 1 TABLESPOON CORNSTARCH

- 1 TABLESPOON DARK RUM (OPTIONAL)
- 3/4 TEASPOON VANILLA EXTRACT
- FRESH LEMON JUICE TO TASTE

> **kitchen note:**
>
> *To save time, prepare the custard mixture ahead of time and keep it in the refrigerator. Cut the bread cubes and store them in a plastic bag or airtight container until you are ready to prepare the pudding.*

1 TO MAKE THE BREAD PUDDING: Combine the eggs, egg yolk, sugar, and salt in a 2½-quart bowl. Whisk vigorously until frothy. Stir in the milk, cream, rum, and vanilla extract. Use a rubber spatula to fold in the bread cubes. Mix well.

2 Spoon the mixture into four 6-ounce ramekins or custard cups. Arrange the ramekins in a circle in a 10-inch microwave-safe glass pie plate. Carefully pour the hot tap water into the pie plate. The water should come halfway up the sides of the ramekins.

3   Microwave on MEDIUM (50 percent) power for 10 to 13 minutes, rotating the puddings a half turn after 5 minutes. If your microwave has no turntable, also rotate the pie plate after 5 minutes. Test the puddings for doneness after 10 minutes by inserting a toothpick into each one; it should come out clean.

4   Let the puddings stand in the water bath on a flat heatproof surface for 10 minutes while you prepare the sauce.

5   TO PREPARE THE CIDER SAUCE: Combine the cider, raisins, and sugar in a 2-cup microwave-safe glass measuring cup.

6   Put the cornstarch in a small cup. Slowly stir in 1 tablespoon of the cider until smooth. Pour this mixture into the measuring cup holding the cider and stir until blended.

7   Cover the measuring cup with waxed paper. Microwave on HIGH (100 percent) power for 1 minute. Whisk until blended.

8   Cover the measuring cup again and continue to microwave on HIGH (100 percent) power for 2 to 4 minutes, whisking every 60 seconds, until the sauce is translucent and comes to a rapid boil. Do not let the sauce boil for more than 30 seconds, or it will become watery.

9   Stir in the rum, if desired, and vanilla extract. Add lemon juice to taste.

10   Run the tip of a small knife around the edge of a warm pudding. Invert the pudding into the palm of your hand and carefully place it right side up in the center of a dessert plate. Spoon some cider sauce around it. Unmold and pour sauce on the remaining puddings in the same way.

Cappuccino Trifle

serves 6

preparation time: ABOUT 30 MINUTES PLUS 5 TO 10 MINUTES COOLING AND 1 HOUR CHILLING

microwave time: 5½ TO 9½ MINUTES

These delicate coffee creams layered with pound cake are as pretty as they are tasty. Our microwave trifle is perfect for serving at the end of a dinner party with coffee or espresso.

Coffee cream:

3 TABLESPOONS COLD WATER

1⅓ TEASPOONS UNFLAVORED GELATIN

¼ CUP CORNSTARCH

2 CUPS MILK (USED IN TWO MEASUREMENTS)

2 LARGE EGG YOLKS

½ CUP GRANULATED SUGAR

⅛ TEASPOON SALT

LARGE PINCH OF GROUND CINNAMON

1 TABLESPOON INSTANT COFFEE GRANULES (SUBSTITUTE DECAFFEINATED IF DESIRED)

1 TABLESPOON VANILLA EXTRACT

5 TABLESPOONS DARK RUM OR BRANDY (USED IN TWO MEASUREMENTS)

2 CUPS ½-INCH-DICED POUND CAKE

¾ CUP HEAVY CREAM

Decoration:

¾ CUP HEAVY CREAM

2 TEASPOONS GRANULATED SUGAR

½ TEASPOON VANILLA EXTRACT

GROUND CINNAMON FOR GARNISH

1   To make the coffee cream: Put the water in a small cup. Sprinkle the gelatin over the water and let the mixture soften for at least 5 minutes.

2   Put the cornstarch in a 1-quart microwave-safe glass measuring cup. Gradually whisk in ¼ cup of milk until smooth. Whisk in the egg yolks, sugar, salt, and cinnamon until blended. Stir in the remaining 1¾ cups of milk.

3   Cover the cup with plastic wrap, turning back a fold over the pouring spout. Microwave the pudding on HIGH (100 percent) power for 3 minutes. Whisk until smooth.

4   Cover the measuring cup again, turning back a fold over the pouring

spout. Microwave on HIGH (100 percent) power for 2 to 5 minutes, whisking every 60 seconds, until the mixture thickens and starts to bubble around the edges. Whisk until smooth.

5   Cover the measuring cup again, turning back a fold over the pouring spout. Microwave on HIGH (100 percent) power for 30 seconds to 1½ minutes, until the mixture comes to a full boil. Note that the mixture will be very thick at first; after it boils its consistency will thin a little.

6   Stir in the softened gelatin and instant coffee, making sure they are completely dissolved.

7   Strain the mixture through a fine-meshed sieve into a noncorrosive 2½-quart metal bowl.

8   Set the bowl over a larger bowl containing ice and ice water for 5 to 10 minutes, stirring frequently, until the mixture is cold and starts to thicken. Remove the bowl from the larger bowl holding the ice water. Stir in the vanilla extract and 2 tablespoons of rum.

9   Put the diced pound cake in a 1½-quart bowl. Sprinkle the remaining 3 tablespoons of rum over the pound cake.

10   Chill a 2½-quart bowl. Whip the cream in the bowl using a hand-held electric mixer or a wire whisk until soft peaks start to form. Using a rubber spatula, fold the cream into the cooled coffee mixture just until it is combined.

11   Put half of the moistened pound cake cubes into the bottom of six 6-ounce martini or stemmed dessert glasses. Spoon half the coffee cream over the cake. Sprinkle the remaining cake over the coffee cream and top with a second layer of coffee cream. Do not fill the glasses more than seven-eighths full to leave room for the topping. Refrigerate the trifle for about 1 hour, until well chilled. The trifle may be prepared up to two days in advance, covered with plastic wrap, and refrigerated.

12   To MAKE THE DECORATION: Combine the cream, sugar, and vanilla extract in a chilled bowl. Using a hand-held electric mixer set at high speed, whip the cream until soft mounds start to form. Spoon the whipped cream over the top of each trifle and sprinkle with cinnamon.

Crème Brûlée

serves 6

preparation time: ABOUT 25 MINUTES PLUS 1 TO 3 HOURS CHILLING

microwave time: 6 TO 9 MINUTES

*T*his recipe was a challenge, but because so many people adore the creamy custard dessert topped with crunchy caramelized sugar, we persevered. At first Adrienne attempted to make a classic baked crème brûlée in the microwave oven, but because of its high fat content, the custard did not cook evenly. She finally decided to make a stirred custard and thicken it with a little gelatin, which works very well. The resulting crème brûlée cooks in less than 10 minutes, as opposed to 30 to 45 minutes for those baked in a conventional oven. With this sort of custard it is very important to chill it thoroughly both before and after caramelizing. (Proper chilling is equally important when making a traditional baked crème brûlée, too.)

Alas, there was no way we could brown the sugar topping in the microwave, and so Adrienne developed two methods for doing this using other kitchen tools. The first requires a household propane torch and the second, an oven broiler. If you have a torch, it is an easy matter to run it over the ramekins and caramelize the sugar to make a thin, delicate crust. With a broiler we use brown sugar spritzed with a little water to make a more robust, thicker topping. Either one is delicious.

Custard:

¼ CUP COLD WATER	1¾ CUPS HEAVY CREAM
2¼ TEASPOONS UNFLAVORED GELATIN	½ CUP MILK
7 LARGE EGG YOLKS	1 LARGE, PLUMP VANILLA BEAN OR 1
⅓ CUP GRANULATED SUGAR	TABLESPOON VANILLA EXTRACT
⅛ TEASPOON SALT	

Caramel topping using a propane torch:

ICE CUBES	6 TEASPOONS GRANULATED SUGAR

Caramel topping using an oven broiler:

ICE CUBES	SPRAY WATER BOTTLE
9 TABLESPOONS LIGHT BROWN SUGAR	

1 To MAKE THE CUSTARD: Put the water in a 6-ounce custard cup. Sprinkle the gelatin over the water and let it soften for at least 5 minutes.

2 Combine the egg yolks, sugar, and salt in a 1-quart microwave-safe glass measuring cup. Using a small wire whisk, stir vigorously until thoroughly blended. Stir in the cream and milk. If using a vanilla bean, split it in half with a small, sharp knife. With the tip of the knife, scrape the tiny black seeds from the inside and add them to the cream mixture. Add the vanilla pods as well. (If using vanilla extract, do *not* add it now.)

3 Microwave, uncovered, on MEDIUM-HIGH (70 percent) power for 3 minutes. Whisk vigorously.

4 Continue to microwave, uncovered, on MEDIUM-HIGH (70 percent) power for 3 to 6 minutes, whisking vigorously every 60 seconds until the custard thickens slightly. Take care the custard does not get so hot that it curdles. Test for doneness by coating the back of a metal spoon with some of the custard: It's done when you can run your finger down the back of the coated spoon and the path remains in the custard. The custard will register 175°F. on an instant-read thermometer.

5 Stir the softened gelatin into the custard and whisk until it dissolves completely.

6 Strain the custard through a fine-meshed sieve into a noncorrosive metal 2½-quart bowl.

7 Set the bowl over a larger bowl containing ice and ice water for 5 to 10 minutes, stirring frequently, until the custard is cool and starts to thicken slightly. If using vanilla extract, stir it in now.

8 Ladle the custard into six 6-ounce ramekins. Put the ramekins in a 9-by-2-inch round metal cake pan and freeze for 45 minutes or refrigerate for at least 2 hours, until the custard is thoroughly chilled. The custard may be prepared up to two days in advance. After the initial chilling, cover the ramekins and refrigerate.

9 To MAKE THE CARAMEL TOPPING USING A PROPANE TORCH: Surround the ramekins, still in the cake pan, with ice cubes that are as small as possible. Sprinkle 1 teaspoon of granulated sugar evenly over the top of each custard. Using a household propane torch, caramelize the top of each custard by heating the sugar with the flame until it melts and turns to a dark amber color.

10 To MAKE THE CARAMEL TOPPING USING AN OVEN BROILER: Preheat the broiler. Surround the ramekins, still in the cake pan, with small ice cubes. Using about 1½ tablespoons of the brown sugar for each ramekin, sprinkle each one with a loose, even layer of sugar. With a spray water bottle, lightly spray the sugar-topped custard. This will help melt the brown sugar which might otherwise burn before melting. Be sure to spray lightly or the sugar will not caramelize properly. Put the cake pan with the ramekins underneath the broiler and broil for 1 to 3 minutes, until the sugar melts and turns to a dark amber color. It may be necessary to spray the tops of the custards again and to turn the pan and rearrange the ramekins halfway through caramelizing for even browning.

11　When the custards are caramelized, drain off any melted water and surround the ramekins with more ice cubes. Put the cake pan holding the ramekins in the freezer for 20 to 30 minutes to reset the custard. Serve, or transfer the crème brulée to the refrigerator. The chilled, caramelized custards should be served within 2 hours or the caramel topping will break down and lose its crunchiness.

Mocha Pots de Crème

serves 6

preparation time: ABOUT 15 MINUTES PLUS 2 TO 3 HOURS CHILLING

microwave time: 6 TO 9 MINUTES

These little desserts, served in fluted white ramekins, make a sophisticated ending to a meal. They are easy to make and, if time is running away from you, may be chilled for 45 to 60 minutes in the freezer until set rather than the longer stint in the refrigerator. We employed the same technique here as with Crème Brulée (page 53), thickening a stirred custard with gelatin to achieve a rich, velvety consistency.

3 TABLESPOONS COLD WATER

1½ TEASPOONS UNFLAVORED GELATIN

6 LARGE EGG YOLKS

1⅓ CUP GRANULATED SUGAR

⅛ TEASPOON SALT

1 CUP HEAVY CREAM

1 CUP MILK

6 OUNCES SEMISWEET CHOCOLATE, FINELY CHOPPED

2 TEASPOONS INSTANT COFFEE GRANULES

1 TABLESPOON VANILLA EXTRACT

WHIPPED CREAM FOR GARNISH

CHOCOLATE COFFEE BEANS FOR GARNISH

1   Put the water in a small cup. Sprinkle the gelatin over the water and let the mixture soften for at least 5 minutes.

2   Combine the egg yolks, sugar, and salt in a 1-quart microwave-safe glass measuring cup. Stir vigorously with a wire whisk until thoroughly blended. Stir in the cream and milk.

3   Microwave, uncovered, on MEDIUM-HIGH (70 percent) power for 3 minutes. Whisk vigorously.

4   Continue to microwave, uncovered, on MEDIUM-HIGH (70 percent) power for 3 to 6 minutes, whisking vigorously every minute, until the custard thickens slightly. Take care that the custard does not get so hot it curdles. Test for doneness by coating the back of a metal spoon with some of the custard; it is done when you can run your finger down the back of the coated spoon and the path remains in the custard. The custard will register 175°F. on an instant-read thermometer.

5   Stir the softened gelatin mixture into the custard and whisk until it is completely dissolved. Add the chocolate and the instant coffee. Let the mixture stand for 1 minute. Whisk until smooth and stir in the vanilla extract.

6   Strain the custard into another 1-quart measuring cup. Put six 6-ounce pots de crème containers or ramekins on a tray or baking sheet. Pour the custard into the containers and refrigerate, uncovered, on the tray for 2 to 3 hours, until set. Decorate with whipped cream rosettes and chocolate coffee beans. The pots de crème may be prepared up to one day in advance. They should be covered after the initial 2 to 3 hours of chilling.

Pumpkin Caramel Custard

serves 4

preparation time: ABOUT 20 MINUTES PLUS 1 TO 2 HOURS CHILLING

microwave time: 18 TO 24 MINUTES PLUS 15 MINUTES STANDING

As we mentioned in the beginning of the chapter, we attempted other kinds of custard in the microwave but were never completely satisfied with any except those that are caramelized. But surely this presents no hardship: The caramel makes the custards more delicious than ever. This one, rich and dark with the flavors of pumpkin, cinnamon, and ginger, is marvelously smooth and satisfying. The sweet caramel enhances the pumpkin flavor, much as a piece of caramel-sweet pecan pie sitting next to the slice of pumpkin pie enhances it after Thanksgiving dinner

¾ CUP GRANULATED SUGAR (USED IN TWO MEASUREMENTS)

2 TABLESPOONS WATER

¼ TEASPOON LEMON JUICE

¾ CUP MILK

⅛ TEASPOON SALT

3 LARGE EGGS PLUS 1 LARGE EGG YOLK

½ CUP UNSWEETENED CANNED PUMPKIN PUREE

¼ TEASPOON GROUND CINNAMON

⅛ TEASPOON GROUND GINGER

⅛ TEASPOON FRESHLY GRATED NUTMEG

2 TEASPOONS VANILLA EXTRACT

1½ CUPS HOT TAP WATER

1 Combine ½ cup of sugar with the water and lemon juice in a high-sided 1½-quart microwave-safe glass ceramic casserole. Cover with waxed paper and microwave on HIGH (100 percent) power for 1½ minutes. Stir with a wooden spoon to dissolve any remaining sugar crystals. Cover the casserole again and microwave on HIGH (100 percent) power for 2 minutes more.

2 Remove the waxed paper and continue to microwave on HIGH (100 percent) power for 1 to 3 minutes, without stirring, until the syrup becomes dark amber. Watch the syrup closely; when it starts to change color, swirl the casserole a couple of times during the cooking process so that the caramel browns evenly. Do not let it become too dark or burn.

3 Immediately pour the caramel into the bottom of four 6-ounce microwave-safe glass custard cups. Set the cups in a 9-inch microwave-safe glass pie plate.

4 Combine the milk with the remaining ¼ cup of sugar and the salt in a 2-cup microwave-safe glass measuring cup. Cover with waxed paper and microwave on HIGH (100 percent) power for 1½ to 2½ minutes, until steaming hot. Stir with a wooden spoon until the sugar is completely dissolved.

5 Put the eggs, egg yolk, pumpkin, cinnamon, ginger, nutmeg, and vanilla extract in a 2½-quart bowl and whisk until blended. While whisking, slowly add the hot milk to the egg-pumpkin mixture, stirring just until combined. Strain the custard through a coarse-meshed sieve back into the measuring cup.

6 Divide the custard equally among the 4 caramel-lined cups. Pour the hot tap water into the pie plate, being careful not to splash the custards. Microwave on MEDIUM (50 percent) power for 6 minutes, turning the cups a quarter turn after 3 minutes.

> **kitchen note:**
>
> *To achieve a smooth, satiny-textured custard, be careful not to overmix the eggs. Too many air bubbles in the mixture makes the texture unpleasant.*

(*CONTINUED*)

7   Continue to microwave on MEDIUM-LOW (30 percent) power for 6 to 9 minutes, turning the cups a quarter turn every 3 minutes, until the edge of each custard is set and the center still quivers. Test for doneness by inserting the tip of a small, sharp knife into the center of each custard; it should come out slightly creamy.

8   Let the custard cups stand in the pie plate on a flat heatproof surface for 15 minutes. Remove them from the water bath and refrigerate for 1 to 2 hours, until well chilled. The custard may be prepared up to two days in advance.

9   Remove the custard from the cups by gently pressing on top of each one with cupped fingers and easing them out onto dessert plates, flat side down. Pour the liquefied caramel from the bottom of the cups over the top of each custard.

Upside-Down Lemon Caramel Custard

serves 4

preparation time: ABOUT 20 MINUTES PLUS 1 TO 2 HOURS CHILLING

microwave time: 18½ TO 27 MINUTES PLUS 15 MINUTES STANDING

*F*or a dessert that is not too heavy but is rich enough to satisfy all cravings, try these pretty, dainty custards that are turned out onto individual plates with amber-colored caramel dripping down their velvety sides. The slight tartness of the lemon nicely offsets the sweetness of the caramel.

1¼ CUPS MILK

¾ GRANULATED SUGAR (USED IN TWO MEASUREMENTS)

1 TEASPOON FINELY GRATED LEMON ZEST

⅛ TEASPOON SALT

2 TABLESPOONS WATER

¼ TEASPOON LEMON JUICE

3 LARGE EGGS PLUS 1 LARGE EGG YOLK

1 TEASPOON VANILLA EXTRACT

1½ CUPS HOT TAP WATER

LEMON SLICES, CUT INTO QUARTERS, FOR GARNISH

1   Combine the milk with ¼ cup of sugar, lemon zest, and salt in a 2-cup microwave-safe glass measuring cup. Cover with waxed paper and microwave on HIGH (100 percent) power for 2 to 3½ minutes, until steaming hot. Let the mixture stand for 10 minutes.

2   Combine the remaining ½ cup of sugar with the water and lemon juice in a high-sided 1½-quart microwave-safe glass ceramic casserole. Cover with waxed paper and microwave on HIGH (100 percent) power for 1½ minutes. Stir with a wooden spoon to dissolve any remaining sugar crystals. Cover the casserole again and microwave on HIGH (100 percent) power for 2 minutes more.

3   Remove the waxed paper and continue to microwave on HIGH (100 percent) power for 1 to 3 minutes, without stirring, until the syrup becomes dark amber. Watch the syrup closely; when it starts to change color, swirl the casserole a couple of times so that the caramel browns evenly. Do not let it become too dark or burn.

4   Immediately pour the caramel into the bottom of four 6-ounce microwave-safe glass custard cups. Put the cups in a 9-inch microwave-safe glass pie plate.

5   Put the eggs, egg yolk, and vanilla extract in a 2½-quart bowl and whisk just until blended.

6   Reheat the milk mixture on HIGH (100 percent) power for 1 to 2 minutes, until steaming hot. Slowly whisk the hot milk into the egg mixture just until blended. Strain the custard through a fine-meshed sieve back into the measuring cup.

7   Divide the custard equally among the 4 caramel-lined cups. Pour the hot tap water into the pie plate, being careful not to splash the custard. Microwave on MEDIUM (50 percent) power for 6 minutes, turning the cups a quarter turn after 3 minutes.

8   Continue to microwave on MEDIUM-LOW (30 percent) power for 6 to 9 minutes, turning the cups a quarter turn every 3 minutes, until the edge of each custard is set and the center still quivers. Test for doneness by inserting the tip of a small, sharp knife into the center of each custard; it should come out slightly creamy.

9   Let the custard cups stand in the pie plate on a flat heatproof surface for 15 minutes. Remove them from the water bath and refrigerate for 1 to 2 hours, until well chilled. This custard may be prepared up to two days in advance.

10   Remove the custard from each by gently pressing on top with cupped fingers and easing it out onto a dessert plate, flat side down. Pour the liquefied caramel from the bottom of the cup over the top of the custard. Garnish with the lemon slices.

kitchen note:

If you notice the custards starting to bubble around the edges at any time, immediately lower the microwave cooking power by 10 to 20 percent. The custards must cook gently to achieve a silky texture.

CHAPTER THREE

Mousses

White Chocolate Mousse

Quick Chocolate Mousse

White and Dark Chocolate Mousse Parfait

Chocolate Mint Semifreddo

Strawberry Mousse

Raspberry Mousse

Raspberry Mousse Hearts with Chocolate Sauce

White Chocolate Raspberry Swirl Mousse

*White Chocolate Lemon Mousse Icebox Cake with
    Strawberry Coulis*

*White Chocolate Orange Mousse Quenelles with
    Fresh Fruit Medley*

Hazelnut Praline Chocolate Mousse

There is no denying that mousses do beautifully in the microwave oven. The glorious mixtures of cream, egg whites, and sugar are a joy to work with and easy to assemble. We thicken our mousses with gelatin, heavy cream, and clouds of whipped egg whites, and flavor them with chocolate, liqueurs, praline, and fruit. The results? Velvety, smooth, rich desserts that are never heavy nor dense. They melt on the tongue and go down oh so easily. Use your prettiest stemmed dessert glasses or wineglasses for these creations and serve them for special dinner parties. Everyone will love them.

Traditionally, mousses are made with whole eggs, separated and uncooked. We have abandoned this practice because of the growing public concern over the danger of salmonella bacteria in a small percentage of eggs. Instead we depend on two completely safe methods for making mousses. The first relies on the natural binding capabilities of heavy cream and dark chocolate. When combined, these two ingredients produce a lovely thick mixture.

The second method works best with fruit mousses such as raspberry and strawberry, which are thickened by egg whites. The whites are simultaneously whipped and heated to 160°F., a temperature considered safe by the Department of Agriculture and the Egg Nutrition Board. The process is not as difficult as it may sound. Hot sugar syrup is poured into the egg whites during beating. The syrup, which has been heated in the microwave to the soft-ball stage at 240°F. cooks the whites.

The microwave oven is the ideal place to make small amounts of sugar syrup, but the cooking goes quickly, so you must use a microwave-safe candy thermometer for accurate results. This method helps avoid many of the frustrations accompanying cooking syrup on top of the stove where the thermometer is often larger than the small saucepan appropriate for the syrup. This makes it hard and cumbersome to get an accurate reading, and the syrup often overheats, which is a distressing event. But as we have found in so many instances, the microwave oven takes all the fuss and bother out of the simple operation.

We use white chocolate in many of our mousses, partly because it looks so pretty and also because we have found that so many people absolutely love white chocolate mousse. White chocolate does not have the same properties as its dark cousin and so must be fortified with a little gelatin to achieve the smooth, satiny texture appropriate for a mousse.

Mousse Tips

*When using gelatin, soften it for at least 5 minutes in liquid before melting it in the microwave or stirring it into the hot mixture. Gelatin that is inadequately softened will not dissolve completely, and the mousse will not set properly.

*Be careful not to overwhip the cream or, when folding it into the mousse mixture, to overwork it. Either excess can result in grainy mousse.

*Many of our mousse recipes require the use of a microwave-safe candy thermometer. When cooking sugar syrup, be sure to use one; a conventional candy thermometer will not do.

*For a successful sugar syrup, the sugar crystals must dissolve completely before the syrup reaches a boil. To help this process along, cover the measuring cup that holds the syrup with waxed paper. The loose cover holds in moisture that accumulates on the sides of the cup and washes down clinging crystals. For this same reason it is crucial that you stir the syrup with a wooden spoon.

*Sugar syrup cooks quickly in the microwave. Watch it carefully, and if the temperature climbs higher than required by the recipe, add about a tablespoon of water to the syrup. Stir it very gently with a wooden spoon and microwave again to the desired temperature.

*Caramel, easily made in the microwave, must be watched carefully during the last minute of cooking to make sure it does not burn. Burned caramel tastes bitter.

*When making caramel be sure to use a high-sided 1½-quart microwave-safe glass ceramic casserole. Even a microwave-safe glass casserole or measuring cup may crack from the heat of the caramel.

White Chocolate Mousse

serves 6

preparation time: ABOUT 15 MINUTES PLUS 10 TO 20 MINUTES COOLING

microwave time: 1½ TO 3½ MINUTES

Because white chocolate can be tricky, we are especially careful when we use it. If it has been incorrectly stored and has absorbed moisture, if the weather is humid, or if the chocolate has been overheated, it can turn gritty or lumpy when melted. These problems can be solved by straining it through a fine-meshed sieve.

Because of its inherent problems we decided to create a white chocolate mousse that was foolproof and that we (fussy grouches that we are when it comes to the sweet chocolate) really, really like.

3 TABLESPOONS COLD WATER	2 TABLESPOONS DARK RUM,
1½ TEASPOONS UNFLAVORED	BRANDY, COGNAC, GRAND
GELATIN	MARNIER, COINTREAU, OR
10 OUNCES WHITE CHOCOLATE,	CREME DE CACAO
FINELY CHOPPED	4 TEASPOONS VANILLA
½ CUP MILK	EXTRACT
5 TEASPOONS VEGETABLE OIL	SEMISWEET CHOCOLATE SHAVINGS
1⅔ CUPS HEAVY CREAM	FOR GARNISH (OPTIONAL)

1   Put the water in a 6-ounce microwave-safe glass custard cup. Sprinkle the gelatin over the water and let the mixture soften for at least 5 minutes.

2   Put the chocolate in a 1½-quart bowl. Put the milk in a 2-cup microwave-safe measuring cup. Cover with waxed paper and microwave on HIGH (100 percent) power for 1 to 2 minutes, until the milk comes to a boil. Pour the hot milk over the bowl of chocolate. Let the mixture stand without stirring.

3   Cover the custard cup containing the softened gelatin mixture with waxed paper. Microwave on MEDIUM (50 percent) power for 30 seconds to 1½ minutes, stirring after 30 seconds, until the gelatin is completely dissolved and the mixture is hot. Do not boil.

(*CONTINUED*)

---

kitchen note:

Do not use white chocolate chips in this recipe. Bars of white baking chocolate, readily available in supermarkets, produce a creamier, smoother mousse than chips. We used Nestlé for this recipe, but you could use imported white chocolate bars such as one made by Lindt.

The satiny texture also depends on gentle folding. Please use light strokes and do not overfold. And once the mousse is mixed, you may—if time is pressing—freeze it for 45 to 60 minutes rather than chilling it in the refrigerator.

4   Slowly whisk the gelatin mixture into the white chocolate mixture and stir until smooth. Stir in the oil until blended. Let the mixture cool for 10 to 20 minutes, until tepid.

5   Put the cream, liqueur, and vanilla extract in a chilled 3-quart bowl. Using a hand-held electric mixer set at high speed, whip just until soft mounds start to form. Do not overwhip.

6   Using a wire whisk, gently stir one-fourth of the cream into the tepid chocolate mixture just until blended. Using a rubber spatula, scrape this misture back into the larger bowl ofwhipped cream and fold together just until combined, being careful not to overfold.

7   Spoon the mousse into six 7-ounce stemmed dessert glasses. Cover them with plastic wrap and refrigerate for 1 to 2 hours, until set. Sprinkle with chocolate shavings before serving, if desired.

Quick Chocolate Mousse

serves 4

preparation time: ABOUT 15 MINUTES PLUS 1 TO 2 HOURS CHILLING

microwave time: 1½ TO 3 MINUTES

Not only is this really *quick—which is saying something since we make no claims of incredible speed when cooking in the microwave oven—but it tastes* really *good. If you like creamy, chocolaty mousse, this is for you. Serve it to your kids or your dinner guests. Try the variations as the months go by. We doubt you will tire of it. We made the mousse with Nestlé and with Lindt chocolate. The texture was silkier with Lindt but excellent nonetheless with Nestlé.*

7 OUNCES SEMISWEET CHOCOLATE, COARSELY CHOPPED

⅓ CUP MILK

2 TABLESPOONS GRANULATED SUGAR

FEW GRAINS OF SALT

2 TABLESPOONS VEGETABLE OIL

1 TABLESPOON COGNAC, BRANDY, OR DARK RUM

1 TABLESPOON VANILLA EXTRACT

1 CUP HEAVY CREAM

WHIPPED CREAM FOR GARNISH

CHOCOLATE CURLS FOR GARNISH

1   Put the chocolate in a food processor fitted with the metal chopping blade. Process for 20 to 30 seconds, until finely ground.

2   Combine the milk, sugar, and salt in a 2-cup microwave-safe glass measuring cup. Cover the cup with waxed paper and microwave on HIGH (100 percent) power for 1 to 3 minutes, until the mixture comes to a boil. Stir with a wooden spoon until the sugar is completely dissolved.

3   With the food processor running, pour the hot milk mixture through the feed tube. Process for 15 to 30 seconds, until the chocolate is melted and the mixture is smooth. Using a spatula, scrape down the sides of the work bowl. Add the oil, liqueur, and vanilla extract. Process for 10 to 20 seconds, until the mixture is creamy. Scrape the mixture into a 2½-quart bowl and cool for 5 to 10 minutes, until tepid.

4   Put the cream in a chilled 3-quart bowl. Using a hand-held electric mixer set at high speed, whip just until soft mounds start to form. Do not overwhip the cream.

5   Using a wire whisk, gently stir one-fourth of the cream into the chocolate mixture just until blended. Using a rubber spatula, scrape this mixture back into the whipped cream and fold together just until combined. Do not overfold.

6   Spoon the mousse into four 6-ounce stemmed dessert glasses. Cover the glasses with plastic wrap and refrigerate for 1 to 2 hours, or until set. The mousse may be prepared up to two days in advance.

7   Just before serving, garnish with whipped cream and chocolate curls.

variations

Mexican Chocolate Mousse

Put ½ teaspoon of instant coffee granules and a pinch of ground cinnamon in the food processor with the chocolate in step 1. Substitute 2 tablespoons of coffee-flavored liqueur such as Kahlua or Tía Maria for the brandy or rum in step 3. Spoon the mousse into four 6-ounce Irish coffee glasses. Garnish with whipped cream and chocolate coffee beans instead of chocolate curls.

Grand Marnier Chocolate Mousse

Add ¼ teaspoon of finely grated orange zest and substitute 2 tablespoons of orange-flavored liqueur such as Grand Marnier, Cointreau, or Triple Sec for the brandy or rum in step 3. Garnish with whipped cream rosettes and an orange slice.

(CONTINUED)

Chocolate Mint Mousse

Add ⅛ teaspoon of peppermint extract in step 3 when adding the liqueur. Garnish with whipped cream rosettes and fresh mint.

White and Dark Chocolate Mousse Parfait

serves 8

preparation time: ABOUT 30 MINUTES PLUS 20 TO 30 MINUTES COOLING AND 1 TO 2 HOURS CHILLING

microwave time: 2 MINUTES AND 5 SECONDS TO 3½ MINUTES

This is one of the richest desserts contained on these pages. Chocolate lovers will go wild. No eggs are used in the recipe, which should please people watching their egg consumption. Again, Lindt chocolate produced the silkiest-textured mousse, but it works very well with Nestlé, too.

White chocolate mousse:

2 TABLESPOONS COLD WATER

1 TEASPOON UNFLAVORED GELATIN

6 OUNCES WHITE CHOCOLATE, FINELY CHOPPED

¼ CUP MILK

1 TABLESPOON VEGETABLE OIL

1 CUP HEAVY CREAM

1 TABLESPOON VANILLA EXTRACT

Dark chocolate mousse:

7 OUNCES SEMISWEET CHOCO-
   LATE, FINELY CHOPPED
⅓ CUP MILK
2 TABLESPOONS GRANULATED
   SUGAR
FEW GRAINS OF SALT

2 TABLESPOONS VEGETABLE OIL
1 TABLESPOON COGNAC, BRANDY,
   OR DARK RUM
1 TABLESPOON VANILLA EXTRACT
1 CUP HEAVY CREAM
CHOCOLATE CURLS FOR GARNISH

kitchen note:

Please be careful not to overwhip the cream or fold it into the mousse with too many strokes or strokes that are too vigorous. Gentleness is the name of the game.

Both mousses may be prepared at the same time. You can also chill the assembled parfaits by putting them in the freezer for 45 to 60 minutes rather than chilling them in the refrigerator.

1 TO MAKE THE WHITE CHOCOLATE MOUSSE: Put the water in a 6-ounce microwave-safe glass custard cup. Sprinkle the gelatin over the water and let the mixture soften for at least 5 minutes. Put the white chocolate in a 2½-quart bowl.

2 Put the milk in a 1-cup microwave-safe measuring cup. Cover with waxed paper and microwave on HIGH (100 percent) power for 45 seconds to 1½ minutes, until the milk comes to a boil. Pour the hot milk over the bowl of chocolate. Let the mixture stand without stirring.

3 Cover the custard cup containing the softened gelatin mixture with waxed paper. Microwave on MEDIUM (50 percent) power for 20 to 30 seconds, stirring after 20 seconds, until the gelatin is completely dissolved and the mixture is hot. Do not boil.

4 Slowly whisk the gelatin into the white chocolate mixture and stir until smooth. Stir in the oil until blended. Let the mixture cool for 10 to 15 minutes, until tepid.

5 Put the cream and vanilla extract in a chilled 3-quart bowl. Using a hand-held electric mixer set at high speed, whip just until soft mounds start to form. Do not overwhip.

6 Using a wire whisk, gently stir one-fourth of the cream into the tepid chocolate mixture just until blended. Using a rubber spatula, scrape this mixture back into the larger bowl of whipped cream and fold together just until combined. Do not overfold.

7 Cover the bowl containing the mousse and keep it at room temperature while preparing the dark chocolate mousse. If you refrigerate it, the mousse will set too quickly.

8 TO MAKE THE DARK CHOCOLATE MOUSSE: Put the chocolate in a 2½-quart bowl. Combine the milk, sugar, and salt in a 1-cup microwave-safe glass measuring cup. Cover the cup with waxed paper and microwave on MEDIUM (50 percent) power for 1 to 3 minutes, until the mixture comes to a boil. Stir with a wooden spoon until the sugar is completely dissolved.

9   Pour the hot milk mixture over the bowl of chocolate. Let the mixture stand for 30 seconds to melt the chocolate. Gently whisk until smooth. Stir in the oil until blended. Stir in the liquor and vanilla extract. Let the mixture cool for 10 to 15 minutes, until tepid.

10   Put the cream in a chilled 3-quart bowl. Using a hand-held electric mixer set at high speed, whip just until soft mounds start to form. Do not overwhip.

11   Using a wire whisk, gently stir one-fourth of the cream into the tepid chocolate mixture just until blended. Using a rubber spatula, scrape this mixture back into the larger bowl of whipped cream and fold together just until combined. Do not overfold.

12   Starting with half the dark chocolate mousse, spoon equal portions into eight 6-ounce parfait flutes or martini glasses. Cover the dark chocolate mousse with equal amounts of white chocolate mousse, using half the total. Top the white chocolate layer with the remaining dark chocolate mousse. Fill the glasses with the remaining white chocolate mousse. Each glass should contain four alternating layers of dark and white chocolate mousse.

13   Cover the glasses with plastic wrap and refrigerate for 1 to 2 hours, until set. The parfaits may be prepared up to two days in advance.

14   Just before serving, garnish the parfaits with chocolate curls.

Chocolate Mint Semifreddo

serves 6

preparation time: 25 MINUTES PLUS 10 TO 15 MINUTES COOLING AND 4 HOURS FREEZING

microwave time: 8½ TO 18½ MINUTES

The Italians have produced some of the best frozen confections of all time, and borrowing from their concept for a semifreddo, we have developed a luscious, fudgy frozen chocolate mousse. With the microwave it is an easy alternative to chocolate ice cream, and no doubt you will serve this time and again after an Italian meal or anytime you need something dark, delicious, and icy cold.

¾ TEASPOON UNFLAVORED GELATIN

⅓ CUP PLUS 4 TEASPOONS COLD WATER
(EACH MEASUREMENT USED
SEPARATELY)

½ CUP UNSWEETENED
DUTCH-PROCESSED COCOA, SUCH AS
HERSHEY'S EUROPEAN STYLE OR
DROSTE (SPOONED INTO A MEASURING
CUP AND LEVELED WITH THE EDGE OF A
KNIFE)

2 TABLESPOONS LIGHT CORN SYRUP

⅔ CUP PLUS 2 TABLESPOONS
GRANULATED SUGAR (EACH
MEASUREMENT USED SEPARATELY)

PINCH OF SALT

1 CUP HEAVY CREAM

2 OUNCES UNSWEETENED CHOCOLATE,
FINELY CHOPPED

2 LARGE EGG WHITES, AT ROOM
TEMPERATURE

1 TABLESPOON VANILLA EXTRACT

⅛ PEPPERMINT EXTRACT

SATINY CHOCOLATE SAUCE (PAGE 288)
(OPTIONAL)

FRESH MINT FOR GARNISH (OPTIONAL)

1   Sprinkle the gelatin over 4 teaspoons of water in a small custard cup. Let the gelatin soften for at least 5 minutes.

2   Combine the cocoa, corn syrup, 2 tablespoons of sugar, and salt in a 2½-quart microwave-safe bowl. Slowly whisk in the cream until the mixture is smooth. Cover the bowl with waxed paper and microwave on HIGH (100 percent) power for 1½ to 2½ minutes, until the mixture is steaming hot. Whisk until blended.

3   Cover the bowl again and continue to microwave on HIGH (100 percent) power for 2 to 4 minutes, stirring every 60 seconds, until the mixture comes to a rapid boil and is slightly thickened. Whisk in the gelatin mixture, stirring, until it is completely dissolved. Add the chocolate and let the mixture stand for 30 seconds. Stir until the chocolate is completely melted and the mixture is smooth. Set the chocolate mixture aside to cool for 10 to 15 minutes, or until tepid.

4   Combine the remaining ⅔ cup of sugar and the remaining ⅓ cup of water in a 2-cup microwave-safe glass measuring cup. Cover with waxed paper and microwave on HIGH (100 percent) power for 2 to 4 minutes, until the syrup is steaming hot. Stir with a wooden spoon to dissolve any remaining sugar crystals.

5   Cover the cup again and microwave on HIGH (100 percent) power for 30 to 60 seconds, until the syrup comes to a rapid boil.

6   Attach a microwave-safe candy thermometer to the side of the measuring cup, making sure that the bulb is completely submerged. Microwave, uncovered, on HIGH (100 percent) power for 2 to 5 minutes, or until the syrup registers

240°F., soft-ball stage. When the syrup registers 225°F., start preparing the egg whites.

7 Beat the egg whites in a grease-free 2½-quart bowl, using a hand-held electric mixer set at low speed. Gradually increase the speed to high and continue to beat until soft peaks start to form.

8 At this point the sugar syrup should register 240°F. on the candy thermometer. While continuing to beat at medium speed, slowly pour the sugar syrup down the side of the bowl into the beaten egg whites. Increase the speed to high and continue beating for 5 to 8 minutes, until the meringue is tepid and forms soft shiny peaks when the beaters are lifted.

9 Using a wire whisk, stir the vanilla and peppermint extracts into the chocolate mixture. Whisk one-third of the meringue into the chocolate mixture until smooth. Stir in the remaining meringue. Do not worry if the mixture deflates.

10 Scrape down the sides of the bowl and cover the surface of the semifreddo mixture with plastic wrap. Freeze for at least 4 hours or overnight until firm.

11 To serve, put scoops of the semifreddo in dessert glasses. Drizzle with Satiny Chocolate Sauce and garnish with fresh mint, if desired.

Strawberry Mousse

serves 6 or 8

preparation time: ABOUT 30 MINUTES PLUS 1 TO 2 HOURS CHILLING

microwave time: 18½ TO 30½ MINUTES

Both this and the Raspberry Mousse that follows are wonderfully light and refreshing. Their pale pink color is especially pretty, too. You will need a microwave-safe candy thermometer to gauge the temperature of the sugar syrup. If time is a problem, chill the mousse in the freezer, rather than in the refrigerator, for 45 to 60 minutes until set.

½ CUP PLUS 3 TABLESPOONS WATER
   (EACH MEASUREMENT USED
   SEPARATELY)
2½ TEASPOONS UNFLAVORED GELATIN
1 20-OUNCE BAG FROZEN, UNSWEETENED
   WHOLE STRAWBERRIES (ABOUT 4
   CUPS)
¾ CUP PLUS 3 TABLESPOONS SUGAR
   (EACH MEASUREMENT USED
   SEPARATELY)
2 LARGE EGG WHITES, AT ROOM
   TEMPERATURE

2 TABLESPOONS ORANGE-FLAVORED
   LIQUEUR SUCH AS GRAND MARNIER,
   COINTREAU, OR TRIPLE SEC
1 TABLESPOON FRESH LEMON JUICE
1 TABLESPOON VANILLA EXTRACT
1 CUP HEAVY CREAM
WHIPPED CREAM FOR GARNISH
3 TO 4 FRESH STRAWBERRIES, CUT IN
   HALF, FOR GARNISH

1 Put 3 tablespoons of water in a 6-ounce custard cup. Sprinkle the gelatin over the water and let it soften for 5 minutes.

2 Combine the frozen strawberries with 3 tablespoons of sugar in a 2½-quart microwave-safe bowl. Cover the bowl with waxed paper and microwave on HIGH (100 percent) power for 3 minutes. Stir with a wooden spoon to dissolve any remaining sugar crystals.

3 Cover the bowl again and microwave on HIGH (100 percent) power for 4 to 7 minutes, until the mixture comes to a rapid boil and the strawberries are very soft.

4 Press the strawberry mixture through a fine-meshed sieve into a 2-quart microwave-safe measuring cup. Discard the pulp and seeds.

5 Microwave the sieved strawberries, uncovered, for 5 to 10 minutes, until the mixture has reduced to 1 cup. Whisk in the softened gelatin, stirring, until it is completely dissolved. Transfer the mixture to a 3-quart noncorrosive metal bowl and set aside to cool.

6 Combine the remaining ¾ cup of sugar with the remaining ½ cup of water in a 2-cup microwave-safe glass measuring cup. Cover with waxed paper and microwave on HIGH (100 percent) power for 1½ to 2 minutes, until the syrup is steaming hot. Stir with a wooden spoon to dissolve any remaining sugar crystals.

7 Cover the measuring cup again and microwave on HIGH (100 percent) power for 30 to 60 seconds, until the syrup comes to a rapid boil.

8 Attach a microwave-safe candy thermometer to the right side of the measuring cup, making sure that the bulb is submerged in the syrup. Microwave, uncovered, on HIGH (100 percent) power for 4 to 7 minutes, until the syrup registers 240°F., soft-ball stage. When the syrup registers 225°F., start preparing the egg whites.

(CONTINUED)

9   Using a hand-held electric mixer set at low speed, beat the egg whites in a grease-free 2½-quart bowl. Gradually increase the speed to high and continue to beat the whites until soft, shiny peaks start to form when the beaters are lifted.

10   At this point the sugar syrup should register 240°F. While continuing to beat at medium speed, slowly pour the sugar syrup down the side of the bowl into the beaten egg whites. Increase the speed to medium-high and continue beating for 6 to 8 minutes, until the meringue is cool and forms stiff peaks when the beaters are lifted.

11   Using a wire whisk, stir one-third of the meringue into the strawberry mixture until smooth. Gently stir in the remaining meringue just until blended. Stir in the liqueur, lemon juice, and vanilla extract.

12   Put the cream in a chilled 3-quart bowl. Using a hand-held electric mixer set at high speed, whip the cream just until soft mounds start to form. Do not overwhip. Gently whisk one-third of the cream into the strawberry mixture to lighten it. Using a rubber spatula, fold in the remaining whipped cream just until blended.

13   Spoon the mousse into eight 6-ounce ramekins or six 8-ounce stemmed glasses. Cover with plastic wrap and refrigerate for 1 to 2 hours until set. The mousse may be prepared up to two days in advance. Garnish with whipped cream rosettes and fresh strawberry halves.

Raspberry Mousse

serves 6

preparation time: ABOUT 30 MINUTES PLUS 1 TO 2 HOURS CHILLING

microwave time: 12½ TO 19½ MINUTES

D*o not let the soft pink color of this mousse fool you; its flavor is intense. Read the note for Strawberry Mousse (page 72) before beginning.*

2 TEASPOONS UNFLAVORED GELATIN

⅓ CUP PLUS 3 TABLESPOONS WATER
(EACH MEASUREMENT USED
SEPARATELY)

1 12-OUNCE BAG FROZEN,
UNSWEETENED RASPBERRIES (ABOUT
3 CUPS)

⅔ CUP PLUS 3 TABLESPOONS SUGAR
(EACH MEASUREMENT USED
SEPARATELY)

2 LARGE EGG WHITES, AT ROOM
TEMPERATURE

3 TABLESPOONS FRAMBOISE (CLEAR
RASPBERRY BRANDY) OR CHAMBORD
(BLACK-RASPBERRY LIQUEUR)

1 TABLESPOON VANILLA EXTRACT

1¼ CUPS HEAVY CREAM

FRESH RASPBERRIES AND MINT LEAVES
FOR GARNISH

1   Sprinkle the gelatin over 3 tablespoons of water in a 6-ounce custard cup. Let the gelatin soften for 5 minutes.

2   Combine the frozen raspberries with 3 tablespoons of sugar in a 2½-quart microwave-safe glass bowl. Cover the bowl with waxed paper and microwave on HIGH (100 percent) power for 3 minutes. Stir with a wooden spoon to dissolve any remaining sugar crystals.

3   Cover the bowl again and microwave on HIGH (100 percent) power for 4 to 7 minutes, until the mixture comes to a rapid boil.

4   Press the raspberry mixture through a fine-meshed sieve into a 3-quart noncorrosive metal bowl. Discard the seeds. Whisk in the gelatin mixture, stirring, until it is completely dissolved. Set the mixture aside to cool.

5   Combine the remaining ⅔ cup of sugar with the remaining ⅓ cup of water in a 2-cup microwave-safe glass measuring cup. Cover with waxed paper and microwave on HIGH (100 percent) power for 1½ to 2 minutes, until the syrup is steaming hot. Stir with a wooden spoon to dissolve any remaining sugar crystals.

6   Cover the cup again and microwave on HIGH (100 percent) power for 30 to 60 seconds, until the syrup comes to a rapid boil.

7   Attach a microwave-safe candy thermometer to the side of the measuring cup, making sure that the bulb is submerged in the syrup. Microwave, uncovered, on HIGH (100 percent) power for 3 to 6 minutes, until the sugar registers 240°F., soft-ball stage. When the syrup registers 225°F., start preparing the egg whites.

8   Using a hand-held electric mixer set at low speed, beat the egg whites in a grease-free, 2½-quart bowl. Gradually increase the speed to high and continue to beat the whites until soft, shiny peaks start to form when the beaters are lifted.

9   At this point the sugar syrup should register 240°F. While continuing to beat at medium speed, slowly pour the sugar syrup down the side of the bowl into the beaten egg whites. Increase the speed to high and continue beating for 6 to 8 minutes, until the meringue is cool and forms stiff peaks when the beaters are lifted.

10   Using a wire whisk, stir one-third of the meringue into the raspberry mixture until smooth. Gently stir in the remaining meringue just until blended. Stir in the liqueur and vanilla extract.

11   Put the cream in a chilled 3-quart bowl. Using a hand-held electric mixer set at high speed, whip the cream just until soft mounds start to form. Do not overwhip. Gently whisk one-third of the cream into the raspberry mixture to lighten it. Using a rubber spatula, fold in the remaining whipped cream just until blended.

12   Spoon the mousse into six 7-ounce stemmed dessert glasses. Cover with plastic wrap and refrigerate for 1 to 2 hours, or until set. The mousse may be prepared up to two days in advance. Garnish with fresh raspberries and mint leaves.

Raspberry Mousse Hearts with Chocolate Sauce

serves 6

preparation time: ABOUT 15 MINUTES PLUS 2 TO 5 HOURS FREEZING, AND TIME TO MAKE THE RASPBERRY MOUSSE AND SATINY CHOCOLATE SAUCE

*T*hese little hearts are pretty and are fun to make, but you can cut the frozen mousse into other shapes if you do not have a heart cutter. Use a sharp knife to make diamonds, triangles, or squares, or try a round cookie cutter.

Once the mousse is spread on the baking sheet, you can wrap it well in plastic and freeze it for as long as two weeks. Or cut out the hearts and transfer them to a waxed-paper-lined baking sheet, cover them with plastic, and freeze until serving time. Do not simply refrigerate the hearts or they will be too soft to transfer to the plates.

RASPBERRY MOUSSE (PAGE 74)

SATINY CHOCOLATE SAUCE FLAVORED
WITH FRAMBOISE (CLEAR RASPBERRY
BRANDY) OR CHAMBORD
(BLACK-RASPBERRY LIQUEUR) (PAGE 288)

FRESH RASPBERRIES AND MINT LEAVES
   FOR GARNISH

1   Make the Raspberry Mousse according to the recipe's instructions. Freeze it in a 2½-quart bowl for 25 to 45 minutes, or until almost set. Do not overchill the mousse. If you do, it will be difficult to spread.

2   Line a flat baking sheet with waxed paper. Scrape the mousse onto the center of the baking sheet. Using an offset (crooked) metal cake spatula, carefully spread it into a 12-by-8-inch rectangle that is about ¾ inch thick. Cover the mousse with waxed paper and freeze it for 2 to 4 hours, until completely frozen.

3   When the time comes to serve the mousse, make the Satiny Chocolate Sauce and flavor it with the liqueur. Keep it warm.

4   Remove the mousse from the freezer. Peel off the waxed paper and let it sit loosely on top of the mousse. Lay another baking sheet over the waxed-paper–covered mousse and invert it. (The loose sheet of waxed paper will now be on the bottom of the mousse.) Lift off the chilled baking sheet and peel off and discard the top piece of waxed paper.

5   Fill a shallow bowl with scalding water. Heat a 4¼-inch heart-shaped cookie cutter by dipping it in the hot water. Dry the cutter and use it to cut out a heart-shaped mousse. Repeat the dipping, drying, and cutting process five more times to make a total of 6 hearts.

6   Spoon some warm chocolate sauce into a paper cone with a ¹⁄₁₆-inch opening or into a pastry bag fitted with a small writing tip (such as Ateco #2). With quick back-and-forth motions, pipe thin lines of chocolate diagonally over the top of each mousse heart.

7   Using a metal pancake spatula, transfer each heart to the center of a dinner-size plate. Arrange 2 small mint leaves and a fresh raspberry on the upper left-hand side of each heart. Spoon some of the chocolate sauce around the base of each heart and serve immediately.

White Chocolate Raspberry Swirl Mousse

serves 4

preparation time: ABOUT 20 MINUTES PLUS 15 TO 20 MINUTES COOLING AND 1 TO 2 HOURS CHILLING, AND TIME TO MAKE THE MELBA SAUCE

microwave time: 2½ TO 4½ MINUTES

*S*pooned into stemmed dessert or wineglasses, the white mousse and the rich raspberry sauce combine to make a pleasing, tantalizingly pretty dessert. The Melba Sauce cuts the sweetness of the white chocolate nicely. Be careful not to overwhip the cream or overfold the mousse; either could make the mousse grainy.

2 TABLESPOONS ORANGE-FLAVORED LIQUEUR SUCH AS GRAND MARNIER, COINTREAU, OR TRIPLE SEC

½ TEASPOON UNFLAVORED GELATIN

6 OUNCES WHITE CHOCOLATE, COARSELY CHOPPED

⅓ CUP MILK

1 TABLESPOON VEGETABLE OIL

¼ TEASPOON FINELY GRATED ORANGE ZEST

1 CUP HEAVY CREAM

2 TEASPOONS VANILLA EXTRACT

MELBA SAUCE (PAGE 282), CHILLED

FRESH RASPBERRIES AND MINT LEAVES FOR GARNISH

1   Put the liqueur in a 6-ounce microwave-safe custard cup. Sprinkle the gelatin over the liqueur and let the mixture soften for at least 5 minutes.

2   Combine the white chocolate and milk in a 1½-quart microwave-safe glass bowl. Cover with waxed paper and microwave on MEDIUM (50 percent) power for 2 to 3 minutes, or until the milk is steaming hot. Do not let the milk boil. Whisk until smooth.

3   Cover the custard cup containing the softened gelatin mixture with waxed paper. Microwave on MEDIUM (50 percent) power for 30 seconds to 1½ minutes, stirring after 30 seconds, until the gelatin is completely dissolved and the mixture is hot. Do not allow the mixture to boil.

4   Slowly whisk the dissolved gelatin mixture into the white chocolate mixture and stir until smooth. Stir in the oil and orange zest until blended. Let the mixture cool for 15 to 20 minutes, until tepid.

5   Put the cream and vanilla extract in a chilled 3-quart bowl. Using a hand-held electric mixer set at medium speed, whip the cream just until soft mounds start to form. Do not overwhip.

6   Using a wire whisk, gently stir one-fourth of the cream into the tepid chocolate mixture just until blended. Using a rubber spatula, scrape this mixture into the bowl of whipped cream and gently fold just until combined. Do not overfold.

7   Spoon 2½ tablespoons of the chilled melba sauce into the bottom of four 7-ounce stemmed glasses. Half-fill the glasses with mousse. Spoon the remaining melba sauce over the mousse and top with the remaining mousse. Cover the glasses with plastic wrap and refrigerate for 1 to 2 hours, or until set. Garnish with fresh raspberries and mint leaves.

variation

White Chocolate Strawberry Swirl Mousse

Follow the instructions for making and assembling the dessert, using 2½ tablespoons of Strawberry Sauce (page 281) for each sauce layer. You will have some sauce left over.

White Chocolate Lemon Mousse Icebox Cake with Strawberry Coulis

serves 10

preparation time: ABOUT 45 MINUTES PLUS 10 MINUTES STANDING, 10 TO 20 MINUTES COOLING, 1 HOUR CHILLING, AND 6½ TO 7 HOURS FREEZING

microwave time: 1 MINUTE 20 SECONDS TO 3 MINUTES

You may remember an icebox cake made with chocolate wafers and sweetened whipped cream. It was so popular in her childhood home that Mary's brothers requested it for Christmas Eve dessert long after they had entered adulthood, and Adrienne's husband David still has a special fondness for it. We have updated the concept here, using a rich, creamy white chocolate mousse delicately flavored with fresh lemon zest in place of whipped cream. And although we call it an icebox cake for old times' sake, its preparation calls for freezing. Serve the dessert with a simple strawberry coulis or, if you prefer, substitute Melba Sauce (page 282).

To make this for children, substitute orange juice or water for the liqueur. You can also omit the orange zest, but do not take any other shortcuts such as trying to use white chocolate chips rather than bar white chocolate.

White chocolate lemon mousse cake:

3 TABLESPOONS WATER

1¾ TEASPOONS UNFLAVORED GELATIN

10 OUNCES WHITE CHOCOLATE, FINELY CHOPPED

½ CUP MILK

6 2-BY-3¼ STRIPS OF LEMON ZEST

1 TABLESPOON VEGETABLE OIL

1¾ TEASPOON FINELY GRATED LEMON ZEST

1¾ CUPS HEAVY CREAM

1 TABLESPOON VANILLA EXTRACT

27 NABISCO CHOCOLATE WAFERS

Strawberry coulis:

4 CUPS HULLED MEDIUM STRAWBERRIES

1 CUP CONFECTIONERS' SUGAR (SPOONED INTO A MEASURING CUP AND LEVELED WITH THE EDGE OF A KNIFE)

1   TO MAKE THE WHITE CHOCOLATE LEMON MOUSSE CAKE: Put the water in a 6-ounce microwave-safe custard cup. Sprinkle the gelatin over the water and let the mixture soften for at least 5 minutes. Put the chocolate in a 1½-quart bowl and set aside.

2   Put the milk and strips of lemon zest in a 2-cup microwave-safe measuring cup. Cover with waxed paper and microwave on HIGH (100 percent) power for 1 to 2 minutes, until steaming hot. Let the mixture stand for 10 minutes.

3   Reheat the milk mixture on HIGH (100 percent) power for 1 to 2 minutes until it comes to a boil. Strain the hot mixture over the chocolate and let it stand without stirring. Discard the strips of lemon zest.

4   Cover the custard cup containing the gelatin mixture with waxed paper. Microwave on MEDIUM (50 percent) power for 15 to 45 seconds, stirring every 15 seconds, until the gelatin is completely dissolved and the mixture is hot. Do not boil.

5   Pour the hot gelatin over the chocolate-milk mixture and whisk until smooth. Stir in the oil and grated lemon zest. Let the mixture cool for 10 to 20 minutes, until tepid.

6   Put the cream and vanilla extract in a chilled 3-quart bowl. Using a hand-held electric mixer set at high speed, whip the cream just until soft mounds start to form. Do not overwhip.

7   Using a wire whisk, gently stir one-fourth of the cream into the tepid chocolate mixture until just blended. Using a rubber spatula, scrape this mixture into the larger bowl of whipped cream and fold just to combine. Do not overfold.

8   Cover the surface of the mousse with plastic wrap and freeze for 30 to 60 minutes, until the mousse starts to set. Do not let the mousse set completely.

9   Line the inside of an 8½-by-4½-by-2-inch glass loaf pan with a double thickness of plastic wrap so that the plastic extends 6 inches beyond both short ends of the pan.

10   Spoon 1¼ cups of the partially set mousse into the bottom of the prepared loaf pan and spread it evenly with a spatula.

11   Take a chocolate wafer and spread it with a heaping tablespoon of mousse. Starting at one end of the loaf pan, stand the wafer upright in the layer of spread mousse, with the coated side pressing gently against the long side of the pan. Take a second wafer, spread it with the same amount of mousse, and position it so that it forms a sandwich with the first wafer, with the tablespoon of mousse between the wafers. Repeat this procedure with 7 more mousse-spread wafers so that a total of 9 wafers form a row filling the width of the pan. Fill the gap between the last chocolate wafer and the side of the loaf pan with mousse.

12   Create 2 more rows of sandwiched wafers in the same manner. They should easily cover the length of the loaf pan.

13   Using a metal cake spatula, cover the sandwiched wafers with the remaining mousse, filling in any gaps between the wafers and the sides of the pan.

14   Fold the overhanging ends of plastic over the top of the mousse. The plastic should cover it completely. Freeze the cake for at least 6 hours or overnight, until firm. If desired, the cake may be kept frozen for up to two weeks before unmolding.

15   To MAKE THE STRAWBERRY COULIS: Combine the strawberries and the confectioner's sugar in a food processor fitted with the metal chopping blade. Process for 30 to 45 seconds to a smooth puree. Scrape the coulis into a bowl, cover, and refrigerate.

16   To ASSEMBLE: Fold back the plastic wrap covering the top of the frozen cake. Put a cutting board on top of the loaf pan and invert the pan onto the board. Gently pull down on the ends of the plastic wrap until the cake releases from the pan and onto the board. Remove the loaf pan.

17 Using a large, sharp knife, cut the cake into 10 pieces. Lay the slices on dessert plates and allow them to soften at room temperature for about 10 minutes. Spoon some of the strawberry coulis around each slice and serve. If desired, the cake can be sliced, put onto plates, and kept refrigerated for up to 1 hour; it will soften nicely in the refrigerator. Spoon the sauce around the slices just before serving.

White Chocolate Orange Mousse Quenelles with Fresh Fruit Medley

serves 6

preparation time: ABOUT 30 MINUTES PLUS 10 TO 20 MINUTES COOLING AND 2 TO 3 HOURS CHILLING, AND TIME TO MAKE THE FRESH FRUIT MEDLEY

microwave time: 1 MINUTE 20 SECONDS TO 3 MINUTES

*O*val-shaped quenelles look elegant, especially when surrounded, as these are, with a colorful fruit medley. Since the quenelles can be formed an hour before serving, this light, refreshing dessert is a perfect make-ahead choice for your next dinner party. The secret to success is gentle mixing and folding, which keeps it light and easy to manipulate. If you have never formed quenelles before, it may take a little practice, but it is a simple operation.

3 TABLESPOONS ORANGE-FLAVORED LIQUEUR SUCH AS GRAND MARNIER, COINTREAU, OR TRIPLE SEC
1 TABLESPOON COLD WATER
2 TEASPOONS UNFLAVORED GELATIN
10 OUNCES WHITE CHOCOLATE, COARSELY CHOPPED
½ CUP MILK
1 TABLESPOON VEGETABLE OIL
¾ TEASPOON FINELY GRATED ORANGE ZEST

1½ CUPS HEAVY CREAM
⅓ CUP SOUR CREAM (SPOONED INTO A MEASURING CUP AND LEVELED WITH THE EDGE OF A KNIFE)
4 TEASPOONS VANILLA EXTRACT
THIN STRIPS OF ORANGE ZEST FOR GARNISH (OPTIONAL)
FRESH FRUIT MEDLEY (PAGE 293), CHILLED

1   Put the liqueur and water in a 6-ounce microwave-safe glass custard cup. Sprinkle the gelatin over the mixture and let it soften for at least 5 minutes. Put the chocolate in a 1½-quart bowl.

2   Put the milk in a 2-cup microwave-safe measuring cup. Cover with waxed paper and microwave on HIGH (100 percent) power for 1 to 2 minutes, until the milk comes to a boil. Pour the hot milk over the bowl of chocolate. Let the mixture stand.

3   Cover the cup of softened gelatin with waxed paper. Microwave on MEDIUM (50 percent) power for 15 to 45 seconds, stirring every 15 seconds, until the gelatin is completely dissolved and the mixture is hot. Do not boil.

4   Pour the hot gelatin mixture over the chocolate-milk mixture and whisk until smooth. Stir in the oil and orange zest. Let the mixture cool for 10 to 20 minutes, or until tepid.

5   Combine the cream, sour cream, and vanilla extract in a chilled 3-quart bowl. Using a hand-held electric mixer at high speed, whip just until soft mounds start to form. Do not overwhip.

6   Using a wire whisk, gently stir one-fourth of the cream into the tepid chocolate mixture just until blended. Using a rubber spatula, scrape this mixture into the larger bowl of whipped cream. Fold together just to combine. Do not overfold.

7   Cover the surface of the mousse with plastic wrap and refrigerate for 2 to 3 hours, or until set. The mousse may be prepared up to two days in advance. If you are short of time, the mousse may be frozen for 1 to 2 hours, until firm enough to form the quenelles.

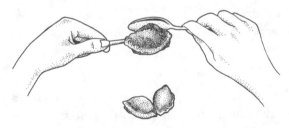

8   Dip two soupspoons in warm water. Scoop a generous spoonful of mousse into one spoon. Form into an oval quenelle by transferring the mousse back and forth between the two spoons several times, scraping the bowl of the spoon over and under the mousse to smooth and shape it. Place each quenelle on a large dessert plate. Dip the spoons in warm water again before forming the next quenelle. Put three quenelles on each plate, forming a star pattern. The quenelles may be shaped ahead of time, put on dessert plates, and refrigerated.

9   Just before serving, spoon some of the fruit medley around the quenelles. If desired, garnish with thin strips of orange zest.

Hazelnut Praline Chocolate Mousse

serves 6

preparation time: ABOUT 30 MINUTES PLUS 15 MINUTES COOLING AND 1 TO 2 HOURS CHILLING

microwave time: 10 MINUTES 15 SECONDS TO 19 MINUTES

*A*drienne's father, an art historian who travels extensively, is keen on the combination of chocolate and roasted hazelnuts, or noisettes, as he calls hazelnuts. She remembers the hazelnut and bittersweet chocolate bars he brought her from Europe when she was a child—special treats that nurtured her own fondness for the flavor combination ("I even prefer it to raspberries and chocolate," she says). Since she began cooking professionally, she has been devising hazelnut and chocolate desserts for her father, particularly at Christmas time. This satiny, indulgent mousse is excellent on the holiday table (or any other, for that matter).

⅓ CUP PLUS 1 TABLESPOON HAZELNUTS

⅓ CUP PLUS 1 TABLESPOON GRANULATED SUGAR (EACH MEASUREMENT USED SEPARATELY)

2 TABLESPOONS WATER

¼ TEASPOON LEMON JUICE

8 OUNCES SEMISWEET CHOCOLATE, COARSELY CHOPPED

⅓ CUP MILK

FEW GRAINS OF SALT

1 TABLESPOON VEGETABLE OIL

1 TABLESPOON COGNAC, BRANDY, OR DARK RUM

1 TABLESPOON VANILLA EXTRACT

1½ CUPS HEAVY CREAM

WHIPPED CREAM FOR GARNISH (OPTIONAL)

1   Spread the hazelnuts in a single layer in a 9-inch microwave-safe glass pie plate and microwave, uncovered, on HIGH (100 percent) power for 2 minutes. Stir the nuts.

2   Continue to microwave on HIGH (100 percent) power for 4 to 7 minutes, stirring every 60 seconds, until the skins crack and the hazelnuts are lightly browned. Test for doneness by cutting a couple of nuts in half; they should be lightly browned on the inside. Do not let the nuts become dark brown on the inside or lightly browned on the outside. Wrap the hot nuts in a clean kitchen towel and cool completely. Transfer the nuts to a large sieve and with your fingers rub them back and forth over the screening to remove the loose skins. Coarsely chop the nuts. Set aside 1 tablespoon of the chopped hazelnuts to decorate the mousse. You will use the remaining ⅓ cup of hazelnuts to make the praline.

3   Lightly oil the bottom of a 9-inch metal cake pan. Set aside.

4   Combine the sugar, water, and lemon juice in a high-sided 1½-quart microwave-safe glass ceramic casserole. Cover with waxed paper and microwave on HIGH (100 percent) power for 1 to 2 minutes, until steaming hot. Stir with a wooden spoon so that the sugar is almost completely dissolved. Cover the casserole again and continue to microwave on HIGH (100 percent) power for 45 seconds to 1½ minutes, until the syrup is boiling rapidly.

5   Remove the waxed paper and continue to microwave on HIGH (100 percent) power for 1 to 3 minutes, without stirring, until the syrup becomes dark amber. Watch the syrup closely: When it starts to change color, swirl the casserole a couple of times during the cooking process so that the caramel browns evenly. Do not let the caramel become too dark or burn.

6   Using a clean wooden spoon, immediately stir in the reserved ⅓ cup of chopped hazelnuts until blended. Quickly scrape the praline into the oiled cake pan and spread it over the bottom of the pan. Put the cake pan on a wire rack and let the praline cool for 15 minutes, until hardened. Chop the praline coarsely with a large, sharp knife.

> **kitchen note:**
>
> *Be sure to use a microwave-safe glass ceramic casserole to make the caramel. A glass casserole might crack. Watch the caramel carefully during the last stages of cooking to be sure it does not burn, which would make the hazelnut praline bitter. Remember to use pot holders and tip the casserole with the hot caramel away from you when swirling it.*

7   Put the chopped praline in a food processor fitted with the metal chopping blade. Process for 45 to 60 seconds, until finely ground. Continue to process for 5 to 6 minutes, until ground to a creamy paste. Scrape the praline paste into a 2-cup microwave-safe glass measuring cup and set aside.

8   Put the chocolate in the food processor (it is not necessary to clean the bowl first). Process for 20 to 30 seconds, until finely ground.

9   Add the milk and salt to the measuring cup containing the hazelnut praline paste. Cover with waxed paper and microwave on HIGH (100 percent) power for 1 to 2 minutes. Stir with a wooden spoon until the praline is almost completely dissolved. Cover the cup again and microwave on HIGH (100 percent) power for 30 seconds to 1½ minutes more, until the mixture comes to a rapid boil.

10   With the food processor running, pour the hot praline–milk mixture through the feed tube. Process for 15 to 30 seconds, until the chocolate is melted and the mixture is smooth. Using a rubber spatula, scrape down the sides of the work bowl. Add the oil, liqueur, and vanilla extract, and process for

10 to 20 seconds, until the mixture is creamy. Scrape the mixture into a 2½-quart bowl.

11   Put the cream and remaining tablespoon of sugar in a chilled 3-quart bowl. Using a hand-held electric mixer set at high speed, whip just until soft mounds start to form. Do not overwhip the cream.

12   Using a rubber spatula, gently fold one-fourth of the cream into the chocolate mixture just until blended. Using a rubber spatula, scrape this mixture back into the larger bowl of whipped cream and fold just until combined. Do not overfold.

13   Spoon the mousse into six 6-ounce stemmed dessert glasses. Cover the glasses with plastic wrap and refrigerate for 1 to 2 hours, until set. The mousse may be prepared up to two days in advance.

14   Just before serving, garnish each glass with whipped cream, if desired, and a sprinkling of chopped hazelnuts.

CHAPTER FOUR

Cakes and Cupcakes

Vanilla Cupcakes
Chocolate Cupcakes
Cream-Filled Chocolate Cupcakes
Black and White Cupcakes
Double-Fudge Brownie Cupcakes
Carrot Pineapple Cupcakes
Applesauce Spice Cupcakes
Walnut Brownie Cake
French Apple Cake
Georgia Peach Cake
Triple Chocolate Sour Cream Cake
Upside-Down Summer Berry Shortcakes
Pumpkin Gingerbread with Lemon Cream
Pumpkin Spice Cake with Rum Cream Frosting
Strawberry Bavarian Cake
Chocolate Raspberry Charlotte

It is only natural to turn to cake recipes when leafing through a dessert cook-book. After all, to many of us, cakes are the ultimate dessert. We make them for birthdays and graduations, to celebrate anniversaries and christenings, and to end special dinner parties. Brides pay nearly as much attention to their wedding cake as to their gown.

Although this chapter may not include cakes fit for a formal wedding, there are a few you could proudly serve at a small informal affair. There is a wide selection of whimsical cupcakes; upside-down fruit-topped cakes; dark, sweet gingerbread and pumpkin spice cake; and a rich chocolate sour cream cake. We also include our "flagship" cake, a luscious chocolate walnut cake that can be eaten out of hand like a brownie or frosted and decorated for the most elegant occasion.

In the microwave, cakes do not form a nice brown crust as they do in the conventional oven. This makes them look unfinished. We have compensated by studding them with nuts and berries, topping them with sliced fruit, chopped nuts, or crumbs, or using ingredients such as whole wheat flour, chocolate, cocoa powder, sweet spices, brown sugar, molasses and pumpkin puree to deepen their color. Frosting a cake solves the crust problem, too.

To ensure good results, we always elevate the cake pan on an inverted pie plate. This gives the microwaves a chance to enter the bottom of the cake at the same rate they enter the sides and top, promoting even baking. Standing time is important, too, to give the bottom of the cake time to finish cooking and the entire cake the opportunity to cool a little before it is unmolded from the pan.

Our cakes measure up to more traditional recipes in every way. They taste wonderful and look pretty—we would not have included them if they did not. And now you have no excuse for not making a cake. Too hot to bake? The microwave does not heat up the kitchen. The chicken is roasting in the oven? Use the microwave. These are quick to bake and assemble and a joy to eat. Let's eat cake.

CAKES and CUPCAKES   **89**

Cupcake Tips

*We begin the chapter with cupcakes because the microwave handles small amounts of batter so well.

*Cupcake batter needs to stand for several minutes for the same reason muffin batter does: to give the leaveners time to begin working, since the actual cooking time is so short. Do not let the batter stand for any longer than specified before baking, otherwise the cupcakes may overflow the cups during baking or lose their lightness.

*Line the cupcake pans with two paper baking cups. The inside liner is to hold the cupcake batter; the outside liner absorbs moisture that forms between the cooking cupcake and the pan.

*Be sure to spoon an equal amount of batter into each cup to ensure that the cupcakes bake evenly. Test each cupcake for doneness after the minimum suggested baking time. Remove any that test done. Continue microwaving the remaining cupcakes, testing after 10-second intervals. Cupcakes that are over-cooked in the microwave will be tough and dry. Visual tests for doneness are as important as they are in conventional baking.

*After baking, immediately remove the outside liners and set the cupcakes, still in the inside liners, on wire racks to cool. Cupcakes left in both liners will absorb excess moisture, which causes them to dry out and harden.

*Wipe the moisture from the cupcake pans with a kitchen or paper towel before baking the second batch of cupcakes.

*Cupcakes baked in the microwave oven do not form a crust, as they do in a conventional oven. This means the cupcakes expand to their full volume and are especially light and moist. It also means that without the protective crust, they can dry out quickly after baking. As soon as they cool, frost the cupcakes or store them in an airtight container.

Vanilla Cupcakes

makes 14 cupcakes

preparation time: ABOUT 15 MINUTES PLUS 5 MINUTES STANDING

microwave time: 3½ TO 8 MINUTES

*P*lain *vanilla cupcakes can be frosted with such an assortment of icings, they surely are one of the most versatile of small, hand-held confections. Check out step 7 of the recipe to see all the frosting ideas. Try these for a child's birthday, an afternoon tea, a picnic, or Sunday night dessert. And be sure to try the variations at the end of the recipe.*

1 CUP PLUS 2 TABLESPOONS SIFTED ALL-PURPOSE FLOUR	6 TABLESPOONS UNSALTED BUTTER
1¼ TEASPOONS DOUBLE-ACTING BAKING POWDER	½ CUP GRANULATED SUGAR
⅛ TEASPOON SALT	2 TEASPOONS VANILLA EXTRACT
	1 LARGE EGG, AT ROOM TEMPERATURE
	½ CUP MILK, AT ROOM TEMPERATURE

1   Put the flour, baking powder, and salt in a 1-quart bowl. Use a wire whisk to complete 12 to 15 strokes to ensure that the ingredients are thoroughly blended.

2   Put the butter in a 2½-quart microwave-safe bowl. Cover with waxed paper and microwave on HIGH (100 percent) power for 20 to 45 seconds, until the butter is slightly softened. Do not let the butter melt or become oily.

3   Using a hand-held electric mixer set at high speed, beat the butter for 30 seconds, until creamy. Add the sugar and continue to beat 1 to 2 minutes more, scraping down the sides of the bowl often until the mixture is nearly white and its texture is light. Beat in the vanilla extract.

4   Add the egg and beat until smooth. At low speed beat in the flour mixture, a third at a time, alternating with the milk. Beat briefly, just until each addition is incorporated into the batter. Scrape down the sides of the bowl with a rubber spatula and beat the batter a few seconds more. Let the batter stand for 5 minutes.

kitchen note:

These small cakes are meant to be moist and delicate. Take care not to overcook them, or they may turn out dry and tough. Do your best to spoon the same amount of batter into each cup so that the cupcakes bake at the same rate.

5   Line each cup of a 6-cup microwave-safe cupcake or muffin pan with 2 paper baking cups. Fill the cups no more than half full of batter. Microwave on HIGH (100 percent) power for 1½ to 3 minutes, rotating the pan, if you do not have a turntable, a half turn after 1 minute. Test for doneness after 1½ minutes by inserting a wooden toothpick in the center of each cupcake; it should come out clean. Any small wet patches on the surface of the cupcakes will dry while standing. If not done, check the cupcakes at 10-second intervals.

6   Immediately remove the outside paper baking cup from each cupcake and set the cupcakes, still in the inner baking cups, on a wire rack to cool and cover them with a clean kitchen towel. Repeat the baking and cooling procedure with the remaining batter. Cook the last 2 cupcakes for 20 seconds to 1½ minutes, testing for doneness after 20 seconds.

7   When the cupcakes are completely cool, frost them with one of the following: Fudgy Chocolate Frosting (page 297), Vanilla Buttercream Frosting (page 300), Chocolate Buttercream Frosting (page 302), Lemon Buttercream Frosting (page 301), Orange Buttercream Frosting (page 301), Chocolate Raspberry Frosting (page 299), or White Chocolate Sour Cream Frosting (page 296). Store the cupcakes in an airtight container in the refrigerator for up to two days.

variations

Lemon Cupcakes

Add 1 teaspoon of finely grated lemon zest in step 4.

Orange Cupcakes

Add ¾ teaspoon of finely grated orange zest in step 4.

Chocolate Cupcakes

makes 12 cupcakes

preparation time: ABOUT 15 MINUTES PLUS 5 MINUTES STANDING

microwave time: 3½ TO 5 MINUTES PLUS 5 MINUTES STANDING

*M*ary *made these early one morning for her daughter Laura to take to day camp for her seventh birthday party. Talk about waiting until the last minute! Not only was she able to mix and bake them while packing a lunch box, finding a dry bathing suit, and serving breakfast, but the cupcakes were a big hit with the campers. Be careful when measuring the dry ingredients—too much leavener will cause the cupcakes to overflow the pan.*

¾ CUP SIFTED ALL-PURPOSE FLOUR

⅔ CUP GRANULATED SUGAR

⅓ CUP PLUS 1 TABLESPOON SIFTED UNSWEETENED ALKALIZED COCOA POWDER, SUCH AS HERSHEY'S EUROPEAN STYLE OR DROSTE

⅛ TEASPOON DOUBLE-ACTING BAKING POWDER

⅛ TEASPOON BAKING SODA

⅛ TEASPOON SALT

½ CUP PLUS 1 TABLESPOON BUTTERMILK, AT ROOM TEMPERATURE

½ CUP VEGETABLE OIL

1 LARGE EGG, AT ROOM TEMPERATURE

1 TABLESPOON VANILLA EXTRACT

1   Put the flour, sugar, cocoa, baking powder, baking soda, and salt in a 2½-quart bowl. Use a wire whisk and complete 12 to 15 strokes to ensure that the ingredients are thoroughly blended.

2   Combine the buttermilk, oil, egg, and vanilla extract in a 2-cup measuring cup and mix with a fork for 20 to 30 seconds, until thoroughly blended.

3   Make a well in the center of the dry ingredients. Pour the buttermilk mixture into the well and whisk just until smooth. Let the batter stand for 5 minutes.

4   Line each cup of a 6-cup microwave-safe cupcake or muffin pan with two paper baking cups. Fill the cups no more than half full of batter. Microwave on HIGH (100 percent) power for 1¾ to 2½ minutes, rotating the pan, if you do not have a

kitchen note:

Use unsweetened alkalized cocoa (also referred to as Dutch processed or European style). In a pinch you can use nonalkalized cocoa, but the flavor will not be quite as good and the color not as dark.

turntable, a half turn after 1 minute. Test for doneness after 1¾ minutes by inserting a wooden toothpick in the center of each cupcake; it should come out clean. Any small wet patches on the tops of the cupcakes will dry while standing. If not done, check the cupcakes at 10-second intervals.

5 Immediately remove the outside paper baking cup from each cupcake and set the cupcakes, still in the inner baking cups, on a wire rack to cool and cover them with a clean kitchen towel to keep them from drying out. Repeat the baking and cooling procedure with the remaining batter.

6 When the cupcakes are completely cool, dust them with confectioner's sugar or frost them with Fudgy Chocolate Frosting (page 297), Vanilla Buttercream Frosting (page 300), Chocolate Buttercream Frosting (page 302), White Chocolate Sour Cream Frosting (page 296), or Chocolate Raspberry Frosting (page 299). Or glaze them with Shiny Chocolate Glaze (page 295). Store the cupcakes in an airtight container in the refrigerator for up to four days.

Cream-Filled Chocolate Cupcakes

makes 12 cupcakes

preparation time: ABOUT 20 MINUTES PLUS 5 TO 10 MINUTES CHILLING AND TIME TO MAKE THE CUPCAKES AND GLAZE

microwave time: 1½ TO 2½ MINUTES

To make this variation on the Chocolate Cupcakes recipe, use a pastry bag to fill each cupcake with sweetened cream. It's easy, but be sure to squeeze enough cream into the cupcakes. Too much will cause them to crack, but too little will barely be noticeable when you bite into them. And that is no fun.

CHOCOLATE CUPCAKES (PAGE 93)
⅔ CUP HEAVY CREAM
2 TEASPOONS GRANULATED SUGAR

¾ TEASPOON VANILLA EXTRACT
SHINY CHOCOLATE GLAZE (PAGE 295)

Decoration:

2 TABLESPOONS WHITE CHOCOLATE
CHIPS

¾ TEASPOON VEGETABLE OIL

1 Make the chocolate cupcakes according to the recipe instructions. Let them cool completely. Chill a 3-quart bowl to use when mixing the cream filling.

2 Using a hand-held electric mixer set at high speed, beat the cream, sugar, and vanilla extract in the chilled bowl until stiff peaks start to form.

3 Fill a pastry bag fitted with a ¼-inch plain tip (such as an Ateco #1) with the cream filling. Using a small, sharp knife, make a small hole in the bottom of each cupcake through the paper baking cup. Insert the pastry bag tip about a ¼ inch into a cupcake through the hole and gently squeeze some filling into the cupcake. Continue filling the cupcake until the cake starts to swell, but stop piping before the top of the cupcake begins to crack. Fill all the cupcakes in the same way.

> ### kitchen note:
>
> *In step 4 we instruct you to dip the tops of the cupcakes into the warm glaze. You may find it easier to use a flat metal spatula to spread a thin coating of glaze on them.*

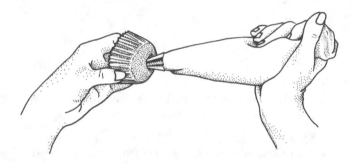

4 Prepare the shiny chocolate glaze according to the recipe instructions. Do not let the glaze cool, but while it is still warm, dip the top of each cupcake in the glaze to coat it. Gently shake the cupcake over the bowl to let any excess glaze drip back into it. Put the glazed cupcakes on a baking sheet covered with waxed paper and refrigerate them for 10 minutes to allow the glaze to set.

5 To DECORATE THE CUPCAKES: Put the white chocolate chips in a 6-ounce microwave-safe custard cup. Microwave on MEDIUM (50 percent) power for 1½ to 2½ minutes, until the chocolate looks shiny. Stir in the oil until blended.

6 Dip the tines of a kitchen fork in the white chocolate and drizzle it in a decorative zigzag pattern over the tops of the cupcakes. Refrigerate the cupcakes for another 5 to 10 minutes to allow the white chocolate to set. Store the cupcakes in an airtight container in the refrigerator for up to two days.

Black and White Cupcakes

makes 12 cupcakes

preparation time: ABOUT 15 MINUTES PLUS 5 MINUTES CHILLING AND TIME TO MAKE THE
CUPCAKES AND FROSTING

microwave time: 2½ TO 3½ MINUTES

Here's a recipe where we combine two existing ones to come up with a third recipe that is special and festive. We decorate the cupcakes with a free-flowing design that allows for great flexibility—and it's easy. Have a good time with it.

WHITE CHOCOLATE SOUR CREAM
FROSTING (PAGE 296), CHILLED BUT NOT
BEATEN UNTIL TIME TO FROST THE
CUPCAKES

CHOCOLATE CUPCAKES (PAGE 93),
COOLED COMPLETELY
1 OUNCE SEMISWEET CHOCOLATE

> **kitchen note:**
>
> *Using an unpleated sealable plastic bag to melt the chocolate in, and then to pipe it, makes the decorating easy, quick, and efficient.*

1   Prepare the frosting and the cupcakes according to their instructions.
2   Whip the frosting and ice the tops of the cupcakes. Put the cupcakes on a baking sheet lined with waxed paper and refrigerate.
3   Put the square chocolate in a bottom corner of a small, unpleated sealable plastic bag. Microwave on MEDIUM (50 percent) power for 1½ to 3 minutes, until the chocolate is melted.
4   Squeeze the melted chocolate so that it gathers in one corner of the bag. Using scissors, cut a tiny hole that is no larger than 1/16 inch at the corner of the bag containing the melted chocolate. Quickly pipe thin, delicate lines of melted chocolate over the top of each cupcake. Refrigerate the cupcakes for 5 minutes to set the chocolate. The cupcakes may be stored in an airtight container in the refrigerator for up to four days.

Double-Fudge Brownie Cupcakes

makes 12 cupcakes

preparation time: ABOUT 15 MINUTES PLUS 5 MINUTES STANDING TIME

microwave time: 3¾ TO 6 MINUTES

Sometimes you simply have to have a moist, fudgy something! When the craving hits—midnight, 10 A.M., after supper—make these brownies, let them cool, and frost them with Fudgy Chocolate Frosting.

6 TABLESPOONS UNSALTED BUTTER

2 OUNCES UNSWEETENED CHOCOLATE

¾ CUP GRANULATED SUGAR

¼ TEASPOON SALT

⅛ TEASPOON BAKING SODA

2 TABLESPOONS COLD WATER

2 TEASPOONS VANILLA EXTRACT

2 LARGE EGGS, CHILLED

¼ CUP SIFTED UNSWEETENED ALKALIZED COCOA POWDER SUCH AS HERSHEY'S EUROPEAN STYLE OR DROSTE

¼ CUP SIFTED ALL-PURPOSE FLOUR

⅔ CUP SEMISWEET MINI CHOCOLATE CHIPS

⅓ CUP PLUS 3 TABLESPOONS FINELY CHOPPED WALNUTS (EACH MEASUREMENT USED SEPARATELY)

FUDGY CHOCOLATE FROSTING (PAGE 297) (OPTIONAL)

kitchen notes:

Be careful when measuring the dry ingredients: Too much baking soda will make the cupcakes overflow in the pan. These cupcakes are meant to be fudgy and moist. Take care not to overcook them, or they will be dry and crumbly. Do your best to spoon an equal amount of batter into each cup so that the cupcakes bake at the same rate. If you prefer to leave out the nuts, note that you will have less batter, enough for 10 or 11 cupcakes instead of 12. We use miniature semisweet chocolate chips in the batter because regular-sized chips are too chunky.

1   Combine the butter and unsweetened chocolate in a 2½-quart microwave-safe glass bowl. Cover the bowl with waxed paper and microwave on MEDIUM-HIGH (70 percent) for 2 to 3 minutes, until the butter is completely melted. Whisk until the mixture is smooth.

2   Whisk in the sugar, salt, and baking soda. Stir in the water and vanilla extract. Add the eggs one at a time, beating well after each addition. Whisk vigorously for 30 seconds. Add the cocoa and flour, and stir until the batter is smooth. Using a rubber spatula, fold in the chocolate chips and ⅓ cup of chopped walnuts. Let the batter stand for 5 minutes.

3 Line each cup of a 6-cup microwave cupcake or muffin pan with 2 paper baking cups. Fill the cups no more than two-thirds full of batter. Microwave on HIGH (100 percent) power for 1¾ to 3 minutes. If you are not using a turntable, rotate the pan a half turn after 1 minute. Test for doneness after 1¾ minutes by inserting a wooden toothpick in the center of each cupcake. It should come out with a few moist crumbs clinging to it. Any small wet patches on the surface of the cupcakes will dry while standing. If the cupcakes are not done after 1¾ minutes, microwave again, checking for doneness every 10 seconds.

4 Remove the outside baking cup from each cupcake. Set the cupcakes, still in the inner paper cup, on a wire rack to cool. Cover the cupcakes with a clean kitchen towel after 10 minutes to prevent them from drying out. Repeat the baking and cooling procedure with the remaining batter.

5 Sprinkle the tops of the cupcakes with the remaining 3 tablespoons of chopped walnuts. Serve the brownie cupcakes while still warm or cool completely and frost with Fudgy Chocolate Frosting. Store the cupcakes in an airtight container in the refrigerator for up to four days.

Carrot Pineapple Cupcakes

makes 12 cupcakes

preparation time: ABOUT 20 MINUTES PLUS 5 MINUTES STANDING AND TIME TO MAKE THE CREAM CHEESE FROSTING

microwave time: 4 TO 7 MINUTES

These moist, sweet cupcakes will remind you of your favorite carrot cake, especially when you ice them with the Cream Cheese Frosting. Unfrosted, they make great muffins.

¾ CUP PLUS 2 TABLESPOONS SIFTED
   WHOLE WHEAT FLOUR

2 TEASPOONS UNSWEETENED
   NONALKALIZED COCOA POWDER, SUCH
   AS HERSHEY'S REGULAR COCOA

¾ TEASPOON GROUND CINNAMON

¼ TEASPOON FRESHLY GRATED NUTMEG

⅛ TEASPOON GROUND CLOVES

¼ TEASPOON DOUBLE-ACTING BAKING
   POWDER

¼ TEASPOON BAKING SODA

¼ TEASPOON SALT

½ CUP VEGETABLE OIL

½ CUP PACKED LIGHT BROWN SUGAR

1 LARGE EGG, AT ROOM TEMPERATURE

⅔ CUP SHREDDED CARROTS

½ CUP CRUSHED PINEAPPLE IN
   UNSWEETENED PINEAPPLE JUICE,
   DRAINED

2 TABLESPOONS PLUS ½ CUP
   SWEETENED FLAKED COCONUT FOR
   DECORATION (OPTIONAL FOR
   DECORATION)

2 TEASPOONS VANILLA EXTRACT

CREAM CHEESE FROSTING (PAGE 298)

1   Put the flour, cocoa, cinnamon, cloves, nutmeg, baking powder, baking soda, and salt in a 1½-quart bowl. Use a wire whisk and complete 12 to 15 strokes to ensure that the ingredients are thoroughly blended.

2   Using a hand-held electric mixer set at high speed, beat the oil, brown sugar, and egg in a 4-quart bowl for 2 minutes, until creamy and a beige color. Using a rubber spatula, stir the carrots, pineapple, 2 tablespoons of coconut, and vanilla extract into the batter. Fold in the flour mixture just until blended. Let the batter stand for 5 minutes.

3   Line each cup of a 6-cup microwave-safe cupcake or muffin pan with 2 paper baking cups. Fill the cups two-thirds full of batter. Microwave on HIGH (100 percent) power for 2 to 3½ minutes, rotating the pan, if you do not have a turntable, a half turn after 1 minute. Test for doneness after 2 minutes by inserting a wooden toothpick in the center of each cupcake; it should come out clean. The tops of the cupcakes will no longer look wet. If not done, check the cupcakes at 10-second intervals.

4   Immediately remove the outside paper baking cup from each cupcake and set the cupcakes on a wire rack to cool. Leave the inside baking cups in place. Repeat the baking and cooling procedure with the remaining batter.

5   Frost the cooled cupcakes with cream cheese frosting. If desired, put the remaining ½ cup of coconut in a small, shallow bowl. Dip the frosted cupcakes in the coconut to coat them. Store the cupcakes in an airtight container in the refrigerator for up to four days.

kitchen note:

Use a fine-meshed sieve to sift the whole wheat flour so that the cupcakes will have a fine, light texture.

Applesauce Spice Cupcakes

makes 12 cupcakes

preparation time: ABOUT 15 MINUTES PLUS 5 MINUTES STANDING AND COOLING

microwave time: 4 TO 7 MINUTES

These are delicious with hot mulled cider or freshly brewed tea on a chilly day. Don't be discouraged by the long ingredient list; many of the items listed are probably already on your spice rack. To frost the cupcakes, try Cream Cheese Frosting (page 298), White Chocolate Sour Cream Frosting (page 296), Orange Buttercream Frosting (page 301), or Vanilla Buttercream Frosting (page 300). All are delicious.

⅔ CUP SIFTED WHOLE WHEAT FLOUR

¼ CUP SIFTED ALL-PURPOSE FLOUR

1 TEASPOON GROUND CINNAMON

½ TEASPOON DOUBLE-ACTING BAKING POWDER

½ TEASPOON BAKING SODA

¼ TEASPOON SALT

¼ TEASPOON GROUND CLOVES

¼ TEASPOON FRESHLY GRATED NUTMEG

½ CUP VEGETABLE OIL

½ CUP PACKED LIGHT BROWN SUGAR

1 LARGE EGG, AT ROOM TEMPERATURE

½ CUP UNSWEETENED APPLESAUCE

2 TEASPOONS VANILLA EXTRACT

¼ CUP FINELY CHOPPED WALNUTS

¼ CUP CURRANTS

1   Put the flours, cinnamon, baking powder, baking soda, salt, cloves, and nutmeg in a 1½-quart bowl and whisk well to combine. Use a wire whisk and complete 12 to 15 strokes to ensure that the ingredients are thoroughly blended.
2   Using a hand-held electric mixer set at high speed, beat the oil, brown sugar, and egg in a 4-quart bowl for 2 minutes, until creamy and a beige color. Reduce the speed to low and add the applesauce and vanilla extract. When they are combined, use a rubber spatula to fold the flour mixture into the applesauce mixture. Stir in the walnuts and currants. Let the batter stand for 5 minutes.
3   Line each cup of a microwave-safe cupcake or muffin pan with 2 paper baking cups. Fill the cups two-thirds full of batter. Microwave on HIGH (100 percent) power for 2 to 3½ minutes, rotating the pan, if you do not have a turntable, a half turn after 1 minute. Test for doneness after 2 minutes by inserting a wooden toothpick in the center of each cupcake; it should come out clean. The tops of the cupcakes will no longer look wet. If not done, check the cupcakes at 10-second intervals.

4 Immediately remove the outside paper baking cup from each cupcake and set the cupcakes on a wire rack to cool. Repeat the baking and cooling procedure with the remaining batter.

5 When the cupcakes are completely cool, frost them with Cream Cheese Frosting, White Chocolate Sour Cream Frosting, Orange Buttercream Frosting, or Vanilla Buttercream Frosting. Store the frosted cupcakes in an airtight container in the refrigerator for up to three days

Cake Tips

*When making microwave cake batters, the ingredients need to be at room temperature, as they do for conventional cake batters (unless otherwise specified in the recipe).

*In recipes calling for room-temperature softened butter, we explain how to do it in the microwave.

*Eggs can be brought to room temperature by immersing them in a bowl of warm water for about 5 minutes. Dry the eggs before cracking them.

*Inaccurate measuring can affect the outcome of the recipe—for instance, too much flour results in a dry cake. We instruct you to sift the flour and then measure. This ensures accuracy of measurement.

*Another way to ensure accuracy is to be sure to use the kind of measuring cup designed for dry ingredients—the kind that allows you to level the ingredients with the sweep of a knife.

*We suggest using Jack Frost or Town House Fine Granulated sugar, which have finer grains than other brands. Other brands work well but should be sifted first. Do not use superfine sugar.

*Unlike cupcake batter, cake batter does not have to stand before baking. The leaveners have ample time to work while the cake is cooking in the microwave.

*In some of the cake recipes we instruct you to line the bottom of the baking dish or casserole with two circles of waxed paper. Lightly oil the bottom of the dish or casserole before lining it with the paper circles. To prevent sticking, be sure the circles cover the entire bottom of the dish or casserole. The circle closest to the bottom of the dish absorbs excess moisture from the batter and the one on top enables you to remove the baked cake from the dish or casserole easily. To cut these circles, lay two sheets of waxed paper on the counter and set the

dish or casserole on top of them. Using the point of a small, sharp knife, trace the outline of the circle and then cut both circles at once.

*For even baking, make sure to spread the cake batter evenly in the pan.

*When we bake cakes, we may regulate the microwave power, starting with the MEDIUM (50 percent) power and ending with HIGH (100 percent) power. This gives the batter time to expand and the crumb opportunity to develop.

*If you do not have a turntable, rotate the cake as instructed in the recipe, being sure you rotate it before increasing the power to HIGH.

*Be diligent about testing the cakes for doneness. After the first time check, test the cakes every 30 seconds. Otherwise, they could overcook and become dry and tough.

*Because microwaves vary according to brand, wattage, model, and size, the visual doneness tests are crucial. Do not rely on time alone. A minute or two may not make much of a difference in a conventional oven, but in the microwave it can spell the difference between success and disaster.

*A paper towel loosely covering the cake as it cooks helps hold in just enough moisture to promote even cooking. It also prevents the batter from drying out. At the same time, the paper towel allows excess moisture to escape. Do not substitute plastic wrap, thinking it must be more efficient; it holds in too much moisture.*We leave the paper towel over the cake as its stands after baking to hold in heat so that the batter on the bottom of the pan can finish cooking. Also, as the cake cools, the paper towel prevents the surface of the cake from drying out.

*Standing time completes the baking. If called for, be sure to allow the cake to stand for as long as specified. Remember that any small wet patches will disappear well before it is time to unmold the cake. Set the cake on a flat heatproof surface rather than a wire rack for the most effective standing time. The heat trapped in the pan will complete the cooking.

*Before the cake is turned out onto a rack or serving plate, we instruct you to sprinkle the top of it with graham cracker or cookie crumbs. The cake does not have a protective crust and this prevents it from sticking to the rack or plate.

*After the specified standing time, the paper towel should be replaced with a clean kitchen towel, which will protect the cake and keep it moist as it cools completely.

*Once cool, keep the cake under a cake dome or upturned bowl to hold in moisture. Remember, these cakes have no protective crust.

*Microwave cakes will be just as crumbly as conventionally baked cakes if cut into while still warm. All cakes slice more easily and neatly if allowed to cool completely.

*We prefer lightweight polyester pastry bags for decorating because they are soft and flexible. They are very easy to control with just the slightest release of pressure. They come in a variety of sizes, but we find the 12-, 14-, and 16-inch to be the most useful. You can also use clear disposable plastic pastry bags. We do not recommend canvas pastry bags as they are too cumbersome for most beginners or occasional users.

*After inserting the decorating tip in the empty pastry bag, twist the portion of the bag that is just above the widest opening of the tip and then tuck the twisted portion in this opening. Once the bag is filled, this will prevent the whipped cream or buttercream frosting from leaking out of the end of the pastry bag before you are ready to pipe.

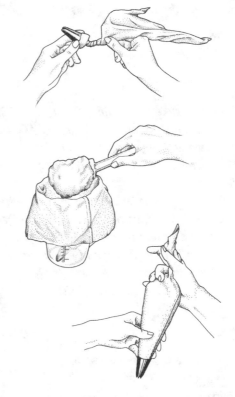

*After inserting the tip, turn down the widest portion of the pastry bag at the top to form a 3- to 4-inch cuff. Suspend the pastry bag in a 2-cup liquid measuring cup before filling it with the frosting. The cup will support the pastry bag, making it easier to fill. When you are ready to pipe, twist the top of the pastry bag above the filling and grasp the bag so that the top of the filled section rests in the palm of your hand. Wrap the excess twisted portion of the bag around your forefinger. Untwist the twisted portion at the pastry-tip end of the bag and begin decorating.

*Wash polyester (and canvas) pastry bags in warm water and mild detergent. Rinse them well and dry them draped over large bottles.

*We suggest using a small, offset (crooked) metal cake spatula or the back of a spoon to frost cupcakes. For a smooth, even coating of frosting on cakes, use a flat 8- to 10-inch metal cake spatula. Do not use a rubber spatula or table knife, which are awkward and do not produce attractive results.

*We developed the Pumpkin Gingerbread (page 118) in a 2-quart Pyrex Originals square glass cake dish with rounded corners. In recent years, Pyrex redesigned its square and oblong dishes with more rounded corners. This promotes more even baking. We recommend using these rather then older-style Pyrex dishes with ''squarer'' corners.

Walnut Brownie Cake

serves 8

preparation time: ABOUT 20 MINUTES PLUS CHILLING

microwave time: 10 MINUTES AND 30 SECONDS TO 14 MINUTES AND 30 SECONDS PLUS
STANDING

*T*his is the cake responsible for our book. Several years ago Adrienne developed a similar one for Chocolatier *magazine. As a skeptical newcomer to the microwave, she was pleased and surprised: She could not believe anything this delicious could be made in the microwave oven. From there it was a logical leap to a few more recipes and a book proposal.*

The cake is wonderful on its own, whether you serve it chilled, warm, or at room temperature. We have tried it with a number of accompaniments, dressing it up or down depending on the occasion. Look at the variations following the master recipe for a few ideas. You might serve it with a sprinkling of confectioner's sugar, frosted with Coffee Rum Buttercream Frosting (page 301), or topped with vanilla ice cream and Satiny Chocolate Sauce (page 288), or with fresh berries and whipped cream. The flavor of the cake will improve if it is left to sit overnight.

½ CUP PLUS 2 TABLESPOONS SIFTED
    CAKE FLOUR (NOT SELF-RISING)

½ CUP GRANULATED SUGAR (USED IN
    TWO MEASUREMENTS)

⅓ CUP WALNUTS

½ TEASPOON BAKING SODA

⅛ TEASPOON SALT

3 OUNCES UNSWEETENED CHOCOLATE,
    COARSELY CHOPPED

⅓ CUP LIGHTLY PACKED DARK BROWN
    SUGAR

¾ TEASPOON INSTANT COFFEE GRANULES

4 TABLESPOONS CHILLED UNSALTED
    BUTTER, CUT INTO ½-INCH CUBES

¼ CUP WATER

½ CUP SOUR CREAM, CHILLED

1 JUMBO EGG, CHILLED

2 TEASPOONS VANILLA EXTRACT

1 TABLESPOON CHOCOLATE WAFER OR
    GRAHAM CRACKER CRUMBS

1   Lightly oil the bottom of an 8¼-inch microwave-safe round glass cake dish. Line the bottom with two circles of waxed paper.

2 Put the flour, 2 tablespoons granulated sugar, walnuts, baking soda, baking powder, and salt in a food processor fitted with the metal chopping blade. Process for 10 to 20 seconds, until the walnuts are coarsely ground. Transfer the flour mixture to a small bowl and set aside.

3 Without washing the container of the food processor, combine the chocolate, ¼ cup plus 2 tablespoons granulated sugar, brown sugar, and coffee. Process for 30 to 40 seconds, until the mixture is finely ground.

4 Combine the butter and water in a 2-cup microwave-safe glass measuring cup. Cover the cup with plastic wrap, turning back a fold over the pouring spout. Microwave on MEDIUM-HIGH (70 percent) power for 1½ to 2½ minutes, until the butter is completely melted and the mixture is steaming hot. Do not let the mixture boil.

5 With the food processor running, pour the hot butter mixture through the feed tube and process for 15 to 25 seconds, until the chocolate mixture is smooth.

6 Add the sour cream, egg, and vanilla extract. Process for no longer than 5 seconds, until the mixture is creamy. Scrape down the sides of the container with a spatula. Add half of the flour mixture and pulse 4 to 6 times, until there is barely a trace of flour left. Scrape down the sides of the container. Add the remaining flour mixture and pulse 4 to 6 times, until there is barely a trace of flour left in the batter. Do not overprocess.

7 Scrape the batter into the prepared cake dish and spread it evenly with the back of a spoon.

8 Put the dish on an inverted 9-inch microwave-safe glass pie plate and microwave, uncovered, on MEDIUM (50 percent) power for 9 to 12 minutes. If your microwave has no turntable, rotate the cake dish a quarter turn every 3 minutes. Test for doneness after 9 minutes by inserting a wooden toothpick into the center of the cake; it should come out with a few moist crumbs clinging to it. Any small wet patches on the cake's surface will disappear as the cake cools. If not done, check the cake at 30-second intervals. Put the cake on a flat heatproof surface, cover with a clean kitchen towel, and let it stand for 15 minutes.

9 Remove the towel and sprinkle the top of the cake with the chocolate wafer or graham cracker crumbs. Run the tip of a knife around the cake to loosen it. Cover the cake dish with a plate. Invert the cake and with a gentle tap, release it, and lift off the dish. Peel off the waxed paper. Serve the cake warm or chill it for 15 to 20 minutes in the freezer to enhance the moist texture. As soon as the cake is cool enough, wrap it well in plastic. The flavor of the

> **kitchen note:**
>
> *Unlike most of our cakes, this one is baked, uncovered at* MEDIUM *(50 percent) power for the full baking time. After the cake has been unmolded and while it is still warm, chill it for 15 to 20 minutes in the freezer. The quick chilling will enhance the moist texture and enable you to frost it sooner.*

CAKES and CUPCAKES   **105**

walnut brownie cake will improve if it is left to sit overnight. The cake may be baked up to two days in advance and kept refrigerated.

variations

Walnut Brownie Cake with Mocha Custard Sauce

1 *Prepare Mocha Custard Sauce (page 286) and refrigerate.*
2 *Lightly dust the top of the warm or cooled walnut brownie cake with confectioners' sugar. Spoon equal amounts of mocha custard sauce onto 8 dessert plates. Put a slice of cake in the center of each plate. If desired, garnish the top of the cake slice with a fresh strawberry half.*

Walnut Brownie Cake with Quick Chocolate Frosting

1 *Prepare Quick Chocolate Frosting (page 304).*
2 *Make the walnut brownie cake and put it on a serving plate. Chill it in the freezer for 15 to 20 minutes, until cold.*
3 *Surround the base of the cake with strips of waxed paper to keep the serving plate clean. Using a small offset (crooked) metal cake spatula, frost the top and the sides of the cake with the quick chocolate frosting.*
4 *Remove the strips of waxed paper from around the cake. Keep the cake refrigerated under a cake dome or large upturned bowl. Bring the cake to room temperature before serving. The frosted cake may be kept refrigerated for up to two days if covered with the bowl.*

Walnut Brownie Cake with Chocolate Chantilly

1 *Make the walnut brownie cake and put in on a serving plate. Chill it in the freezer for 15 to 20 minutes, until cold. Cover it with plastic wrap.*
2 *Make chocolate curls or shavings (page 26).*
3 *Make the Chocolate Chantilly (page 303).*
4 *Surround the base of the cake with strips of waxed paper to keep the serving plate clean. Using a small offset (crooked) metal cake spatula, frost the top and the sides of the cake with the chocolate chantilly. Refrigerate the cake.*
5 *Put a 1-ounce square of semisweet chocolate in a bottom corner of a small unpleated sealable plastic bag. Microwave on* MEDIUM *(50 percent) power for 1½ to 3½ minutes, until the chocolate is melted. Squeeze the melted chocolate so that it gathers in one corner of the bag. Using scissors, cut a tiny hole that is no longer than ¹/₁₆ of an*

inch at the corner of the bag containing the melted chocolate. Quickly pipe delicate lines of dark chocolate over the top of the frosted cake. Refrigerate the cake for 5 minutes to set the chocolate.

6   Using a bakers' scraper or a metal cake spatula, scoop up some of the curls or shavings and press them against the sides of the frosted cake.

7   If desired, decorate the top of the cake with 8 walnuts that have been halved and dipped in melted semisweet chocolate.

8   Remove the strips of waxed paper from around the cake. Keep the cake refrigerated under a cake dome or large upturned bowl. Let the cake stand for 15 minutes at room temperature before serving. The frosted cake may be kept refrigerated for up to two days if covered with the bowl.

French Apple Cake

serves 8

preparation time: ABOUT 25 MINUTES

microwave time: 10 MINUTES AND 5 SECONDS TO 13 MINUTES AND 15 SECONDS PLUS 15 MINUTES STANDING

*W*e set out with high expectations for this book, knowing we could come up with delicious desserts just right for cooking in the microwave oven. As with any work in progress, we ran into a few snags. Then the phone calls would start: countless conversations in which we tossed around ideas. But this single-layer apple cake was perfect from the start—a rousing success as the perfect sort of cake for microwave baking. Try it and you will immediately see why.

Apple layer:

- 2 TABLESPOONS UNSALTED BUTTER
- 1/4 CUP PACKED LIGHT BROWN SUGAR
- 2 TEASPOONS COGNAC
- 1/8 TEASPOON GROUND CINNAMON
- 1/2 POUND COOKING APPLES, SUCH AS MCINTOSH, EMPIRE, GOLDEN DELICIOUS, OR ROME (ABOUT 1 OR 2 MEDIUM APPLES)

Cake:

- 1 CUP PLUS 2 TABLESPOONS SIFTED ALL-PURPOSE FLOUR
- 1½ TEASPOONS DOUBLE-ACTING BAKING POWDER
- 1/8 TEASPOON SALT
- 1/2 CUP SOUR CREAM (SPOONED INTO A MEASURING CUP AND LEVELED WITH THE EDGE OF A KNIFE)
- 2 TABLESPOONS MILK
- 5 TABLESPOONS UNSALTED BUTTER
- 1/2 CUP GRANULATED SUGAR
- 2 TEASPOONS VANILLA EXTRACT
- 1 TEASPOON FINELY GRATED LEMON ZEST
- 1 JUMBO EGG, AT ROOM TEMPERATURE (LIGHTLY BEATEN)
- 1 TABLESPOON GRAHAM CRACKER CRUMBS
- VANILLA CUSTARD SAUCE (PAGE 285), CHILLED, CARAMEL RUM SAUCE (PAGE 292), OR CINNAMON SPICE ICE CREAM (PAGE 198)

1   TO MAKE THE APPLE LAYER: Put the butter in a high straight-sided 2-quart microwave-safe round glass casserole. Cover with waxed paper and microwave on MEDIUM-HIGH (70 percent) power for 45 seconds to 1½ minutes, until melted.

2 Add the brown sugar, cognac, and cinnamon to the melted butter and stir vigorously with a wooden spoon until the mixture is creamy. Use the back of a spoon to spread the mixture into an even layer over the bottom of the casserole.

3 Cut the apples into quarters. Peel and core them with a small sharp knife. Cut the apple quarters into ⅛-inch thick slices. Make them as neat as possible; they will adorn the top of the cake.

4 Starting from the outside edge of the casserole, arrange the apples in slightly overlapping concentric circles. Fill in the center of the ring with more apple slices. Set aside.

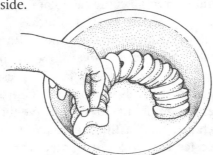

5 TO MAKE THE CAKE: Combine the flour, baking powder, and salt in a 1½-quart bowl. Use a wire whisk and complete 12 to 15 strokes to ensure that the ingredients are thoroughly blended.

6 Put the sour cream and milk in a 1-cup microwave-safe glass measuring cup. Microwave uncovered on MEDIUM-LOW (30 percent) power for 1 to 2 minutes, stirring until the chill is off. Do not let the sour cream mixture get hot. Set aside.

7 Put the butter in a 2½-quart microwave-safe bowl. Cover with waxed paper and microwave at HIGH (100 percent) power for 15 to 45 seconds, until the butter is slightly softened. Do not let the butter melt or become oily.

8 Using a hand-held electric mixer set at high speed, beat the butter for 30 seconds, until creamy. Add the sugar and continue to beat for 1 to 2 minutes, scraping down the sides of the bowl often until the mixture is nearly white and its texture is light. Beat in the vanilla and lemon zest.

9 While continuing to beat at medium speed, slowly add the egg. Beat until smooth. At low speed beat in the flour mixture, a third at a time, alternating with the sour cream mixture. Beat briefly, just until each addition is incorporated into the batter. Scrape down the sides of the bowl with a rubber spatula and beat a few seconds more.

10 Carefully spoon the batter over the apple slices. Spread the batter in an

even layer over the apples, being careful not to disturb the design created by the overlapping apple slices.

11　Cover the top of the casserole with a microwave-safe paper towel. Set the casserole on an inverted 9-inch microwave-safe glass pie plate and microwave on MEDIUM (50 percent) power for 5 minutes. If not using a turntable, rotate the casserole a quarter turn every 2½ minutes.

12　Continue to microwave on HIGH (100 percent) power for 3 to 6 minutes. If not using a turntable, rotate the casserole every 1½ minutes. Test for doneness after 3 minutes by inserting a wooden toothpick in the center of the cake; it should come out clean. The surface of the cake will appear dry. If not done, check the cake at 30-second intervals. Let the cake stand, still covered with the paper towel, on a flat heatproof surface for 15 minutes.

13　Sprinkle the cake with the graham cracker crumbs. Run the tip of a knife around the edge of the cake to loosen it. Cover the casserole with a serving plate and invert the cake onto it, using a gentle tap, if necessary, to release it. Cover the cake with a large bowl that is propped up about ½ inch above the counter to allow heat to escape until time to serve. Serve the cake warm or at room temperature with chilled Vanilla Custard Sauce, warm Caramel Rum Sauce, or Cinnamon Spice Ice Cream. Store any leftover cake under a cake dome or large upturned bowl for up to one day.

Georgia Peach Cake

serves 8

preparation time: ABOUT 30 MINUTES PLUS COOLING

microwave time: 15 MINUTES AND 5 SECONDS TO 22 MINUTES AND 15 SECONDS PLUS 15 MINUTES STANDING

*T*he method used here is similar to that for the French Apple Cake. This winner features all-American ingredients: juicy, sweet Georgia peaches (or any ripe peaches), pecans, and bourbon whiskey.

Peach layer:

¼ CUP PLUS 2 TABLESPOONS PECANS

2 TABLESPOONS UNSALTED BUTTER

¼ CUP PACKED LIGHT BROWN SUGAR

2 TEASPOONS BOURBON

2 MEDIUM FIRM, RIPE PEACHES, PEELED AND CUT IN ⅜-INCH WEDGES OR 1¼ CUPS FROZEN, SLICED, UNSWEETENED PEACHES

Cake:

1 CUP PLUS 1 TABLESPOON SIFTED ALL-PURPOSE FLOUR

¼ CUP FINELY CHOPPED TOASTED PECANS, RESERVED FROM PEACH LAYER

1½ TEASPOONS DOUBLE-ACTING BAKING POWDER

⅛ TEASPOON SALT

⅔ CUP SOUR CREAM (SPOONED INTO A MEASURING CUP AND LEVELED WITH THE EDGE OF A KNIFE)

1 TABLESPOON MILK

5 TABLESPOONS UNSALTED BUTTER

½ CUP LIGHTLY PACKED LIGHT BROWN SUGAR

2 TEASPOONS VANILLA EXTRACT

1 JUMBO EGG, AT ROOM TEMPERATURE (LIGHTLY BEATEN)

1 TABLESPOON GRAHAM CRACKER CRUMBS

Vanilla-bourbon cream:

1 CUP HEAVY CREAM

1 TABLESPOON GRANULATED SUGAR

1 TABLESPOON BOURBON

½ TEASPOON VANILLA EXTRACT

1   FOR THE PEACH LAYER: Spread the pecans in a single layer in a 9-inch microwave-safe glass pie plate. Microwave on HIGH (100 percent) power for 3 minutes and then stir with a wooden spoon. Continue to microwave on HIGH (100 percent) power for 3 to 6 minutes more, until the nuts are lightly toasted and fragrant. Spread the nuts on a plate to cool. When cool, finely chop ¼ cup and reserve for the cake batter. Coarsely chop the rest of the pecans and set aside separately.

2   Put the butter in a 2-quart microwave-safe round glass-knob covered casserole or a high, straight-sided 2-quart microwave-safe round glass casserole. Cover with waxed paper and microwave on MEDIUM-HIGH (70 percent) power for 45 seconds to 1½ minutes, until melted.

3   Add the brown sugar and bourbon to the melted butter and stir vigorously with a wooden spoon until the mixture is creamy. Use the back of a spoon to spread the mixture into an even layer over the bottom of the casserole. Sprinkle the coarsely chopped pecans over the brown sugar mixture.

4   Starting from the outside edge of the casserole, arrange the peaches in concentric circles similar to the spokes of a wheel. Fill the center with more peach slices. Set aside.

5   TO MAKE THE CAKE: Combine the flour, ¼ cup finely chopped pecans, baking powder, and salt in a 1½-quart bowl. Use a wire whisk and complete 12 to 15 strokes to ensure that the ingredients are thoroughly blended.

6   Put the sour cream and milk in a 1-cup microwave-safe glass measuring cup. Microwave uncovered on MEDIUM-LOW (30 percent) power for 1 to 2 minutes, stirring until the chill is off. Do not let the sour cream mixture get hot. Set aside.

7   Put the butter in a 2½-quart microwave-safe bowl. Cover with waxed paper and microwave at HIGH (100 percent) power for 15 to 45 seconds, until the butter is slightly softened. Do not let the butter melt or become oily.

8   Using a hand-held electric mixer set at high speed, beat the butter for 30 seconds, until creamy. Add the brown sugar and continue to beat for 1 to 2 minutes, scraping down the sides of the bowl often until the mixture is light in texture and color. Beat in the vanilla extract.

9   While continuing to beat at medium speed, slowly add the egg. Beat until smooth. At low speed beat in the flour mixture, a third at a time, alternating with the sour cream mixture. Beat briefly, just until each addition is incorporated into the batter. Scrape down the sides of the bowl with a rubber spatula and beat a few seconds more.

10   Spread the batter in an even layer, being careful not to disturb the design created by the peach slices.

11   Cover the casserole with a microwave-safe paper towel and set the casserole on an inverted 9-inch microwave-safe glass pie plate. Microwave on MEDIUM (50 percent) power for 5 minutes. If not using a turntable, rotate the casserole a quarter turn every 2½ minutes.

12   Continue to microwave on HIGH (100 percent) power for 3 to 6 minutes more. If not using a turntable, rotate the casserole a quarter turn every 1½ minutes. Test for doneness after 3 minutes by inserting a wooden toothpick in the center of the cake; it should come out clean. The surface of the cake will appear dry, and the edges will have started to pull away from the sides of the casserole. If not done, check the cake at 30-second intervals. Let the cake stand, still covered with the paper towel, on a flat heatproof surface for 15 minutes.

13   To MAKE THE BOURBON-VANILLA CREAM: Chill a 3-quart bowl. Pour the cream in the bowl, and using a hand-held electric mixer set at high speed, whip the cream with sugar, bourbon, and vanilla extract until it starts to thicken but is still pourable. Keep the cream refrigerated until ready to serve.

14   To SERVE: Sprinkle the top of the cake with the graham cracker crumbs. Run the tip of a knife around the sides of the casserole to loosen the cake. Cover the casserole with a serving plate and invert the cake onto it, using a gentle tap, if necessary, to release it. Cover the cake with a large bowl that is propped up about ½ inch above the counter to allow heat to escape, until it is time to serve the cake.

15   Serve the cake warm or at room temperature. Ladle the chilled bourbon-vanilla cream onto 8 dessert plates and set a slice of cake on each plate. Store any leftover cake under a cake dome or large upturned bowl for up to one day.

Triple Chocolate Sour Cream Cake

serves 8 to 10

preparation time: ABOUT 1 HOUR PLUS COOLING AND CHILLING

microwave time: 10 TO 12 MINUTES PLUS STANDING

When you are in the mood for a deep, dark, chocolate cake, try this one. It's rich and moist, generously studded with mini chocolate chips, and made all the more delicious by a coating of fruity apricot preserves and a shiny chocolate glaze. Finally the dark, deluxe dessert is striped with delicate threads of sweet white chocolate. Try it glazed and decorated or serve it warm from the oven with no more embellishment than whipped cream or vanilla ice cream. Or how about using the chocolate glaze as a sauce for the ice cream and cake? This was one of the last cakes Adrienne developed and with the fondness often reserved for the youngest child it became a fast favorite.

Sour cream chocolate cake:

4 TABLESPOONS CHOCOLATE WAFER CRUMBS (USED IN TWO SEPARATE MEASUREMENTS)

1 CUP PLUS 1 TABLESPOON GRANULATED SUGAR (USED IN TWO SEPARATE MEASUREMENTS)

1 CUP SOUR CREAM

½ CUP VEGETABLE OIL

2 LARGE EGGS

2 TABLESPOONS VANILLA EXTRACT

1 CUP SIFTED ALL-PURPOSE FLOUR

½ CUP PLUS 2 TABLESPOONS SIFTED UNSWEETENED ALKALIZED COCOA POWDER, SUCH AS HERSHEY'S EUROPEAN STYLE OR DROSTE

1¾ TEASPOONS DOUBLE-ACTING BAKING POWDER

¼ TEASPOON SALT

¼ CUP MINI SEMISWEET CHOCOLATE CHIPS

Apricot coating:

½ CUP APRICOT PRESERVES

Chocolate glaze:

6 OUNCES SEMISWEET CHOCOLATE, FINELY CHOPPED

¾ CUP HEAVY CREAM

FEW GRAINS OF SALT

3 TABLESPOONS LIGHT CORN SYRUP

1½ TEASPOONS VANILLA EXTRACT

Decoration:

1½ OUNCES WHITE CHOCOLATE

1   To MAKE THE SOUR CREAM CHOCOLATE CAKE: Using a pastry brush, thoroughly coat the bottom and sides of a 6-cup microwave-safe Bundt pan with vegetable shortening. Combine 3 tablespoons chocolate wafer crumbs and 1 tablespoon sugar in a small bowl until blended. Sprinkle the pan with the wafer mixture and turn it to coat it evenly. Set aside.

2   Combine the sour cream, oil, eggs, and vanilla extract in a 2½-quart bowl and whisk vigorously for 30 seconds until thoroughly blended. Set the bowl over a larger bowl of hot water, stirring the sour cream mixture occasionally for 3 to 5 minutes, until the chill is off.

3   Meanwhile, put the flour, 1 cup sugar, cocoa, baking powder, and salt in a 3-quart bowl. Use a wire whisk and complete 12 to 15 strokes to ensure that the ingredients are thoroughly blended.

4   Remove the bowl containing the sour cream mixture from the bowl of water. Make a well in the center of the dry ingredients. Pour the sour cream mixture into the well and whisk just until smooth. Stir in the chocolate chips.

5   Scrape the batter into the prepared pan and spread it evenly with the back of a spoon.

6   Cover the pan with a microwave-safe paper towel and set it on an upturned 9-inch microwave-safe glass pie plate. Microwave on MEDIUM (50 percent) power for 8 minutes, rotating the pan, if you do not have a turntable, a quarter turn every 4 minutes.

7   Microwave on HIGH (100 percent) power for 2 to 4 minutes, rotating the pan if you do not have a turntable, a quarter turn every 2 minutes. Test for doneness after 2 minutes by inserting a wooden toothpick in the center of the cake; it should come out clean. The surface of the cake will appear dry. If not done, check the cake at 30-second intervals. Let the cake stand, still covered with the paper towel, on a flat heatproof surface for 20 minutes.

8   Sprinkle the top of the cake with 1 tablespoon chocolate wafer crumbs. Run the tip of a knife around the center tube and around the edge of the cake pan to loosen the cake. Cover the cake with a wire rack. Invert the cake and gently tap to release the cake. Keep the cake covered with a clean kitchen towel until cool.

9   To PREPARE THE APRICOT COATING: Put the apricot preserves in a 1-cup microwave-safe glass measuring cup. Cover with waxed paper and microwave on MEDIUM-HIGH (70 percent) power for 45 seconds to 1½ minutes, until steaming hot. Strain the hot preserves into a small cup. Immediately brush the hot apricot preserves over the cooled cake. Let the cake stand uncovered while

---

kitchen note:

We set the combined liquid ingredients over a bowl of hot water to take the chill off. This improves the texture of the baked cake. Coating the cooled cake with the warm apricot preserves not only adds flavor, it prevents the glaze from soaking into the cake and losing its gloss.

CAKES and CUPCAKES   **115**

preparing the chocolate glaze.

10   To PREPARE THE CHOCOLATE GLAZE: Put the chocolate in a 1-quart measuring cup. Combine the cream, salt, and corn syrup in a 2-cup microwave-safe glass measuring cup. Cover with waxed paper and microwave on HIGH (100 percent) power for 1½ to 3 minutes, until the mixture comes to a full boil.

11   Pour the hot cream mixture over the chocolate and let the mixture stand for 30 seconds. Whisk gently until smooth. Stir in the vanilla extract.

12   Put the cake set on the wire rack onto a baking sheet. Pour the warm chocolate glaze over the cake, completely coating it with the glaze. Refrigerate the cake on the baking sheet for 5 to 10 minutes to set the glaze.

13   To DECORATE THE CAKE: Put the white chocolate in a bottom corner of a small unpleated sealable plastic bag. Microwave on MEDIUM (50 percent) power for 1½ to 3½ minutes, until the chocolate is melted. Squeeze the melted chocolate so that it gathers in one corner of the bag. Using scissors, cut a tiny hole that is no larger than 1/16 of an inch at the corner of the bag containing the melted chocolate. Quickly pipe slightly curved delicate lines of white chocolate over the glazed cake. Refrigerate the cake for 5 minutes to set the white chocolate. Store the cake in the refrigerator under a cake dome or a large, upturned bowl for up to 4 days. Bring the cake to room temperature before serving.

Upside-Down Summer Berry Shortcakes

serves 4

preparation time: ABOUT 25 MINUTES PLUS STANDING

microwave time: 5 MINUTES AND 20 SECONDS TO 8 MINUTES AND 45 SECONDS PLUS STANDING

We cannot think of summertime without thinking about shortcake. These mini upside-down cakes are at their absolute best when the blueberries and raspberries are fresh, plump, and juicy, and tasting of sunshine. The berries are topped with a light, *moist, golden cake and then served, still warm, with a little orange-flavored cream. They would be wonderfully good with plain whipped cream, too.*

Shortcakes:

⅔ CUP FRESH RASPBERRIES

⅔ CUP FRESH BLUEBERRIES

½ CUP PLUS 2 TABLESPOONS
  GRANULATED SUGAR (EACH
  MEASUREMENT USED SEPARATELY)

1 CUP PLUS 2 TABLESPOONS SIFTED
  ALL-PURPOSE FLOUR

1½ TEASPOONS DOUBLE-ACTING BAKING
  POWDER

⅛ TEASPOON SALT

6 TABLESPOONS UNSALTED BUTTER

1 LARGE EGG

1 TEASPOON VANILLA EXTRACT

½ TEASPOON FINELY GRATED ORANGE
  ZEST

½ CUP MILK

Orange cream:

¾ CUP HEAVY CREAM

1 TABLESPOON GRANULATED SUGAR

¼ TEASPOON FINELY GRATED ORANGE
  ZEST

½ TEASPOON VANILLA EXTRACT

ORANGE ZEST, CUT INTO THIN STRIPS, FOR
  GARNISH (OPTIONAL)

1   Combine the berries with 2 tablespoons of sugar in a 1-quart bowl. Stir gently until the berries are coated with sugar. Divide the berry mixture equally among four 10-ounce microwave-safe deep pie dishes, then set aside.

2   Put the flour, baking powder, and salt in a 1-quart bowl. Using a wire whisk, complete 12 to 15 strokes to ensure that the ingredients are thoroughly mixed.

3   Put the butter in a 2½-quart microwave-safe bowl. Cover with waxed paper and microwave on HIGH (100 percent) power for 20 to 45 seconds, until the butter is slightly softened. Do not let the butter melt or become oily.

4   Using a hand-held electric mixer set at high speed, beat the butter for 30 seconds, until creamy. Add the ½ cup of sugar and continue to beat for 1 to 2 minutes, scraping down the sides of the bowl often, until the mixture is nearly white and light in texture. Beat in the vanilla extract and orange zest.

5   Add the egg and beat until smooth. At low speed, beat in the flour mixture, a third at a time, alternating with the milk. Beat briefly after each addition, just

> ### kitchen note:
>
> *If it's easier (or the wrong season), substitute frozen berries for fresh. Do not thaw the berries but allow for a slightly longer cooking time.*

until the added ingredients are incorporated. Scrape down the sides of the bowl with a rubber spatula and beat the batter a few seconds more. Let the batter stand for 5 minutes.

6   Divide the batter equally among the berry-lined dishes and smooth with the back of a spoon. Arrange the pie dishes in a circle in the microwave, making sure they do not touch one another. Cover the dishes with a microwave-safe paper towel and microwave on HIGH (100 percent) power for 5 to 8 minutes, rotating each dish a half turn after 3 minutes. Test for doneness after 5 minutes by inserting a wooden toothpick in the center of each shortcake; it should come out clean. Any small wet patches on the surface of the shortcakes will dry while standing. If the shortcakes are not done, microwave them for 30 seconds at a time until they are. Let the shortcakes stand, still covered with the towel, on a flat heatproof surface for 10 minutes.

7   To MAKE THE ORANGE CREAM: Using a hand-held electric mixer set at high speed, whip the cream, sugar, orange zest, and vanilla extract in a chilled 3-quart bowl until slightly thickened but still pourable.

8   To SERVE: Run a knife around the edge of each shortcake to loosen it from the side of the dish. Invert each shortcake onto a dessert plate so that the fruit is on top. Spoon some of the orange cream around each shortcake. Garnish the cream with a sprinkling of orange zest, if desired. Serve the shortcakes while still warm.

Pumpkin Gingerbread with Lemon Cream

serves 9

preparation time: ABOUT 20 MINUTES

microwave time: 8 TO 11 MINUTES PLUS 10 MINUTES STANDING

The pumpkin puree, so easy to find in the market, makes the gingerbread especially moist and flavorful, and the lightly scented lemon cream is the perfect accompaniment. The Rhubarb Applesauce on page 132 tastes awfully good with it, too.

Unbelievable Microwave Desserts

Gingerbread:

¾ CUP PLUS 2 TABLESPOONS SIFTED
  ALL-PURPOSE FLOUR

1½ TEASPOONS GROUND GINGER

¾ TEASPOON GROUND CINNAMON

¼ TEASPOON GROUND CLOVES

¼ TEASPOON FRESHLY GRATED NUTMEG

1 TEASPOON DOUBLE-ACTING BAKING
  POWDER

½ TEASPOON BAKING SODA

¼ TEASPOON SALT

⅔ CUP PACKED DARK BROWN SUGAR

½ CUP VEGETABLE OIL

1 JUMBO EGG, AT ROOM TEMPERATURE

2 TABLESPOONS MOLASSES

2 TEASPOONS VANILLA EXTRACT

¾ CUP CANNED UNSWEETENED PUMPKIN
  PUREE

Lemon cream:

¾ CUP HEAVY CREAM

¼ CUP SOUR CREAM (SPOONED INTO A
  MEASURING CUP AND LEVELED WITH
  THE EDGE OF A KNIFE)

5 TEASPOONS GRANULATED SUGAR

½ TEASPOON FINELY GRATED LEMON
  ZEST

½ TEASPOON VANILLA EXTRACT

1   Lightly oil the bottom of a 2-quart microwave-safe square glass cake dish with rounded corners. (This dish promotes more even baking than the older ones, which have more angular corners).

2   Combine the flour, ginger, cinnamon, cloves, nutmeg, baking powder, baking soda, and salt in a 1½-quart bowl. Use a wire whisk to complete 12 to 15 strokes to ensure that the ingredients are thoroughly blended.

3   Put the brown sugar, oil, egg, molasses, and vanilla extract in a 4-quart bowl. Using a hand-held electric mixer set at high speed, beat the mixture until creamy and a beige color.

4   Reduce the speed to low and mix in the pumpkin puree until blended. Whisk the flour mixture into the batter until smooth.

5   Scrape the batter into the prepared baking dish and spread it evenly with the back of a spoon.

6   Wrap each corner of the dish with 2-inch-wide strips of aluminum foil, shiny side facing up. Cover the dish with a microwave-safe paper towel and set it on an inverted 9-inch microwave-safe glass pie plate. Microwave on MEDIUM (50 percent) power for 5 minutes. If not using a turntable, rotate the baking dish a quarter turn every 2½ minutes.

7   Continue to microwave on HIGH (100 percent) power for 3

> **kitchen note:**
>
> *Although metal pans are not supposed to be used in the microwave, it is all right to use foil to shield the corners of the baking dish in this recipe. If you do not, the corners of the gingerbread will overcook. Take care that the foil strips do not touch each other and that they are not folded back on themselves; this could cause arcing. The shiny side of the foil should face up.*

to 6 minutes. If not using a turntable, rotate the baking dish a quarter turn every 1½ minutes. Test for doneness after 3 minutes by inserting a wooden toothpick into the center of the gingerbread: it should come out clean. The surface of the gingerbread will appear dry. If not done, check the cake at 30-second intervals. Remove the foil strips and let the gingerbread stand, covered with the paper towel, on a flat heatproof surface for 10 minutes.

8 To make the lemon cream: Chill a 3-quart bowl. Using a hand-held electric mixer set at high speed, whip the cream with the sour cream, sugar, lemon zest, and vanilla extract until soft peaks start to form.

9 Serve the gingerbread still warm, topped with a spoonful of the lemon cream. Store leftover gingerbread in an airtight container at room temperature for up to three days.

Pumpkin Spice Cake with Rum Cream Frosting

serves 8

preparation time: ABOUT 30 MINUTES

microwave time: 12 TO 18 MINUTES PLUS STANDING

This cake is similar to Pumpkin Gingerbread on page 118 but contains less ginger, no molasses, and is baked in a round rather than square dish. We also frost the cake and take the time to decorate it, making it fit for the most elegant occasion. You might opt to serve it without frosting, especially if time is a factor. You won't be disappointed. The cake is delicious served warm with a dollop of the rum cream or a scoop of Ginger Pecan Ice Cream (page 200).

These two recipes (along with the Pumpkin Ginger Tea Ring on page 241) demonstrate the affinity between canned unsweetened pumpkin puree and the microwave oven. The puree provides just the right moisture and consistency. What's more, it is easy to find in the supermarket all year round.

Pumpkin spice cake:

¾ CUP PLUS 2 TABLESPOONS SIFTED
  ALL-PURPOSE FLOUR
¾ TEASPOON GROUND GINGER
¾ TEASPOON GROUND CINNAMON
¼ TEASPOON GROUND CLOVES
¼ TEASPOON FRESHLY GRATED NUTMEG
1 TEASPOON DOUBLE-ACTING BAKING
  POWDER
½ TEASPOON BAKING SODA

¼ TEASPOON SALT
⅔ CUP PACKED LIGHT BROWN SUGAR
½ CUP VEGETABLE OIL
1 JUMBO EGG, AT ROOM TEMPERATURE
2 TEASPOONS VANILLA EXTRACT
¾ CUP CANNED UNSWEETENED PUMPKIN
  PUREE
1 TABLESPOON GRAHAM CRACKER OR
  COOKIE CRUMBS

Decoration and rum cream frosting:

⅔ CUP PECAN HALVES
1¼ CUPS HEAVY CREAM
5 TEASPOONS GRANULATED SUGAR

1 TABLESPOON DARK RUM
¾ TEASPOON VANILLA EXTRACT

1   To make the pumpkin spice cake: Lightly oil the bottom of an 8¼-inch microwave-safe round glass baking dish. Line the bottom with two circles of waxed paper.

2   Combine the flour, ginger, cinnamon, cloves, nutmeg, baking powder, baking soda, and salt in a 1½-quart bowl. Use a wire whisk to complete 12 to 15 strokes to ensure that the ingredients are thoroughly blended.

3   Combine the brown sugar, oil, egg, and vanilla extract in a 4-quart bowl. Using a hand-held electric mixer set at high speed, beat for 2 minutes, until the mixture is creamy and a beige color.

4   With the mixer at low speed, beat in the pumpkin until blended. Whisk in the flour mixture until smooth.

5   Scrape the batter into the prepared baking dish and spread evenly with the back of a spoon.

6   Cover the top of the cake dish with a microwave-safe paper towel. Put the dish on an inverted 9-inch microwave-safe glass pie plate and microwave on MEDIUM (50 percent) power for 5 minutes. If your microwave has no turntable, rotate the cake dish a half turn every 2½ minutes.

7   Continue to microwave on HIGH (100 percent) power for 2 to 5 minutes. Test the cake for doneness after 3 minutes by inserting a wooden toothpick into

> **kitchen note:**
>
> *Before frosting, surround the base of the cake with strips of waxed paper to keep the serving plate neat, then remove the waxed paper before serving. This is a good trick when frosting any cake directly on the serving plate.*

the center of the cake; it should come out clean. The surface of the cake will appear dry. If not done, check the cake at 30-second intervals. Let the cake stand, still covered with the paper towel, on a flat heatproof surface for 15 minutes.

8   Remove the towel and sprinkle the top of the cake with the cookie crumbs or graham cracker crumbs. Run the tip of a knife around the edge of the cake dish to loosen the cake. Cover the cake dish with a serving dish. Invert the cake onto the plate and, with a gentle tap, remove the dish. Peel off the waxed paper. Keep the cake covered with a clean kitchen towel until cool.

9   TO MAKE THE DECORATION AND RUM CREAM FROSTING: Spread the pecans in a single layer in a 9-inch microwave-safe glass pie plate. Microwave on HIGH (100 percent) power for 2 minutes. Stir with a wooden spoon.

10   Continue to microwave on HIGH (100 percent) power for 3 to 6 minutes, stirring every 60 seconds, until the nuts are lightly toasted and fragrant. Transfer the nuts to a plate and cool completely. Reserve 8 of the best pecans and set aside.

11   Chill a 3-quart bowl. Using a hand-held electric mixer set at high speed, beat the cream and sugar until soft peaks start to form. Add the vanilla extract and rum, and continue to beat until stiff peaks start to form.

12   Surround the base of the cake with strips of waxed paper. Reserve ¾ cup of the whipped cream frosting for piping and keep it refrigerated. Using a metal cake spatula, frost the top and sides of the cake with the remaining frosting.

13   Scoop up some of the chopped pecans in the palm of your hand and gently press them against the sides of the frosted cake.

14   Fit a pastry bag with a closed star tip (such as Ateco #4) and fill with the reserved whipped cream. Pipe 8 evenly spaced, swirled rosettes around the edge of the cake. Top each rosette with a pecan half.

15   Remove the strips of waxed paper from the plate. Keep the cake refrigerated, covered with a large bowl, until ready to serve. The frosted cake may be kept refrigerated for up to two days covered with an upturned bowl.

Strawberry Bavarian Cake

serves 8 to 10

preparation time: 1½ HOURS PLUS 4 HOURS CHILLING

microwave time: 17 MINUTES AND 15 SECONDS TO 28½ MINUTES

This truly spectacular dessert is one to make for a special party or event. Ladyfingers, trimmed to fit inside a springform pan, are topped with a smooth, airy bavarian, and then the cake is chilled until set. The decorating may take a little time, but the result is well worth the effort. We promise raves when the cake is carried to the table.

Orange syrup:

¼ CUP WATER

2 TABLESPOONS GRANULATED SUGAR

2 TABLESPOONS ORANGE-FLAVORED LIQUEUR, SUCH AS GRAND MARNIER, COINTREAU, OR TRIPLE SEC

Strawberry bavarian:

3 TABLESPOONS ORANGE-FLAVORED LIQUEUR, SUCH AS GRAND MARNIER, COINTREAU, OR TRIPLE SEC

2½ TEASPOONS UNFLAVORED GELATIN

1 20-OUNCE BAG FROZEN STRAWBERRIES

¾ CUP GRANULATED SUGAR

1¾ CUPS HEAVY CREAM

1 TABLESPOON VANILLA EXTRACT

Assembly and decoration:

2 8-OUNCE PACKAGES LADYFINGERS

1½ YARDS ½-INCH-WIDE RED RIBBON

¾ CUP HEAVY CREAM

2 TEASPOONS GRANULATED SUGAR

1 PINT MEDIUM STRAWBERRIES, HULLED AND CUT IN HALF LENGTHWISE

½ STRAWBERRY, CUT LENGTHWISE, WITH GREEN HULL ATTACHED

1   To MAKE THE ORANGE SYRUP: Combine the water and sugar in a 1-cup microwave-safe glass measuring cup. Cover with waxed paper and microwave on HIGH (100 percent) power for 45 seconds to 1½ minutes, until steaming hot. Stir with a wooden spoon until the sugar is almost completely dissolved. Cover the cup again and continue to microwave on HIGH (100 percent) power for 30 to 60 seconds, until the syrup comes to a rapid boil. Keep the syrup covered and let cool. Stir in the liqueur.

2   To MAKE THE STRAWBERRY BAVARIAN: Put the liqueur in a 6-ounce custard cup. Sprinkle the gelatin over the liqueur and let it soften for 5 minutes.

3   Combine the frozen strawberries and sugar in a 2½-quart microwave-safe bowl. Cover the bowl with waxed paper and microwave on HIGH (100 percent) power for 6 to 8 minutes, until the mixture is steaming hot. Stir with a wooden spoon until the sugar is almost completely dissolved.

4   Cover the bowl again and microwave on HIGH (100 percent) power for 5 to 8 minutes, until the mixture comes to a rapid boil and the strawberries are very soft.

5   Press the strawberry mixture through a fine-meshed sieve into a 2-quart microwave-safe measuring cup. Discard the pulp and seeds.

6   Microwave the sieved strawberries, uncovered, for 5 to 10 minutes, until reduced to 1 cup. Whisk in the softened gelatin, stirring until completely dissolved. Transfer the strawberry mixture to a 2-quart noncorrosive metal bowl. Set the bowl over a large bowl of ice water and stir for 3 to 5 minutes, until the strawberry mixture is cold and slightly thickened. Remove the bowl from the bowl of ice water. Stir in the vanilla extract.

7   Using a hand-held electric mixer at high speed, whip the cream in a chilled 3-quart bowl just until soft mounds start to form. Do not overwhip the cream.

8   Using a rubber spatula, gently fold one-fourth of the whipped cream into the strawberry mixture just until blended. Scrape this mixture back into the larger bowl of whipped cream. Fold the two mixtures together just until combined. Do not overfold. Keep the bavarian at room temperature while lining the pan with the ladyfingers.

9   To ASSEMBLE AND DECORATE: Undo the clamp on a 9-inch round springform pan and separate the side from the bottom. Set the bottom of the pan aside. Refasten the side of the pan and put it on a serving plate. The plate will serve as the bottom of the mold.

10   Trim enough ladyfingers to cover the plate snugly. Trim the bottom of enough ladyfingers to fit snugly around the side of the pan. The rounded side of each ladyfinger should face the side of the pan, and the rounded tip, or untrimmed end, of the ladyfinger should be almost level with the top of the pan. Brush the ladyfingers with the orange syrup, using it all.

11   Scrape the strawberry bavarian into the prepared mold and smooth the surface with a spatula. Cover with plastic wrap and refrigerate for at least 4 hours or overnight.

12   Undo the side of the springform pan and carefully remove it. Wrap the ribbon around the cake and tie it in a bow.

13   Using a hand-held mixer set at high speed, whip the cream and sugar just until stiff peaks start to form. Scrape the whipped cream into a pastry bag fitted with a closed star tip (such as Ateco #5). Pipe a shell border within the border of ladyfingers. Arrange a ring of overlapping strawberry halves within the ring of whipped cream. Pipe a second ring of whipped cream within the strawberry ring and within that a second ring of overlapping strawberry halves. Pipe a large rosette of whipped cream in the center of the cake and top with the unhulled strawberry half. Keep the cake refrigerated until ready to serve.

Chocolate Raspberry Charlotte

serves 8

preparation time: 45 MINUTES PLUS 4 HOURS CHILLING

microwave time: 9 TO 14 MINUTES AND 15 SECONDS, INCLUDING THE RASPBERRY COULIS

Like Strawberry Bavarian Cake (page 123), this chilled cake calls for commercial ladyfingers for the ''cake'' part of the dessert. The chocolate raspberry mousse filling for the cake is wonderful on its own. However, when the entire dessert is assembled and served on a delectable pool of not-too-sweet raspberry coulis, the total effect—visually and tastewise—is fantastic.

Raspberry syrup:

¼ CUP WATER

2 TABLESPOONS GRANULATED SUGAR

2 TABLESPOONS CHAMBORD
(BLACK-RASPBERRY LIQUEUR)

Chocolate raspberry mousse:

9 OUNCES SEMISWEET CHOCOLATE, COARSELY CHOPPED

1/3 CUP MILK

FEW GRAINS OF SALT

1/4 CUP SEEDLESS RASPBERRY PRESERVES

1 TABLESPOON VEGETABLE OIL

5 TEASPOONS VANILLA EXTRACT

1 CUP HEAVY CREAM

Assembly:

2 8-OUNCE PACKAGES LADYFINGERS

Raspberry coulis:

1 12-OUNCE BAG FROZEN UNSWEETENED RASPBERRIES

1/2 CUP GRANULATED SUGAR

1 TABLESPOON CHAMBORD (BLACK-RASPBERRY LIQUEUR)

FRESH MINT LEAVES FOR GARNISH (OPTIONAL)

RASPBERRIES FOR GARNISH (OPTIONAL)

1   To make the raspberry syrup: Combine the water and sugar in a 1-cup microwave-safe glass measuring cup. Cover with waxed paper and microwave on high (100 percent) power for 45 seconds to 1½ minutes, until steaming hot. Stir with a wooden spoon until the sugar is almost completely dissolved. Cover the cup again and continue to microwave on high (100 percent) power for 30 to 60 seconds, until the syrup comes to a rapid boil. Keep the syrup covered and let it cool. Stir in the liqueur.

2   To make the chocolate raspberry mousse: Put the chocolate in a processor fitted with the metal blade. Process for 20 to 30 seconds, until finely ground.

3   Combine the milk and salt in a 2-cup microwave-safe glass measuring cup. Cover with waxed paper and microwave on high (100 percent) power for 1 to 2 minutes, until the milk comes to a boil.

4   With the food processor running, pour the hot milk mixture through the feed tube. Process for 15 to 30 seconds, until the chocolate is almost completely melted. Scrape down the sides of the bowl with a spatula.

5   Put the raspberry preserves in a 6-ounce microwave-safe custard cup. Microwave, uncovered, on medium (50 percent) power for 15 to 45 seconds, until hot. Add the hot preserves, oil, and vanilla extract to the chocolate mixture. Process for 10 to 20 seconds, until the mixture is smooth and creamy. Scrape the chocolate-raspberry mixture into a 2½-quart bowl and cool for 5 minutes, until tepid.

6 Using a hand-held electric mixer set at high speed, whip the cream in a chilled 3-quart bowl just until soft mounds start to form. Do not overwhip the cream.

7 Using a rubber spatula, gently fold one-fourth of the whipped cream into the chocolate mixture just until blended. Scrape this mixture back into the larger bowl of whipped cream. Fold the two mixtures together just until combined. Do not overfold the mousse. Keep the mousse at room temperature while lining the loaf pan with ladyfingers.

8 To ASSEMBLE: Line the inside of an 8½-by-4½-by-2-inch glass loaf pan with plastic wrap. Trim enough ladyfingers to fit snugly on the bottom and around the sides of the pan. The rounded side of each ladyfinger should face the bottom and side of the pan, and the rounded tip should be even with the top of the pan. Brush the ladyfingers with three-quarters of the raspberry syrup.

9 Scrape the chocolate-raspberry mousse into the loaf pan and smooth the surface with a spatula. Using the remaining raspberry syrup, brush the undersides of enough trimmed ladyfingers to fit snugly over the top of the mousse. Cover the charlotte with plastic wrap and refrigerate for at least 4 hours or overnight.

10 To MAKE THE RASPBERRY COULIS: Combine the frozen raspberries and sugar in a 2-quart microwave-safe glass measuring cup. Cover the cup with waxed paper and microwave on HIGH (100 percent) power for 4 minutes. Stir to dissolve any remaining sugar crystals.

11 Cover the cup again and microwave on HIGH (100 percent) power for 2½ to 5 minutes, or until the mixture is hot and the berries are soft. Do not let the mixture boil. Strain the raspberry mixture through a fine-meshed sieve into a bowl. Discard the seeds. Stir in the liqueur. Cover and refrigerate the coulis.

12 To serve, spoon a pool of raspberry coulis onto a dessert plate. Put a slice of charlotte on top of the coulis and garnish with fresh mint leaves and a raspberry, if desired.

CHAPTER FIVE

Fruit Desserts

Rhubarb Applesauce

Apricot Delight

Poached Apricots

Vanilla-Scented Peaches

Brandied Peaches

Rosy Poached Pears

Lemon-Poached Pears

Poached Pears with Caramel Ice Cream and
    Chocolate Sauce

Baked Plums with Port

Blushing Peaches with Melba Sauce

Nectarines and Summer Berries with Orange
    Cream

Gingered Fruit Compote

Rum-Raisin Stuffed Apples

Apple and Pear Crumble

In this chapter we run the gamut from applesauce to fruit crumble. In between are recipes for poached pears and peaches, baked plums, apples, and a smooth, sublime dessert we named Apricot Delight (the title may be a tad trite, but the dish is truly wonderful).

Fruit, with its high moisture content and natural sweetness, is a great match with the microwave oven. It attracts microwaves and cooks evenly and thoroughly without much loss of color, texture, or nutrients. For best flavor buy ripe fruit in season—when the distance from orchard or berry patch to market is shortest.

Fruit-Dessert Tips

*Fruits of equal size cook more evenly than different-sized specimens. When poaching pears, be sure to choose fruits that are of the same degree of ripeness.

*Use a melon-baller for coring apples and pears; it does a neater job than a vegetable peeler or small knife.

*To obtain strips of citrus zest, use a swivel vegetable peeler, which does a good job of peeling away the zest without including the bitter white pith. A sharp paring knife is efficient, too, but more often picks up some of the pith.

*Do not crowd pieces of fruit in a dish or casserole. Allow ample room for the microwaves to penetrate them on all sides to ensure even cooking.

*Using waxed paper over some of the poached fruit while it cooks provides a loose cover that holds in moisture. It requires no venting, as does plastic, and decomposes more quickly.

*In some recipes we instruct you to cover the surface of the poaching liquid with parchment paper to keep the fruit submerged as it poaches. This promotes even color and prevents discoloring. Weighting the parchment paper with a plate ensures gentle, even cooking in the hot syrup, which promotes even color and prevents discoloring, and makes fruits such as peaches easy to peel.

Rhubarb Applesauce

serves 6

preparation time: ABOUT 15 MINUTES

microwave time: 12 TO 20 MINUTES PLUS 5 MINUTES STANDING

The microwave oven is the perfect place for stewing juicy fruit into tasty sauce. Here we team apples and rhubarb for a tangy applesauce with a rosy hue. Serve it warm or chilled, with vanilla yogurt and crushed cookies. Or consider serving the piquant sauce with roast pork.

Botanically speaking, rhubarb is a leaf stem, but it is generally thought of and used as a fruit. It is most often stewed and always requires a little sweetening to counteract its natural sourness. Rhubarb is fresh in the early spring, but if you have a hankering to make this sauce in the fall when apples are at their best, use frozen rhubarb. To use fresh rhubarb, trim the brown tips from the stalks; and remember that the leaves are poisonous—so be careful to remove all of them. We found that with very crisp, firm apples, this applesauce requires about 20 minutes to cook fully.

1½ POUNDS WELL-TRIMMED FRESH RHUBARB STALKS

1 POUND MCINTOSH APPLES (ABOUT 4 MEDIUM APPLES)

½ CUP GRANULATED SUGAR

1 3-INCH CINNAMON STICK, BROKEN IN HALF

WHIPPED CREAM OR VANILLA YOGURT FOR GARNISH (OPTIONAL)

CRUSHED COOKIES, CHOPPED NUTS, OR GRANOLA CEREAL FOR GARNISH (OPTIONAL)

1   Cut the rhubarb into ½-inch chunks. Cut the apples into quarters and then into ½-inch chunks. Do not peel or core the apples.

2   Combine the rhubarb, apples, sugar, and cinnamon stick in a high-sided 3-quart microwave-safe casserole. Cover with the casserole lid and microwave on HIGH (100 percent) power for 12 to 20 minutes, stirring every 3 minutes, until the rhubarb is stringy and the apples are soft. Let stand for 5 minutes on a flat heatproof surface.

3   Force the mixture through a food mill or coarse sieve. Serve warm or refrigerate the rhubarb applesauce for 1 to 2 hours, until chilled. Serve in wine goblets or dessert glasses, garnished with a dollop of whipped cream or vanilla yogurt and sprinkled with crushed cookies, chopped nuts, or granola cereal, if desired.

Apricot Delight

serves 8

preparation time: ABOUT 20 MINUTES PLUS 15 MINUTES STANDING AND 1 TO 2 HOURS CHILLING

microwave time: 12 TO 15 MINUTES PLUS 15 MINUTES STANDING

*T*his layered, satiny dessert is almost but not quite a pudding. As such it is marvelously creamy, and since apricots develop their fullest flavor when cooked, tastes impeccably of the fruit. If the apricots are very tart, you may decide to increase the sugar a little; calorie watchers can substitute low-fat vanilla yogurt for the whipped cream.

2 POUNDS FRESH, RIPE APRICOTS

¾ CUP PLUS 3 TABLESPOONS GRANULATED SUGAR (USED IN TWO SEPARATE MEASUREMENTS)

3 TABLESPOONS FRESH LEMON JUICE

2 TABLESPOONS QUICK-COOKING TAPIOCA

2 CUPS HEAVY CREAM

½ TEASPOON VANILLA EXTRACT

CARAMELIZED ALMONDS (PAGE 309) OR TOASTED SLICED ALMONDS (PAGE 25) FOR GARNISH

1   Using a small, sharp knife, cut the apricots in half. Remove the pits. Reserve 2 pits and discard the rest. Cut the apricot halves into ¼-inch-thick wedges. Cut each wedge in half crosswise. Put the apricots into a high-sided 2-quart microwave-safe casserole.

2   With a large, sharp knife, crack open the 2 reserved apricot pits and remove the kernels. Finely chop the kernels and sprinkle them over the apricots.

3   Add the ¾ cup of sugar, lemon juice, and tapioca to the apricots. Stir with a wooden spoon until the apricot slices are evenly coated. Let the mixture stand for 15 minutes.

4   Cover the casserole with its lid and microwave on HIGH (100 percent) power for 12 to 15 minutes, stirring gently every 3 minutes, until the mixture comes to a full boil. The mixture is cooked when the beads of tapioca become translucent. (Do not confuse the tapioca beads with the chopped apricot kernels.) Let the mixture stand, covered, for 10 minutes on a flat heatproof surface. Remove the lid and cool to room temperature. Cover and refrigerate for 1 to 2 hours, until very cold.

> **kitchen note:**
>
> *We add a small amount of chopped apricot kernel from the cracked pits to provide a subtle hint of bitter almond. We also add them to the Poached Apricots on page 134 for the same reason.*

(CONTINUED)

5 Chill a 3-quart bowl. Whip the cream with the remaining 3 tablespoons of sugar and the vanilla extract in the bowl until stiff peaks start to form.

6 Fill eight 7-ounce champagne flutes or dessert glasses about one-third full with the apricot mixture. Cover the apricot layer in each glass with about 3 tablespoons of whipped cream. Cover the cream layer with the remaining apricot mixture.

7 Fill a pastry bag fitted with a closed star tip (such as Ateco #6) with the remaining whipped cream. Pipe a large swirled rosette over the top of each glass. Garnish with caramelized or toasted sliced almonds. Alternatively, top with a dollop of whipped cream and a sprinkling of almonds. Serve immediately.

Poached Apricots

serves 6

preparation time: ABOUT 20 MINUTES

microwave time: 18 TO 21 MINUTES PLUS COOLING

*P*oaching fruit in the microwave oven is easy and nearly foolproof. And poached fruit is a lovely change from heavier desserts. These apricots are simple, straightforward, and absolutely delicious. Do not substitute peaches or nectarines, which won't work in this recipe. If you want something a little more substantial, serve the fruit over pound cake and dress it up with chocolate sauce, stirred custard, whipped cream, vanilla yogurt, or ice cream.

2 CUPS WATER	1½ POUNDS SMALL, FIRM APRICOTS
1¾ CUPS GRANULATED SUGAR	(ABOUT 16)
¼ CUP FRESH LEMON JUICE	
½ VANILLA BEAN, CUT IN HALF LENGTHWISE	

1   Combine the water, sugar, lemon juice, and vanilla bean in a 3-quart microwave-safe casserole and stir with a wooden spoon until blended. Cover with the casserole lid or waxed paper and microwave on HIGH (100 percent) power for 5 minutes. Stir to dissolve any remaining sugar crystals.

2   Cover again and microwave on HIGH (100 percent) power for 2 to 4 minutes, until the syrup is steaming hot. Let the syrup stand on a flat heatproof surface while you prepare the apricots.

3   Using a small, sharp knife, cut the apricots in half along the crease line of the fruit. Pull the fruit apart and remove the pits. Discard all but 2 of the pits.

4   Crack the reserved pits in half with a large, sharp knife and remove the kernels. Put the apricot kernels in the syrup and then add the apricot halves. Gently stir them in the syrup.

5   Cut a piece of parchment paper about 1½ inches larger than the lid of the casserole. Cut a ½-inch hole in the middle of the paper. Lay the paper on the surface of the syrup, arranging it so that the excess presses up the side of the bowl. Gently press the paper down over the fruit but do not submerge it.

6   Microwave the apricots on MEDIUM-HIGH (70 percent) power for 8 to 12 minutes, until the fruit is tender when pierced with the tip of a paring knife. Gently stir the apricots every 4 minutes with a wooden spoon.

7   Keep the apricots covered with the parchment paper and let them cool to room temperature. With a wooden spoon, transfer them to a wide-mouthed 1-quart jar. Ladle enough syrup over the apricots to cover them. Be sure to include the kernels and vanilla bean.

8   Press a small square of parchment paper over the syrup. Cover the jar with its lid and refrigerate for at least 1 hour. The apricots will keep for up to 5 days in the refrigerator. Serve them with ice cream, pound cake, or yogurt.

kitchen note:

When we poach the apricots in the microwave oven, we cover them with a piece of baking parchment cut a little larger than the casserole so that it will go a little way up its sides. This ensures that the fruit is completely covered with the poaching liquid. Do not use waxed paper; it will fall apart.

Vanilla-Scented Peaches

serves 6

preparation time: ABOUT 20 MINUTES PLUS 20 MINUTES STANDING

microwave time: 15 TO 20 MINUTES

When Mary tested this recipe, she had some raspberry sauce in the refrigerator left over from the previous day's testing. Friends stopped by, and after a take-out meal of spicy Indian Food, she served the peaches with the sauce. Her friends were as impressed with the dessert—which tasted exactly right after their fiery meal—as with the fact that she "just happened" to have dessert in the refrigerator. Use firm but ripe, flavorful peaches for this and all the poached peach recipes.

3½ CUPS WATER

3 CUPS SUGAR

½ CUP FRESH LEMON JUICE (ABOUT 3 LEMONS)

1 VANILLA BEAN, SPLIT IN HALF LENGTHWISE

6 LARGE, FIRM, RIPE PEACHES (ABOUT 2 POUNDS)

1   Combine the water, sugar, lemon juice, and vanilla bean in a 3-quart microwave-safe casserole. Stir with a wooden spoon until blended. Cover with the casserole lid and microwave on HIGH (100 percent) power for 5 minutes. Stir to dissolve any remaining sugar crystals.

2   Cover the casserole again and microwave on HIGH (100 percent) power for 10 to 15 minutes, until the syrup starts to boil. Remove the casserole from the microwave and put it on a flat heatproof surface.

3   Using a small, sharp knife, cut a peach in half along the crease line of the fruit. Twist the peach gently, pull it apart, and remove the pit. Do not peel the peach halves at this point. Put the halves in the hot syrup. Cut the remaining five peaches in the same way, removing the pits. Add them to the hot syrup.

4   Cut a piece of parchment paper about 1½ inches larger than the lid of the casserole. Lay the paper on the surface of the syrup, arranging it so that the excess presses up the sides of the casserole. Put a plate on top of the paper to weight the peaches, keeping them submerged in the syrup. Let the peaches stand for 20 minutes.

5   Using a slotted spoon, remove the peach halves from the syrup one at a time. Peel each peach half with a small, sharp knife and return it to the syrup

before peeling the next one. Cover the peeled peaches with the baking parchment and the plate again. Let the peaches cool to room temperature.

6 Using a slotted spoon, transfer the peaches to a wide-mouthed 1-quart glass jar. Ladle enough of the syrup, including the vanilla bean, over the peaches to cover them completely. There will be some syrup left over, which you can discard or use for more peaches. Keep in mind, however, that there must be ample syrup to cover the peaches completely as they cool.

7 Press a small square of baking parchment over the surface of the syrup. Cover the jar with a lid and refrigerate for at least 1 hour. The peaches will keep for up to five days in the refrigerator.

Brandied Peaches

serves 6

preparation time: ABOUT 20 MINUTES

microwave time: 1 HOUR AND 4 MINUTES TO 1 HOUR AND 12 MINUTES

*T*his *delicious variation of Vanilla-Scented Peaches has a little more punch. The peaches are doused with brandy and covered with a reduced vanilla-flavored sugar syrup. They make a wonderful adult dessert and a great gift—pack them in a pretty sterilized jar and refrigerate until you give them away. Try tying a bright, festive ribbon around the neck of the jar. Always use firm, ripe, unblemished peaches.*

4 CUPS WATER

3 CUPS GRANULATED SUGAR

⅓ CUP FRESH LEMON JUICE (ABOUT 2 LEMONS)

1 VANILLA BEAN, SPLIT IN HALF LENGTHWISE

6 LARGE, FIRM, RIPE, UNBLEMISHED PEACHES (ABOUT 2 POUNDS)

¼ CUP BRANDY OR COGNAC

1   Combine the water, sugar, lemon juice, and vanilla bean in a 3-quart microwave-safe casserole. Stir with a wooden spoon until blended. Cover with the casserole lid and microwave on HIGH (100 percent) power for 5 minutes. Stir to dissolve any remaining sugar crystals.

2   Cover the casserole again and microwave on HIGH (100 percent) power for 10 to 15 minutes, until the syrup starts to boil. Remove the casserole from the oven and put it on a flat heatproof surface.

3   Using a small, sharp knife, cut a peach in half along the crease line of the fruit. Twist the peach gently, pull it apart, and remove the pit. Do not peel the peach halves at this point. Put the halves in the hot syrup. Cut the remaining 5 peaches in the same way, removing the pits. Add them to the hot syrup.

4   Cut a piece of parchment paper about 1½ inches larger than the lid of the casserole. Lay the paper on the surface of the syrup, arranging it so that the excess presses up the sides of the casserole. Put a plate on top of the paper to weight the peaches, keeping them submerged in the syrup. Let the peaches stand for 20 minutes.

5   Using a slotted spoon, remove the peach halves from the syrup one at a time. Peel each peach half with a small, sharp knife and return it to the syrup before peeling the next one.

6   Using a slotted spoon, transfer the peaches to a wide-mouthed 1-quart glass jar. Ladle enough of the syrup, including the vanilla bean, over the peaches to cover them completely. Press a small square of baking parchment over the surface of the syrup. Cover the jar with a lid and set aside.

7   Cover the casserole containing the remaining syrup with the lid and microwave on HIGH (100 percent) power for 9 to 12 minutes, until the syrup starts to boil. Remove the lid and microwave on HIGH (100 percent) power for 40 to 50 minutes, or until the syrup reduces to 1¾ cups. Take the casserole from the microwave oven and let the syrup cool for 15 to 20 minutes, until tepid.

8   Carefully pour off the syrup covering the peach halves in the jar and discard it or save it for another use. Pour the brandy over the peaches in the jar. Ladle enough of the cooled, reduced syrup into the jar to cover the peaches completely.

9   Press a small square of parchment paper over the surface of the syrup. Cover the jar with its lid and refrigerate for at least 1 hour. The peaches will keep in the refrigerator for up to three weeks. Serve the peaches with ice cream or pound cake.

Rosy Poached Pears

serves 6

preparation time: ABOUT 20 MINUTES PLUS 1 HOUR CHILLING

microwave time: 11½ TO 16 MINUTES PLUS 10 MINUTES STANDING

*H*ow pretty these fanned pears look sitting on a pool of rose-colored sauce. And the flavor of the pears combined with the piquant cranberry-raspberry juice gives this dessert an intensely fruity flavor without being overwhelming. For the best effect, try to cut the pound cake as close to the shape of the fanned pear as possible. If you prefer eating the pears solo, without the pound cake, please do. They're delicious either way.

3 MEDIUM FIRM, RIPE ANJOU OR
BARTLETT PEARS, CORED, PEELED,
AND HALVED LENGTHWISE, LEAVING
STEMS INTACT

2⅓ CUPS CRANBERRY-RASPBERRY JUICE

6 WHOLE CLOVES

1 3-INCH CINNAMON STICK

1 SMALL ORANGE

1 TABLESPOON GRANULATED SUGAR

2¼ TEASPOON LEMON JUICE

½ TEASPOON VANILLA EXTRACT

6 SLICES HOMEMADE OR
STORE-BOUGHT POUND CAKE, EACH
ABOUT ⅜ INCH THICK

1   Put the pears, cut side up, in a 2-quart microwave-safe square glass baking dish. Add the juice, cloves, and cinnamon stick.

2   Using a swivel vegetable peeler, peel off 6 strips of orange zest, each about ¾ by ½ inch. Be careful not to include any of the bitter white pith. Add the zest to the baking dish.

3   Cover with waxed paper and microwave on HIGH (100 percent) power for 9 to 12 minutes, until the pears are tender when pierced with the tip of a paring knife. If not using a turntable, rotate the baking dish a half turn after 5 minutes. Let the pears stand, uncovered, for 10 minutes. Cover loosely and refrigerate for about 1 hour, until chilled. The pears may be prepared up to this point a day in advance.

4   Drain the pears, reserving 1 cup of the poaching liquid. Save the excess liquid for another use but discard the orange zest and spices. Keep the pears covered and refrigerated until ready to serve.

> **kitchen note:**
>
> *Use a melon-baller to core the pears. Heed our warning not to let the sauce boil for more than 30 seconds. The cornstarch can easily break down, and the sauce will thin to a watery consistency.*

(*CONTINUED*)

5 Put the sugar and cornstarch in a 2-cup microwave-safe glass a measuring cup and slowly whisk in the reserved cup of poaching liquid. Cover with waxed paper and microwave on HIGH (100 percent) power for 2½ to 4 minutes, whisking every 30 seconds, until the sauce is translucent and comes to a rapid boil. Do not let the sauce boil for more than 30 seconds, or it will lose its thickness and turn watery.

6 Cover the sauce and refrigerate for about 1 hour, until chilled. Stir in the lemon juice and vanilla extract.

7 Spoon the sauce onto 6 dessert plates, reserving a little to spoon over the pears.

8 Lay the pound cake slices on a clean work surface. Take the pears from the refrigerator and, using a small, sharp knife, make lengthwise slits in each one running from the stem end to ½ inch from the core end. With the palm of your hand, flatten the pear half, fanning slightly. Use a pancake spatula to place each pear fan on a slice of pound cake. Use the same knife to trim the pound cake slices so that they are the same shape as the pear fans and then transfer each one to a plate. Spoon the remaining sauce over the pears and serve.

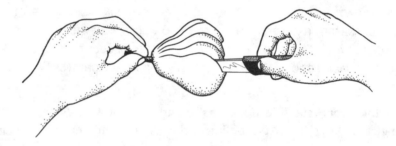

Lemon-Poached Pears

serves 6

preparation time: ABOUT 10 MINUTES

microwave time: 9 TO 12 MINUTES PLUS 10 MINUTES STANDING

This refreshing dessert is simple and elegant, tasting lightly of lemon with only a hint of sweetness. Select slim pears that are all about the same size and the same degree of ripeness. That way they will fit easily but not too snugly in the casserole and will poach evenly.

6 MEDIUM FIRM, RIPE ANJOU, BARTLETT, OR BOSC PEARS

1 TABLESPOON GRANULATED SUGAR

1 SMALL LEMON

1 TABLESPOON PEAR BRANDY OR COGNAC (OPTIONAL)

1   Slice about ⅛ inch off the bottom of each pear so that it stands upright. Using a melon-baller, core the pears from the bottom. Peel the pears, leaving the stems intact.

2   Stand the pears in a circle in a 3-quart casserole. Sprinkle with sugar.

3   Using a swivel vegetable peeler, peel off six ¾-by-2½-inch strips of lemon zest from the lemon, being careful not to include any of the bitter white pith. Add 4 of the strips to the casserole. Cut the remaining 2 strips of zest into very thin strips. Put these in a small cup, cover, and refrigerate.

4   Cover the casserole containing the pears with a lid or a piece of waxed paper. Microwave on HIGH (100 percent) power for 9 to 12 minutes, just until the pears are tender when pierced with the tip of a paring knife. Rotate the casserole, if not using a turntable, a half turn after 5 minutes.

5   Let the pears stand, uncovered, for 10 minutes. Add the pear brandy or cognac to the juices in the casserole and spoon over the pears. Discard the strips of lemon zest. Serve the pears warm or cover loosely and refrigerate until chilled. Garnish the pears with the reserved slivers of lemon zest.

Poached Pears with Caramel Ice Cream and Chocolate Sauce

serves 6

preparation time: ABOUT 20 MINUTES PLUS CHILLING AND TIME TO MAKE THE CARAMEL ICE CREAM AND SATINY CHOCOLATE SAUCE

microwave time: 9 TO 12 MINUTES PLUS 10 MINUTES STANDING

As with the Lemon-Poached Pears on page 141, these pears are cooked in their own juice rather than in sugar syrup. We add a little lemon juice, sugar, and pear brandy or cognac. The result is an intense-tasting fruit that goes well with ice cream and chocolate sauce. We highly recommend making this sundae with our Caramel Ice Cream, but if time is precious, buy high-quality vanilla.

3 MEDIUM FIRM, RIPE ANJOU OR BARTLETT PEARS, CORED, PEELED, AND HALVED LENGTHWISE, LEAVING STEMS INTACT

1 TABLESPOON GRANULATED SUGAR

2 TEASPOONS FRESH LEMON JUICE

1 TABLESPOON PEAR BRANDY OR COGNAC

½ TEASPOON VANILLA EXTRACT

CARAMEL ICE CREAM (PAGE 195) OR STORE-BOUGHT VANILLA ICE CREAM

SATINY CHOCOLATE SAUCE (PAGE 288)

> **kitchen note:**
>
> *Use pears of similar size and ripeness so that they will poach evenly. To core the pears, use a melon-baller or a small, sharp knife.*

1 Put the pears, cut side down, in a 2-quart square or oblong microwave-safe glass baking dish. Sprinkle the sugar and lemon juice over the pears.

2 Cover with waxed paper and microwave on HIGH (100 percent) power for 9 to 12 minutes, just until the pears are tender when pierced with the tip of a paring knife. Rotate the dish a half turn, if not using a turntable, after 5 minutes.

3 Let the pears stand, uncovered, for 10 minutes. Add the pear brandy or cognac and vanilla extract to the juices in the casserole and spoon over the pears. Serve warm or at room temperature. The pears may be prepared up to one day in advance, covered and kept refrigerated.

4 Prepare the Satiny Chocolate Sauce, using cognac or brandy.

5   Spoon some of the chocolate sauce into the bottom of 6 stemmed dessert glasses. Add a large scoop of ice cream to each glass. Top each scoop of ice cream with a pear half. Drizzle chocolate sauce over each pear.

Baked Plums with Port

serves 6

preparation time: ABOUT 15 MINUTES PLUS COOLING

microwave time: 12 TO 16 MINUTES

We developed this recipe to take advantage of the small elliptical freestone or Italian purple plums that are inexpensive and plentiful midsummer to early fall. Try these plums over ice cream or on their own.

2 POUNDS FIRM, RIPE FREESTONE OR ITALIAN PLUMS (ABOUT 28 SMALL PLUMS)

½ CUP GRANULATED SUGAR

½ VANILLA BEAN, SPLIT IN HALF LENGTHWISE

¼ CUP YOUNG PORT

1   Using a small knife, make a slit along the crease line of each plum and remove the pit. Do not cut the plums in half. Reserve 3 of the pits and discard the rest.

2   Using a large, sharp knife, crack the reserved pits in half, then remove the kernels.

3   Combine the plums, sugar, vanilla bean, and plum kernels in a shallow 2-quart microwave-safe casserole. Cover with a lid and microwave on HIGH (100 percent) power for 6 minutes. Stir gently with a wooden spoon to dissolve any remaining sugar crystals.

4   Cover the casserole again and microwave on HIGH (100 percent) power for 6 to 10 minutes, stirring gently every 2 minutes, until the plums are tender and the juice is syrupy.

5   Pour the port over the plums and let the mixture stand on a flat heatproof surface, with the lid half off, until cooled. Serve at room temperature or chilled.

Blushing Peaches with Melba Sauce

serves 4

preparation time: ABOUT 20 MINUTES AND TIME TO MAKE MELBA SAUCE

microwave time: 9 TO 11 MINUTES

*M*ake *this pretty dessert in the summertime with fragrant, delicious peaches with rosy patches of color on their skins. This recipe is simple, but it requires a little time to assemble on the individual plates. The effort is worth it; the presentation is especially nice—and not at all difficult.*

MELBA SAUCE (PAGE 282)
  ½ CUP HEAVY CREAM
4½ CUPS HOT TAP WATER

4 LARGE, FIRM, RIPE PEACHES, CHILLED
  (ABOUT 1½ POUNDS)

kitchen note:

Blanching peaches in boiling water makes them easy to peel. Remember that any bruises on the skin will still show up after the fruit is peeled, so look for perfect specimens for this dessert where appearance counts.

1   Make the melba sauce, flavoring it with either kirsch or an orange-flavored liqueur such as Grand Marnier, Cointreau, or Triple Sec. Refrigerate the sauce.

2   Put the cream in a chilled 2-quart bowl. Using a hand-held electric mixer set at high speed, whip the cream until it starts to thicken but can still be poured. Refrigerate the cream until ready to assemble the dessert.

3   Put the water in a 2-quart microwave-safe measuring cup. Cover with waxed paper and microwave on HIGH (100 percent) power for 9 to 11 minutes, until the water boils.

4   Remove the boiling water from the microwave and put it on a heatproof surface. Put the peaches in the water and let them stand for 1 minute.

5   Using a slotted spoon, remove the peaches from the hot water and drain them on a clean kitchen towel.

6   While the peaches are still hot, remove the skins using a small, sharp knife. Be careful not to nick the flesh. If the skins do not peel off easily, put the peaches back in the hot water, one at a time, for 15 or more seconds. Try again.

7   Put the peeled peaches onto four dessert plates. Spoon enough of the chilled melba sauce around each peach to reach the rim of the plate.

8   Using a small spoon, put six small rounds (about ½ inch) of the softly

whipped cream in a circle on top of the sauce, about ½ inch from the edge of the plate. Using another small spoon, put a drop of melba sauce in the center of each round of cream. Draw the tip of a wooden toothpick through each round of cream to form a heart shape. Serve the dessert at once.

Nectarines and Summer Berries with Orange Cream

serves 8

preparation time: ABOUT 20 MINUTES

microwave time: 6½ TO 10½ MINUTES

If you have made any of the puddings in Chapter 2, you will recognize the method for the light, tasty orange cream we use to top a delicious mixture of summer fruits. It is essentially the same as that for the puddings. As we caution in the recipe, don't mix the nectarines and berries together until an hour or less before serving. Otherwise they will become mushy.

Orange cream:

⅓ CUP CORNSTARCH (LIGHTLY SPOONED INTO A MEASURING CUP AND LEVELED WITH THE EDGE OF A KNIFE)

2 CUPS MILK (USED IN TWO SEPARATE MEASUREMENTS)

2 LARGE EGG YOLKS

½ CUP GRANULATED SUGAR
PINCH OF SALT

1 TEASPOON FINELY GRATED ORANGE ZEST

1 TABLESPOON VANILLA EXTRACT

1 TABLESPOON ORANGE-FLAVORED LIQUEUR SUCH AS GRAND MARNIER, COINTREAU, OR TRIPLE SEC

1 CUP HEAVY CREAM

Nectarines and summer berries:

4 RIPE NECTARINES (ABOUT 1¼ POUNDS)

2 CUPS BLUEBERRIES OR BLACKBERRIES

2 CUPS RASPBERRIES

¾ CUP FRESH ORANGE JUICE

1 TABLESPOON ORANGE-FLAVORED LIQUEUR SUCH AS GRAND MARNIER, COINTREAU, OR TRIPLE SEC

1   To MAKE THE ORANGE CREAM: Put the cornstarch in a 1-quart microwave-safe glass measuring cup. Slowly add ¼ cup of milk, whisking until smooth. Whisk in the egg yolks, sugar, and salt until smooth. Stir in the remaining 1¾ cups of milk until blended.

2   Cover the cup with plastic wrap, turning back a fold over the pouring spout. Microwave on HIGH (100 percent) power for 3 minutes. Whisk until smooth.

3   Cover the cup again and turn back a fold over the pouring spout. Microwave on HIGH (100 percent) power for 3 to 6 minutes, whisking every 60 seconds, or until the mixture thickens and starts to bubble around the edges. Whisk until smooth.

4   Cover the cup again and turn back a fold over the pouring spout. Microwave on HIGH (100 percent) power for 30 seconds to 1½ minutes, until the mixture comes to a full boil. Note that the mixture will be very thick at first; after it boils, its consistency will thin a little. Whisk until smooth.

5   Strain the mixture through a fine-meshed sieve into a noncorrosive metal 2-quart bowl. Push the mixture through the sieve with a rubber spatula. Whisk in the orange zest.

6   Set the bowl over a larger bowl containing ice water for 5 to 10 minutes, stirring frequently, until the mixture is cold and starts to thicken. Whisk in the vanilla extract and orange-flavored liqueur.

7   Chill a 3-quart bowl. Whip the cream in the bowl using a hand-held electric mixer or a wire whisk until soft peaks start to form. Gently whisk a third of the cream into the chilled orange mixture to lighten it. Using a rubber spatula, fold in the remaining whipped cream just until blended. Cover and refrigerate the orange cream while preparing the fruit. The cream may be made up to two days in advance and kept refrigerated.

8   To PREPARE THE NECTARINES AND SUMMER BERRIES: Do not prepare this part of the dessert more than 1 hour before serving. Hold the nectarines over a 2-quart serving bowl as you cut them into ⅛-inch-thick slices. Let the juices drip into the bowl as you put the slices in it.

9   Add the blueberries and raspberries to the bowl. Pour the orange juice and liqueur over the fruit and toss gently. Cover and refrigerate until ready to serve.

10   Just before serving, spoon the fruit into 8 stemmed dessert glasses and top each one with a large dollop of orange cream.

Gingered Fruit Compote

serves 8

preparation time: ABOUT 10 MINUTES

microwave time: 13 TO 19 MINUTES PLUS 15 MINUTES STANDING

*T*his *compote of dried fruit tastes delicious topping plain yogurt or vanilla ice cream at times when you want "something" but don't want it to be too sweet or too complicated. We specify California dried apricots, which are dried in halves, rather than whole Turkish dried apricots. California apricots are not as sweet or as plump as the others and work well here.*

1 SMALL LEMON

3 CUPS UNSWEETENED APPLE JUICE

1 CUP DRIED CALIFORNIA APRICOTS

1 CUP PITTED PRUNES

1 CUP DRIED FIG HALVES

3 TABLESPOONS MINCED CRYSTALLIZED GINGER

2 3-INCH CINNAMON STICKS

1 Using a swivel vegetable peeler, peel off 8 strips of lemon zest, each about ¾ by 2½ inches wide. Be careful not to include the white pith.

2 Combine the apple juice, apricots, prunes, figs, ginger, cinnamon sticks, and lemon zest strips in a 2-quart microwave-safe casserole. Cover the casserole with a lid and microwave on HIGH (100 percent) power for 7 to 10 minutes, until the juice starts to boil. Stir the mixture with a wooden spoon.

3 Cover the casserole again and continue to microwave on MEDIUM-HIGH (70 percent) power, simmering gently, for 6 to 9 minutes, or until the fruits are plump and tender.

4 Let the compote stand with the lid slightly ajar for 15 minutes. Discard the cinnamon sticks and lemon zest strips. Serve the compote warm or refrigerate it for about 1 hour, until chilled. The flavor of the compote improves if left to chill overnight.

Rum-Raisin Stuffed Apples

serves 4

preparation time: ABOUT 15 MINUTES

microwave time: 13½ TO 20 MINUTES PLUS 15 MINUTES STANDING

Baked stuffed apples are an autumn tradition. The fall harvest is delicious and abundant—especially in our native New England—and we find ourselves coming up with one variation after another. This recipe is so easy and quick that we hope you will be tempted, as we are, to make it time and again as the days grow cooler and the nights longer. Of course it's wonderful other times of the year, too.

kitchen note:

When you read through this recipe, you may wonder why we add the vanilla extract at the end. Why not stir it into the rum-raisin sauce with the brown sugar, lemon zest, and cinnamon? Simply because it tastes better this way. The extract loses a little punch if cooked with the apples and sauce.

2 TABLESPOONS PECANS
¼ CUP DARK RUM
2 TABLESPOONS APPLE CIDER OR UNSWEETENED APPLE JUICE
⅓ CUP PLUS 1 TABLESPOON DARK RAISINS
2 TEASPOONS LIGHT BROWN SUGAR
¼ TEASPOON FINELY GRATED LEMON ZEST

⅛ TEASPOON GROUND CINNAMON
4 MEDIUM BAKING APPLES, SUCH AS ROME, CORTLAND, EMPRESS, OR WINESAP
2 TEASPOONS UNSALTED BUTTER (OPTIONAL)
½ TEASPOON VANILLA EXTRACT

1   Put the pecans in a 6-ounce microwave-safe custard cup and microwave on HIGH (100 percent) power for 2 minutes. Stir the nuts and continue to microwave on HIGH (100 percent) power for 2 to 4 minutes more, or until the nuts are lightly toasted and fragrant. Spread the nuts on a plate to cool. When cool, coarsely chop them and set aside.

2   Combine the rum and cider in a 2-cup microwave-safe glass measuring cup. Cover with waxed paper and microwave on HIGH (100 percent) power for 1½ to 3 minutes, until the mixture boils. Add the raisins and let the mixture stand for 5 minutes to give the raisins time to plump a little. Stir in the brown sugar, lemon zest, and cinnamon.

3   Use a melon-baller or small, sharp knife to core the apples. Peel the top third of each one. Arrange the apples in a 2-quart microwave-safe casserole so that they are standing upright with the cored cavities open at the top.

4   Spoon the rum-raisin mixture into the apple cavities and pour the excess liquid over the apples. If desired, top each apple with ½ teaspoon of butter.

5   Cover the casserole with a lid and microwave on HIGH (100 percent) power for 8 to 11 minutes, until the apples are tender but not mushy. If not using a turntable, rotate the casserole a half turn after 4 minutes.

6   Tilt the casserole slightly so that the sauce pools on one side. Stir in the vanilla extract. Spoon the sauce over the hot apples and let them stand, uncovered, for 10 minutes. Sprinkle with the toasted chopped nuts and serve each apple with a generous spoonful of sauce.

Apple and Pear Crumble

serves 6

preparation time: ABOUT 15 MINUTES

cooking time: 8 TO 12 MINUTES PLUS 10 MINUTES STANDING

This bubbling hot fruit dessert could not be easier or faster—the microwave really makes quick work of it. Be sure to use firm, flavorful fruit. Granny Smiths are the best choice for the apples, and either Anjous or Bartletts will do for the pears. Take note that we specify unsifted *flour for this recipe since precise measuring is not as important here as in other recipes. Note, too, that all the sweetening and spices are in the crumble topping, not on the fruit. The fruit is left practically unadulterated for its pure, good flavor.*

The crumble tastes just fine on its own, but it tastes even better with a scoop of Cinnamon Spice Ice Cream (page 198) or Ginger Pecan Ice Cream (page 200). Or try it with a dollop of Lemon Cream (page 119), or whip up some heavy cream with a little sugar, a splash of dark rum, and a little vanilla extract. Calorie watchers can top the crumble with a spoonful of plain or vanilla yogurt.

2 MEDIUM GRANNY SMITH APPLES,
PEELED, CORED, AND CUT INTO
⅛-INCH-THICK SLICES (ABOUT 2 CUPS)

2 MEDIUM, FIRM, RIPE PEARS, PEELED,
CORED, AND CUT INTO ⅛-INCH-THICK
SLICES (ABOUT 2 CUPS)

¼ CUP DARK RAISINS

1 TEASPOON FRESH LEMON JUICE

1 TEASPOON VANILLA EXTRACT

½ TEASPOON FINELY GRATED LEMON
ZEST

⅓ CUP UNCOOKED QUICK-COOKING OATS

⅓ CUP UNSIFTED ALL-PURPOSE FLOUR
(LIGHTLY SPOONED INTO A MEASURING
CUP AND LEVELED WITH THE EDGE OF A
KNIFE)

2 TABLESPOONS DARK BROWN SUGAR

3 TABLESPOONS COARSELY CHOPPED
PECANS OR WALNUTS

½ TEASPOON GROUND CINNAMON

⅛ TEASPOON FRESHLY GRATED NUTMEG

⅛ TEASPOON GROUND GINGER

⅛ TEASPOON SALT

⅛ TEASPOON DOUBLE-ACTING BAKING
POWDER

3 TABLESPOONS CHILLED UNSALTED
BUTTER, CUT INTO ½-INCH
CUBES

1 Toss together the apples, pears, raisins, lemon juice, vanilla extract, and lemon zest in a 2½-quart bowl. Spread the mixture evenly into a 9-inch microwave-safe glass pie plate.

2 Combine the oats, flour, sugar, nuts, cinnamon, nutmeg, ginger, salt, baking powder, and butter in a food processor fitted with the metal chopping blade. Process for 30 to 45 seconds, until the mixture is crumbly.

3 Sprinkle the oat mixture evenly over the fruit.

4 Microwave, uncovered, on HIGH (100 percent) power for 8 to 12 minutes, until the dessert is bubbly around the edges. If your microwave oven does not have a turntable, rotate the pie plate a half turn after 4 minutes. Let the crumble stand on a heatproof surface for 10 minutes before serving.

CHAPTER SIX

Pies and Tarts

Double-Dark Chocolate Cream Pie
Chocolate Wafer Pie Crust or Tart Shell
Banana Cream Pie
Pecan Graham Cracker Pie Crust
Sublime Coconut Lime Pie
Coconut Graham Cracker Pie Crust
White Chocolate Strawberry Tart
Blueberry Tart
Vanilla Wafer Pie Crust or Tart Shell
Graham Cracker Pie Crust or Tart Shell
Butterscotch Pie
Chocolate Peanut Butter Pie
Mocha Mousse Brownie Pie
Caramel Satin Cream Pie
Brownie Sundae Pie
English Toffee Ice Cream Pie
Strawberry Ice Cream Pie
Chocolate Mint Oreo Ice Cream Pie

While researching this book we read somewhere that pies and tarts ought not to be made in a microwave oven. Nonsense! We have developed a number of excellent recipes—some of our favorites in the whole book.

While it is true that traditional pie crusts, meant to brown to a golden turn, cannot be made in a microwave oven, you can make delicious cookie and cracker crumb crumbs that beg for fillings of pudding, pastry cream, mousse, or ice cream. Adrienne also mastered a devilishly decadent brownie-based pie "crust" that we top once with ice cream and another time with a velvety mocha mousse.

We make all pies in either 9- or 10-inch glass pie plates. Tarts are prettiest if made in a ceramic tart pan, although you can use the 10-inch pie plate. Top crusts are out, but we explain how best to decorate the pies so that they will look festive. In some instances you may decide to forgo the garnish. This is fine, but remember that they add flavor as well as luster; if you take the extra time, you will be richly rewarded.

Pie and Tart Tips

Measure cornstarch by spooning it lightly into a measuring cup and then leveling it with the straight edge of a knife. This ensures that you do not overmeasure the cornstarch.

When using gelatin, soften it for at least 5 minutes in liquid before melting it in the microwave or stirring it into the hot mixture. Gelatin that is inadequately softened will not dissolve completely, and the pie filling will not set properly.

For a silky texture we recommend straining some of the pie fillings. You may skip this step, but the fillings will not be as velvety and smooth.

---

*In many of the following recipes we instruct you to whip cream in a chilled metal bowl. To save time use the same bowl that contained the ice and ice water used to chill the pie filling. After emptying it of ice and ice water, completely dry the bowl and use it to whip the cream.

*Ice cream pies are wonderful for those times when you want to plan ahead. Before they are decorated they can be kept in the freezer for as long as two weeks.

*When we call for store-bought ice cream, we hope you will buy the best brand available. These high-quality products have far less air incorporated in them than others, and taste creamier and richer, too. They actually feel heavier (ice cream is packed by volume, not weight). And yes, they generally cost a little more.

*Softening ice cream in the microwave is more efficient than letting it soften on the counter or in the refrigerator. It gives you more control and less mess.

*We do not recommend a food processor for pulverizing cookie or cracker crumbs for crusts. It is too easy to overprocess the crumbs, which should be a little coarse. We suggest putting the cookies or crackers into a sealable plastic bag and crushing them with a rolling pin.

*Oil the pie and tart plates well, or the pie crusts will stick.

*Crusts baked in glass pie plates cook a little faster than those baked in ceramic tart plates. The thinner glass transmits the microwaves more quickly than the relatively thick ceramic.

*For the best results elevate the pie plate on a microwave-safe glass pie plate so that the microwaves can easily reach the bottom of the plate and cook the crust evenly.

*Take care not to overbake the crusts. When you take them from the micro- wave oven, they should be a little soft on the bottom and bounce back when gently pressed with a fingertip. They will become firm when standing.

*For decorating we prefer lightweight polyester pastry bags to the more cum- bersome canvas bags. The soft and flexible polyester bags are easy to control with just a little pressure. They come in a variety of sizes; we find 12, 14, and 16 inches the most useful. You can also use clear disposable plastic pastry bags.

*After inserting the decorating tip in the empty pastry bag, twist the portion of the bag that is just above the widest opening of the tip and then tuck the twisted portion in this opening. Once the bag is filled, this will prevent the whipped cream from leaking out of the end of the pastry bag before you are ready to pipe.

*After inserting the tip, turn down the widest portion of the pastry bag at the top to form a 3- to 4-inch cuff. Suspend the pastry bag in a 2-cup liquid measuring cup before filling it with the frosting. The cup will support the *pastry bag, making it easier to fill. When you are ready to pipe, twist the top of the pastry bag above the filling and grasp the bag so that the top of the filled section rests in the palm of your hand. Wrap the excess twisted portion of the bag around your forefinger. Untwist the twisted portion at the pastry-tip end of the bag and begin decorating.*

*Wash pastry bags in warm water and mild detergent. Rinse them well and dry them draped over large bottles.

Double-Dark Chocolate Cream Pie

makes one 9-inch pie; serves 10 to 12

preparation time: ABOUT 25 MINUTES PLUS 10 TO 15 MINUTES COOLING AND TIME TO MAKE THE PIE CRUST PLUS 1 TO 3 HOURS CHILLING

microwave time: 7 MINUTES AND 45 SECONDS TO 11½ MINUTES

We *set out to create a typical chocolate cream pie using the microwave oven. What we ended up with is super rich and thick. This pie is for chocolate lovers* extraordinaire. *The cream topping is needed to balance the chocolate, but you could serve the unadorned pie with fresh raspberries or strawberries. Most 9-inch pies serve six to eight people; this one, because of its richness, easily takes care of ten or twelve. Chocolate lovers, rejoice.*

1 CHOCOLATE WAFER PIE CRUST (PAGE 157), COOLED

Chocolate filling:

3 TABLESPOONS COLD WATER

1¾ TEASPOONS UNFLAVORED GELATIN

¼ CUP CORNSTARCH (LIGHTLY SPOONED INTO A MEASURING CUP AND LEVELED WITH THE EDGE OF A KNIFE)

2½ CUPS MILK (USED IN TWO MEASUREMENTS)

3 LARGE EGG YOLKS

½ CUP GRANULATED SUGAR

⅛ TEASPOON SALT

10 OUNCES SEMISWEET CHOCOLATE, FINELY CHOPPED

2 TABLESPOONS UNSALTED BUTTER, SOFTENED

4 TEASPOONS VANILLA EXTRACT

(*INGREDIENTS CONTINUED*)

Whipped cream topping:

1¼ CUPS HEAVY CREAM

4 TEASPOONS GRANULATED SUGAR

½ TEASPOON VANILLA EXTRACT

CHOCOLATE CURLS FOR GARNISH (PAGE 26)

kitchen note:

You will have to check the chocolate filling mixture several times during cooking for consistency. After the initial cooking, look at the filling to see if it is bubbling around the edges. The mixture must also be stirred three or four times during cooking.

1 TO MAKE THE CHOCOLATE FILLING: Put the water in a small custard cup. Sprinkle the gelatin over the water and let the mixture soften for at least 5 minutes.

2 Put the cornstarch in a 2-quart microwave-safe glass measuring cup. Gradually whisk in ¼ cup of milk until completely smooth. Whisk in the egg yolks, sugar, and salt until blended. Stir in the remaining 2¼ cups of milk.

3 Cover the cup with plastic wrap, turning back a fold over the pouring spout. Microwave on HIGH (100 percent) power for 4 minutes. Whisk until smooth.

4 Cover the cup again, turning back a fold over the pouring spout, and microwave on HIGH (100 percent) power for 3 to 6 minutes, whisking every 60 seconds, until the mixture thickens and starts to bubble around the edges. Whisk until smooth.

5 Cover the cup again, turning back a fold over the pouring spout, and microwave on HIGH (100 percent) power for 45 seconds to 1½ minutes, until the mixture comes to a full boil. Note that the filling will be very thick at first; after it boils its consistency will thin a little.

6 Stir the softened gelatin into the hot mixture, making sure it dissolves completely. Add the chocolate, stir to blend, and let the mixture stand for 30 seconds. Add the butter and whisk until smooth.

7 Strain the chocolate filling through a fine-meshed sieve into a noncorrosive metal 2½-quart bowl. Push the filling through the sieve with a rubber spatula.

8 Set the bowl over a larger bowl containing ice and ice water for 10 to 15 minutes, stirring frequently, until the filling is cold and starts to thicken. Remove the bowl from the larger bowl holding the ice water. Whisk in the vanilla extract.

9 Scrape the filling into the prepared crust and smooth the top with a spatula. Cover and refrigerate the pie for 1 to 3 hours, until set. The pie can be prepared a day in advance up to this point.

10 TO MAKE THE WHIPPED CREAM TOPPING: Combine the cream, sugar, and vanilla extract in a chilled 3-quart bowl. Using a hand-held electric mixer set at high

speed, whip the cream until stiff peaks start to form. If desired, reserve 1 cup of the whipped cream for piping a border around the edge of the pie. Scrape the remaining whipped cream over the chocolate filling and spread it evenly with a rubber spatula.

11　If piping a border, fill a pastry bag fitted with a closed star tip (such as Ateco #5) with the reserved whipped cream. Pipe a decorative border around the edge of the pie.

12　Scoop up some chocolate curls with a spoon and sprinkle them on top of the whipped cream. Refrigerate the pie until serving time.

Chocolate Wafer Pie Crust or Tart Shell

makes one 9-inch pie crust or one 9½-inch tart shell

preparation time: ABOUT 10 MINUTES

microwave time: 2 MINUTES AND 45 SECONDS TO 5 MINUTES

You will find countless uses for this simple crust. You probably have made similar ones in the conventional oven, but the microwave oven works just as well and takes less time. We use this for the Double-Dark Chocolate Cream Pie and White Chocolate Strawberry Tart, but you could spoon any one of your favorite cream pie or tart fillings into it.

7 TABLESPOONS UNSALTED BUTTER
1¾ CUPS FINELY CRUSHED CHOCOLATE
WAFER CRUMBS (ABOUT 35 WAFERS)

1   Oil the bottom and sides of a 9-inch microwave-safe glass pie plate or a 9½-inch microwave-safe fluted ceramic tart plate.

2   Put the butter in a 1½-quart microwave-safe glass bowl. Cover with waxed paper and microwave on MEDIUM-HIGH (70 percent) power for 1 to 2 minutes, until the butter is melted.

3   Add the cookie crumbs to the melted butter. Stir with a wooden spoon until the mixture is crumbly.

4   Scrape the crumbs into the oiled pie or tart plate. Using your fingers, press the crumb mixture firmly and evenly into the bottom and up the sides of the pie or tart plate.

5   Set the pie or tart plate on an inverted 9-inch microwave-safe glass pie plate and microwave on HIGH (100 percent) power for 1 minute and 45 seconds to 3 minutes, until the bottom of the crust bounces back when gently pressed with a finger. If not using a turntable, rotate the plate a half turn after 1 minute. Do not overbake. The crust will become firm while standing.

6   Let the crust or tart shell stand on a flat heatproof surface for 10 minutes. Cool completely before filling.

Banana Cream Pie

makes one 10-inch pie: serves 10 to 12

preparation time: ABOUT 25 MINUTES PLUS 5 TO 10 MINUTES COOLING AND TIME TO MAKE THE PIE CRUST PLUS 1 TO 3 HOURS CHILLING

microwave time: 10½ TO 15½ MINUTES

This is the sort of pie that was once displayed under shiny glass domes in out-of-the-way diners serving honest, homey food. Since those places hardly exist anymore, we came up with an honest banana cream pie for the microwave oven. If you made the Caribbean Banana Rum Pudding on page 42, you will (almost) recognize the filling for this pie. They are similar in that they both require the addition of diced pound cake. The cake provides bulk as well as flavor, which explains why this pie is a 10-incher. Serve the pie the day it is made; otherwise the bananas will begin to brown.

1 10-INCH PECAN GRAHAM CRACKER PIE
CRUST (PAGE 161), COOLED

Banana filling:

3 TABLESPOONS COLD WATER

2 TEASPOONS UNFLAVORED GELATIN

¼ CUP CORNSTARCH (LIGHTLY SPOONED INTO A MEASURING CUP AND LEVELED WITH THE EDGE OF A KNIFE)

2 CUPS MILK (USED IN TWO MEASUREMENTS)

2 LARGE EGG YOLKS

½ CUP GRANULATED SUGAR

⅛ TEASPOON SALT

1 TABLESPOON VANILLA EXTRACT

2 CUPS ½-INCH-DICED POUND CAKE

3 TABLESPOONS DARK RUM OR FRESH ORANGE JUICE

¾ CUP HEAVY CREAM

2 CUPS ¼-INCH-DICED RIPE BANANAS (ABOUT 4 MEDIUM BANANAS)

Toasted pecans and whipped cream topping:

2 TABLESPOONS PECAN HALVES

1¼ CUPS HEAVY CREAM

4 TEASPOONS SUGAR

½ TEASPOON VANILLA EXTRACT

1 LARGE, RIPE BANANA

1   TO MAKE THE BANANA FILLING: Put the water in a small cup. Sprinkle the gelatin over the water and let the mixture soften for at least 5 minutes.

2   Put the cornstarch in a 1-quart microwave-safe glass measuring cup. Gradually whisk in ¼ cup of milk until smooth. Whisk in the egg yolks, sugar, and salt until blended. Stir in the remaining 1¾ cups of milk.

3   Cover the cup with plastic wrap, turning back a fold over the pouring spout. Microwave on HIGH (100 percent) power for 3 minutes. Whisk until smooth.

4   Cover the cup again, turning back a fold over the pouring spout, and microwave on HIGH (100 percent) power for 2 to 5 minutes, whisking every 60 seconds, until the mixture thickens and starts to bubble around the edges. Whisk until smooth.

5   Cover the cup again, turning back a fold over the pouring spout, and microwave on HIGH (100 percent) power for 30 seconds to 1½ minutes, until the mixture comes to a full boil. Note that the filling will be very thick at first; after it boils its consistency will thin a little.

6   Stir the softened gelatin into the mixture, making sure it dissolves completely.

7   Strain the filling through a fine-meshed sieve into a noncorrosive metal 2-quart bowl. Push the filling through the sieve with a rubber spatula.

8   Set the bowl over a larger bowl containing ice and ice water for 5 to 10 minutes, stirring frequently, until the filling is cold and starts to thicken. Remove the bowl from the larger bowl holding ice water. Whisk in the vanilla extract.

9   Put the diced pound cake into a 1½-quart bowl. Sprinkle with rum or orange juice and toss gently.

10   Chill a 2½-quart bowl. Whip the cream in the bowl using a hand-held electric mixer until soft peaks start to form. Using a rubber spatula, fold the cream into the cooled filling just until blended. Gently fold the diced bananas and pound cake into the filling.

11   Scrape the filling into the prepared crust and spread it evenly with a spatula. Cover the surface of the pie and refrigerate for 1 to 3 hours, until set.

12   TO PREPARE THE TOASTED PECANS AND WHIPPED CREAM TOPPING: Put the pecan halves in a 6-ounce microwave-safe custard cup. Microwave, uncovered, on HIGH (100 percent) power for 2 minutes. Stir and continue to microwave on HIGH (100 percent) power for 2 to 4 minutes, until the nuts are lightly toasted and fragrant. Transfer the nuts to a plate to cool.

13   Combine the cream, sugar, and vanilla extract in a chilled 3-quart bowl. Using a hand-held electric mixer set at high speed, whip the cream until stiff peaks start to form. Spread 1 cup of the whipped cream over the filling in a thin, even layer.

14   Fill a pastry bag fitted with a closed star tip (such as Ateco #5) with the remaining whipped cream. Pipe a shell border around the edge of the pie.

15   Chop the cooled nuts very fine and sprinkle them lightly over the top of the pie. Refrigerate the pie until ready to serve.

16   Just before serving, peel the banana and cut it on the diagonal into slices ⅛ inch thick. Lay the slices in an overlapping ring within the whipped cream border. Serve immediately.

Pecan Graham Cracker Pie Crust

makes one 10-inch pie crust

preparation time: ABOUT 10 MINUTES

microwave time: 6 TO 13 MINUTES PLUS 10 MINUTES STANDING

*R*ead the kitchen note for the Chocolate Wafer Pie Crust, page 157, before crushing the graham crackers into crumbs for this recipe. Remember, they should be slightly coarse. Be sure to oil the pie plate well to prevent sticking.

1 CUP PECAN HALVES
7 TABLESPOONS UNSALTED BUTTER
3 TABLESPOONS LIGHT BROWN SUGAR
PINCH OF SALT

1¾ CUPS SLIGHTLY COARSE GRAHAM CRACKER CRUMBS (ABOUT 13 CRACKERS)

1   Put the pecans in a 9-inch microwave-safe glass pie plate. Microwave, uncovered, on HIGH (100 percent) power for 3 minutes. Stir the pecans. Continue to microwave, uncovered, on HIGH (100 percent) power for 2 to 5 minutes, stirring every 60 seconds, until the nuts are lightly toasted and fragrant. Transfer the nuts to a plate and cool completely.

2   Oil the bottom and sides of a 10-inch microwave-safe glass pie plate.

3   Put the butter in a 2-cup glass measuring cup. Cover with waxed paper and microwave on MEDIUM-HIGH (70 percent) power for 1 to 2 minutes, until melted.

4   Combine the pecans, brown sugar, and salt in a food processor fitted with the metal chopping blade. Process for 20 to 30 seconds, until the pecans are finely ground.

5   Distribute the graham cracker crumbs and the melted butter evenly around the chopping blade. Pulse 4 to 6 times, until the mixture is crumbly. Scrape the mixture into the oiled pie plate. Using your fingers, press the crumbs firmly and evenly into the bottom and up the sides of the plate.

6   Set the pie crust on an inverted 9-inch microwave-safe glass pie plate and microwave on HIGH (100 percent) power for 3 to 6 minutes, until the bottom of the crust bounces back when gently pressed with a finger. If not using a turntable, rotate the crust a half turn after 1 minute. Do not overbake. The crust will become firm while standing.

7   Let the crust stand on a flat heatproof surface for 10 minutes. Cool completely before filling.

Sublime Coconut Lime Pie

makes one 9-inch pie; serves 8 to 10

preparation time: ABOUT 25 MINUTES PLUS 5 TO 10 MINUTES COOLING AND TIME TO MAKE THE PIE CRUST PLUS 1 TO 3 HOURS CHILLING

microwave time: 6 MINUTES AND 45 SECONDS TO 10½ MINUTES

This is one of our prettiest pies, but since everyone knows that ''handsome is as handsome does,'' we made sure it tasted extremely good, too. The seductive combination of lime and coconut works well in this tropical-style dessert guaranteed to brighten even the most snowbound kitchen. And the light fresh flavor makes it perfect for summertime, too.

1   COCONUT GRAHAM CRACKER PIE
    CRUST (PAGE 164), COOLED

Coconut-lime pie filling:

3 TABLESPOONS COLD WATER

1½ TEASPOONS UNFLAVORED GELATIN

¼ CUP CORNSTARCH (LIGHTLY
   SPOONED INTO A MEASURING CUP
   AND LEVELED WITH THE EDGE OF A
   KNIFE)

1½ CUPS MILK (USED IN TWO
   MEASUREMENTS)

2 LARGE EGG YOLKS

1½ TEASPOONS FINELY GRATED LIME
   ZEST (USED IN TWO MEASUREMENTS)

⅛ TEASPOON SALT

1 CUP SWEETENED CREAM OF
   COCONUT SUCH AS COCO LOPEZ

⅓ CUP PLUS 2 TABLESPOONS FRESH
   LIME JUICE

2 TEASPOONS VANILLA EXTRACT

½ CUP HEAVY CREAM

Coconut cream and garnish:

1 CUP HEAVY CREAM

¼ CUP CREAM OF COCONUT SUCH AS
   COCO LOPEZ, CHILLED

½ TEASPOON VANILLA EXTRACT

LIME SLICES CUT INTO QUARTERS FOR
GARNISH

1   To make the coconut-lime filling: Put the water in a small cup. Sprinkle the gelatin over the water and let the mixture soften for at least 5 minutes.

2   Put the cornstarch in a 1-quart microwave-safe glass measuring cup. Gradually whisk in ¼ cup of milk until smooth. Whisk in the egg yolks, 1 teaspoon of lime zest, and salt until blended. Stir in the remaining 1¼ cups of milk and cream of coconut.

3   Cover the cup with plastic wrap, turning back a fold over the pouring spout. Microwave on HIGH (100 percent) power for 3 minutes. Whisk until smooth.

4   Cover the cup again, turning back a fold over the pouring spout, and microwave on HIGH (100 percent) power for 3 to 6 minutes, whisking every 60 seconds, until the mixture thickens and starts to bubble around the edges. Whisk until smooth.

5   Cover the cup again, turning back a fold over the pouring spout, and microwave on HIGH (100 percent) power for 45 seconds to 1½ minutes, until the mixture comes to a full boil. Note that the filling will be very thick at first; after it boils its consistency will thin a little.

6   Stir the softened gelatin into the mixture, making sure it dissolves completely.

7   Strain the filling through a fine-meshed sieve into a noncorrosive metal 2-quart bowl. Push the filling through the sieve with a rubber spatula. Stir in the remaining ½ teaspoon of lime zest and the lime juice.

8   Set the bowl over a larger bowl containing ice and ice water for 5 to 10 minutes, stirring frequently, until the filling is cold and starts to thicken. Remove the bowl from the larger bowl holding the ice water. Whisk in the vanilla extract.

9   Chill a 2½-quart bowl. Whip the cream in the bowl using a hand-held electric mixer set at high speed until soft peaks start to form. Using a rubber spatula, fold the cream into the cooled filling just until blended.

10   Scrape the filling into the prepared crust and spread it evenly with a spatula. Cover the surface of the pie with plastic wrap and refrigerate for 1 to 3 hours, until set. The pie may be prepared to this point up to one day in advance.

11   To PREPARE THE COCONUT CREAM AND GARNISH: Combine the heavy cream, cream of coconut, and vanilla extract in a chilled 3-quart bowl. Using a hand-held electric mixer set at high speed, whip until stiff peaks start to form.

12   Fill a pastry bag fitted with a closed star tip (such as Ateco #5) with the whipped cream. Pipe lines diagonally across the surface of the pie about an inch apart. Pipe more lines on the diagonal to intersect the first, creating a lattice effect. Pipe a shell border around the edge of the pie. Arrange the lime quarters so that they are evenly spaced on top of the shell border. Refrigerate until ready to serve.

Coconut Graham Cracker Pie Crust

makes one 9-inch pie crust

preparation time: ABOUT 10 MINUTES

microwave time: 8 TO 13 MINUTES

This delicious crust, subtly flavored with toasted coconut, is the ideal base for the Sublime Coconut Lime Pie (page 162). But, as with all our crusts, you might want to use it with other fillings, too. For instance, try combining it with your favorite lemon meringue or key lime recipe. You won't be disappointed.

½ CUP SWEETENED FLAKED COCONUT   2 TABLESPOONS GRANULATED SUGAR

6 TABLESPOONS UNSALTED BUTTER

1¼ CUPS COARSE GRAHAM CRACKER
    CRUMBS (ABOUT 11 CRACKERS)

1 Put the coconut in a 9-inch microwave-safe glass pie plate. Microwave, uncovered, on HIGH (100 percent) power for 1 minute. Stir with a wooden spoon. Continue to microwave, uncovered, on HIGH (100 percent) power for 4 to 7 minutes, stirring every 30 seconds, until the coconut turns golden brown. Transfer the coconut to a plate to cool.

2 Oil the bottom and sides of a 9-inch microwave-safe glass pie plate.

3 Put the butter in a 1½-quart microwave-safe glass bowl. Cover with waxed paper and microwave on MEDIUM-HIGH (70 percent) power for 1 to 2 minutes, until melted.

4 Add the graham cracker crumbs, toasted coconut, and sugar to the bowl of melted butter. Mix with a wooden spoon until the mixture is crumbly.

5 Scrape the crumbs into the prepared pie plate. Using your fingers, press the crumbs firmly and evenly into the bottom and up the sides of the plate.

6 Set the pie plate on an inverted 9-inch microwave-safe glass pie plate and microwave on HIGH (100 percent) power for 2 to 3 minutes, until the bottom of the crust bounces back when gently pressed with a finger. If not using a turntable, rotate the crust a half turn after 1 minute. Do not overbake. The crust will become firm while standing.

7 Let the crust stand on a flat heatproof surface for 10 minutes. Cool completely before filling.

> **kitchen note:**
>
> *Read the note preceding the recipe for Chocolate Wafer Pie Crust, page 157, on how to make the graham crackers into crumbs. They should be finely crushed—not powdery—to work well here. Be sure to oil the pie plate well to prevent sticking.*

White Chocolate Strawberry Tart

makes one 9½-inch tart; serves 6 to 8

preparation time: ABOUT 30 MINUTES PLUS 10 TO 20 MINUTES COOLING AND 1 TO 2 HOURS CHILLING

microwave time: 1 MINUTE AND 5 SECONDS TO 2½ MINUTES

It was Halloween. Mary had just finished testing and putting the finishing touches on this tart that afternoon. Invited to stay for supper at a neighbor's after trick-or-treating, she took along the tart for dessert. ''Ohs'' and ''ahs'' accompanied the pretty creation to the table but were nothing compared to the comments on the tart as it was eaten. As much as everyone liked it, the question asked most often was, ''How long did this take?''

In truth, making the white chocolate mousse and the crust does take a while, as do slicing and arranging the strawberries, demonstrating that the microwave oven does not turn every culinary exercise into a speedy event. But the combination of creamy white chocolate, fresh strawberries, and rich chocolate crust is unbeatable—even after an evening of stealing candy from your child's trick-or-treat sack.

1 CHOCOLATE WAFER TART SHELL
(PAGE 157), COOLED

White chocolate mousse filling:

2 TABLESPOONS COLD WATER

1 TABLESPOON ORANGE-FLAVORED LIQUEUR SUCH AS GRAND MARNIER, COINTREAU, OR TRIPLE SEC

1¼ TEASPOONS UNFLAVORED GELATIN

6 OUNCES WHITE CHOCOLATE, FINELY CHOPPED

⅓ CUP MILK

1 TABLESPOON VEGETABLE OIL

¼ TEASPOON FINELY GRATED ORANGE ZEST

1 CUP HEAVY CREAM

1 TABLESPOON VANILLA EXTRACT

Topping and assembly:

4 CUPS MEDIUM STRAWBERRIES, HULLED AND SLICED

2 TABLESPOONS STRAWBERRY OR RED CURRANT JELLY

1   TO MAKE THE WHITE CHOCOLATE MOUSSE FILLING: Put the water and liqueur in a 6-ounce microwave-safe glass custard cup. Sprinkle the gelatin over the liquid and let the mixture soften for at least 5 minutes.

2   Put the white chocolate in a 2½-quart bowl. Put the milk in a 1-cup microwave-safe measuring cup. Cover with waxed paper and microwave on HIGH (100 percent) power for 45 seconds to 1½ minutes, until the milk comes to a boil. Pour the hot milk over the bowl of chocolate. Let the mixture stand without stirring.

3   Cover the custard cup containing the softened gelatin mixture with waxed paper. Microwave on MEDIUM (50 percent) power for 15 to 45 seconds, stirring every 20 seconds, until the gelatin is completely dissolved and the mixture is hot. Do not let it boil.

4   Pour the dissolved gelatin mixture over the white chocolate mixture and whisk until smooth. Add the oil and orange zest, and stir to blend. Let the mixture cool for 10 to 20 minutes, until tepid.

5   Chill a 3-quart bowl. Using a hand-held electric mixer set at high speed, whip the cream and vanilla extract in the chilled bowl just until soft mounds start to form. Do not overwhip the cream.

6   Gently whisk a quarter of the cream into the tepid chocolate mixture just until blended. Using a rubber spatula, scrape this mixture back into the bowl of whipped cream and fold together just until blended. Do not overfold.

7   Spread the mousse into the baked and cooled tart shell. Cover with plastic wrap and refrigerate for 1 to 2 hours, until set. The tart may be prepared to this point up to one day in advance.

8   To make the topping and assemble: Starting from the outside edge, arrange the sliced strawberries on the mousse in concentric, overlapping circles with the tips pointing outward. Or, if desired, alternate the direction of each circle.

9   Press the jelly through a sieve into a small bowl to liquefy. Lightly coat the strawberries with the jelly using a pastry brush and dabbing motions. Serve immediately or keep the tart refrigerated for no longer than 2 hours.

variation

White Chocolate Raspberry Tart

1   *Follow the instructions of the White Chocolate Strawberry Tart through step 7.*

2   *Starting from the outside edge of the filled tart shell, cover the mousse with 3 cups of fresh raspberries. Glaze the tart with raspberry or red currant jelly.*

Blueberry Tart

makes one 9½-inch tart; serves 6 to 8

preparation time: ABOUT 10 MINUTES PLUS TIME TO MAKE THE PASTRY CREAM AND GRAHAM
CRACKER TART SHELL

microwave time: SEE LIME PASTRY CREAM (PAGE 307) AND GRAHAM CRACKER TART SHELL
(PAGE 170)

Here again our penchant for blueberries and lime is evident. The chilled pie is pretty and refreshing in the summer when the berries are in season. Use large, plump berries; they are easy to arrange on top of the pastry cream and look bright and inviting. Do not refrigerate the tart for longer than 2 hours, or the pastry cream may become rubbery. If you make the pastry cream ahead of time, whisk it well before spreading it in the tart shell.

LIME PASTRY CREAM (PAGE 307)
1 9½-INCH GRAHAM CRACKER TART SHELL
    (PAGE 170) OR VANILLA WAFER TART
    SHELL (PAGE 169), COOLED

3 CUPS LARGE, FRESH BLUEBERRIES
2 TABLESPOONS RED CURRANT JELLY

1   Spread the pastry cream in the cooled tart shell. Starting from the outside edge, arrange the blueberries on the tart in concentric circles. Make sure the berries stand on their sides and touch each other.

2   Press the jelly through a sieve into a small bowl to liquefy. Lightly coat the berries with the jelly using a pastry brush and dabbing motions. Serve immediately or keep the tart refrigerated for no longer than 2 hours.

Vanilla Wafer Pie Crust or Tart Shell

makes one 9-inch pie crust or one 9½-inch tart shell

preparation time: ABOUT 10 MINUTES

microwave time: 3 TO 7 MINUTES PLUS 10 MINUTES STANDING

6 TABLESPOONS UNSALTED BUTTER
2 CUPS VANILLA WAFER CRUMBS (ABOUT
   60 NABISCO VANILLA WAFERS)

1 Oil the bottom and sides of a 9-inch microwave-safe glass pie plate or 9½-inch microwave-safe fluted ceramic tart plate.

2 Put the butter in a 1½-quart microwave-safe glass bowl. Cover with waxed paper and microwave on MEDIUM-HIGH (70 percent) power for 1 to 2 minutes, until melted.

3 Add the wafer crumbs to the bowl of melted butter. Mix with a wooden spoon until the mixture is crumbly.

4 Scrape the crumbs into the oiled pie or tart plate. Using your fingers, press the crumbs firmly and evenly into the bottom and up the sides of the plate.

5 Set the pie or tart plate on an inverted 9-inch microwave-safe glass pie plate and microwave on HIGH (100 percent) power for 2 to 5 minutes, until the crust bounces back when gently pressed with a finger. If not using a turntable, rotate the crust a half turn after 1 minute. Do not overbake. The crust will become firm on standing.

6 Let the crust stand on a flat heatproof surface for 10 minutes. Cool completely before filling.

Graham Cracker Pie Crust or Tart Shell

makes one 9-inch pie crust or one 9½-inch tart shell

preparation time: ABOUT 10 MINUTES

microwave time: 3½ TO 8 MINUTES PLUS 10 MINUTES STANDING

You will find numerous uses for this basic graham cracker pie crust. We like it with the Blueberry Tart (page 168), Butterscotch Pie (page 171), and Chocolate Peanut Butter Pie (page 173), but you could also substitute it for the Chocolate Wafer Crust in the recipe for Double-Dark Chocolate Cream Pie (page 155).

7 TABLESPOONS UNSALTED BUTTER

1¾ CUPS GRAHAM CRACKER CRUMBS
(ABOUT 13 CRACKERS)

2 TABLESPOONS GRANULATED SUGAR

1   Oil the bottom and sides of a 9-inch microwave-safe glass pie plate or 9½-inch microwave-safe fluted ceramic tart plate.

2   Put the butter in a 1½-quart microwave-safe glass bowl. Cover with waxed paper and microwave on MEDIUM-HIGH (70 percent) power for 1 to 2 minutes, until the butter melts.

3   Add the cracker crumbs and sugar to the bowl of melted butter. Mix with a wooden spoon until the mixture is crumbly.

4   Scrape the crumbs into the oiled pie or tart plate. Using your fingers, press the crumbs firmly and evenly into the bottom and up the sides of the pie or tart plate.

5   Set the pie or tart plate on an inverted 9-inch microwave-safe glass pie plate and microwave on HIGH (100 percent) power for 2½ to 6 minutes, until the bottom of the crust bounces back when gently pressed with a finger. If not using a turntable, rotate the crust a half turn after 1½ minutes. Do not over-bake. The crust will become firm while standing.

6   Let the crust or tart shell stand on a flat heatproof surface for 10 minutes. Cool completely before filling.

Butterscotch Pie

makes one 10-inch pie; serves 10

preparation time: ABOUT 45 MINUTES PLUS 5 TO 10 MINUTES COOLING AND 1 TO 3 HOURS CHILLING AND TIME TO MAKE THE PECAN GRAHAM CRACKER PIE CRUST

microwave time: 21 MINUTES AND 15 SECONDS TO 30 MINUTES

To us, just the name *"butterscotch pie"* sounds comforting and inviting, like something that should be served at a children's tea party—or for dessert right now. As with our *Butterscotch Velvet Pudding (page 36)* and *Butterscotch Sauce (page 284)*, this tastes deeply and satisfyingly of true, creamy butterscotch.

1 PECAN GRAHAM CRACKER PIE
  CRUST (PAGE 161), COOLED

Butterscotch filling:

1 CUP HEAVY CREAM

¾ CUP PACKED LIGHT BROWN SUGAR

⅛ TEASPOON SALT

3 TABLESPOONS COLD WATER

2 TEASPOONS UNFLAVORED GELATIN

3 CUPS SKIM MILK (USED IN TWO
  MEASUREMENTS)

⅓ CUP CORNSTARCH (LIGHTLY SPOONED
  INTO A MEASURING CUP AND LEVELED
  WITH THE EDGE OF A KNIFE)

3 LARGE EGG YOLKS

4 TEASPOONS VANILLA EXTRACT

Decoration:

⅓ CUP PECAN HALVES

1 CUP HEAVY CREAM

1 TABLESPOON GRANULATED SUGAR

½ TEASPOON VANILLA EXTRACT

> **kitchen note:**
>
> *For the right texture, be sure to use skim milk. You will need a microwave-safe candy thermometer. If time is a factor, chill the filled pie in the freezer for about 1 hour to set the butterscotch filling.*

1 TO MAKE THE BUTTERSCOTCH FILLING: Combine the heavy cream, brown sugar, and salt in a 1-quart microwave-safe glass measuring cup. Stir with a wooden spoon until the lumps of sugar are broken up. Cover with a piece of waxed paper and microwave on HIGH (100 percent) power for 1½ to 3 minutes, until the mixture is steaming hot. Stir with a wooden spoon until the sugar is almost completely dissolved.

(*CONTINUED*)

2 Cover the cup again and microwave on HIGH (100 percent) power for 1 to 3 minutes, until the mixture starts to boil.

3 Attach a microwave-safe candy thermometer to the side of the measuring cup, making sure the bulb is submerged. Micro- wave, uncovered, on HIGH (100 percent) power for 7 to 9 minutes, until the thermometer registers 250°F., hard-ball stage.

4 Meanwhile, put the cold water in a small cup. Sprinkle the gelatin over the water and let the mixture stand for at least 5 minutes.

5 Using a long-handled wooden spoon, slowly stir 2¾ cups of milk into the hot butterscotch mixture until blended.

6 Put the cornstarch in a 2-quart microwave-safe glass measuring cup. Grad- ually whisk in the remaining ¼ cup of milk until smooth. Whisk in the egg yolks until smooth. Stir in the butterscotch-milk mixture until blended.

7 Cover the top of the measuring cup with plastic wrap, turning back a fold over the pouring spout. Microwave on HIGH (100 percent) power for 4 minutes. Whisk until smooth.

8 Cover the cup again, turning back a fold over the pouring spout, and microwave on HIGH (100 percent) power for 2 to 5 minutes, whisking every 60 seconds, until the mixture starts to bubble around the edges. Whisk until smooth.

9 Cover the cup again, turning back a fold over the pouring spout, and microwave on HIGH (100 percent) power for 45 seconds to 1½ minutes, until the mixture comes to a full boil. Note that the filling will be very thick at first; after it boils its consistency will thin a little. Whisk until smooth.

10 Stir the softened gelatin into the mixture, making sure it dissolves com- pletely.

11 Using a rubber spatula, press the filling through a fine-meshed sieve into a noncorrosive metal 2½-quart bowl. Set the bowl over a larger bowl contain- ing ice and ice water for 5 to 10 minutes, stirring frequently, until the filling is cold and starts to thicken. Remove the bowl from the larger bowl holding the ice water. Whisk in the vanilla extract.

12 Scrape the filling into the prepared pie crust and spread it evenly with a spatula. Cover the surface of the pie and refrigerate for 1 to 3 hours, until set.

13 FOR THE DECORATION: Put the pecans in a 9-inch microwave-safe glass pie plate and spread in a single layer. Microwave on HIGH (100 percent) power for 2 minutes. Stir with a wooden spoon.

14 Continue to microwave on HIGH (100 percent) power for 3 to 6 minutes, until the nuts are lightly toasted and fragrant. Transfer the nuts to a plate to cool completely. Reserve 10 pecan halves to decorate the top of the cake. Coarsely chop the remaining pecans and set aside.

15　Put the cream, sugar, and vanilla extract in a chilled 3-quart bowl. Using a hand-held electric mixer set at high speed, whip until stiff peaks start to form.

16　Using a small offset (crooked) metal cake spatula, spread 1 cup of the whipped cream in a thin, even layer over the pie filling.

17　Fit a pastry bag with a closed star tip (such as Ateco #5) and fill with the remaining whipped cream. Pipe 10 swirled rosettes around the top edge of the pie. Top each rosette with a pecan half.

18　Lightly sprinkle the chopped, toasted pecans over the top of the pie, within the piped border. Keep the pie refrigerated until ready to serve.

Chocolate Peanut Butter Pie

makes one 9-inch pie; serves 10

preparation time: ABOUT 30 MINUTES PLUS 20 TO 30 MINUTES FREEZING, 10 TO 20 MINUTES
　　　　　　　　　　　COOLING, 1 TO 3 HOURS CHILLING, AND TIME TO MAKE THE GRAHAM
　　　　　　　　　　　CRACKER PIE CRUST

microwave time: 5 TO 8 MINUTES PLUS STANDING

We like the different textures in this sensational dessert: a crumbly pie crust, topped by the fudgy chocolate layer, and then mounds of billowing peanut butter mousse. We will always be indebted to Ray Freeze, who as the pastry chef at the Mad Batter in Cape May, New Jersey, inspired this pie. We have altered the recipe and adapted it for the microwave.

1 GRAHAM CRACKER PIE CRUST (PAGE
　170), CHILLED

Chocolate layer:

1 CUP HEAVY CREAM

7 OUNCES SEMISWEET CHOCOLATE

FEW GRAINS SALT

2 TEASPOONS VANILLA EXTRACT

(INGREDIENTS CONTINUED)

PIES and TARTS　　**173**

Peanut butter mousse:

2 CUPS HEAVY CREAM (USED IN TWO
  MEASUREMENTS)
1⅔ CUPS PEANUT BUTTER CHIPS

1 TEASPOON VEGETABLE OIL
2 TEASPOONS VANILLA EXTRACT

Decoration:

¾ CUP HEAVY CREAM
2 TEASPOONS GRANULATED SUGAR
¼ TEASPOON VANILLA EXTRACT

3 TABLESPOONS CHOPPED UNSALTED
  PEANUTS

---

kitchen note:

When making the peanut butter mousse for this pie, it is extremely important to whip the cream just until soft mounds start to form. When folding the cream into the peanut butter mixture, take great care not to overmix. Either excess will result in a grainy mousse rather than a smooth, satiny one. If time is a factor, freeze the pie for 45 minutes, until the filling is set.

1   To make the chocolate layer: Put the cream, chocolate, and salt in a 1½-quart microwave-safe glass bowl. Cover with waxed paper and microwave on MEDIUM-HIGH (70 percent) power for 2½ to 4 minutes, until the cream is steaming hot. Do not let the mixture boil. Let the mixture stand for 1 minute. Whisk until smooth. Stir in the vanilla extract.

2   Pour the chocolate mixture into the chilled pie crust and smooth the top with the back of a spoon. Put the filled pie crust in the freezer and chill for 20 to 30 minutes, until set. Meanwhile, prepare the peanut butter mousse.

3   To make the peanut butter mousse: Combine ¾ cup of the cream with the peanut butter chips in a 1½-quart bowl. Cover with waxed paper and microwave on MEDIUM-HIGH (70 percent) power for 2½ to 4 minutes, until the cream is steaming hot. Let the mixture stand for 1 minute. Whisk until smooth. Stir in the oil and vanilla extract. Let the mixture cool for 10 to 20 minutes, stirring occasionally, until tepid.

4   Pour the remaining 1¼ cups of cream into a chilled 4-quart bowl. Using a hand-held electric mixer set at high speed, whip just until soft mounds start to form. Do not overwhip. Using a large rubber spatula, fold one-third of the whipped cream into the peanut butter mixture just until blended. Fold this mixture into the whipped cream just until combined. Do not overfold.

5   Using a small offset (crooked) metal cake spatula or the back of a spoon, spread the mousse on top of the chilled chocolate layer and smooth it so that it mounds slightly in the center. Cover the surface of the mousse with plastic wrap and freeze the pie for about 45 minutes or refrigerate it for up to 3 hours,

until the mousse is firm. The pie may be prepared to this stage and kept refrigerated for two days or frozen for up to two weeks.

6 To MAKE THE DECORATION: Combine the cream, sugar, and vanilla extract in a chilled 3-quart bowl. Using a hand-held electric mixer set at high speed, whip the cream until stiff peaks start to form. Spread the cream on top of the chilled pie using a small offset (crooked) metal cake spatula or the back of a spoon. Sprinkle the chopped peanuts over the top of the pie. Keep the pie refrigerated until ready to serve.

Mocha Mousse Brownie Pie

makes one 10-inch pie; serves 10

preparation time: ABOUT 20 MINUTES PLUS AT LEAST 6 HOURS CHILLING AND TIME TO MAKE THE BROWNIE PIE

microwave time: 2 TO 3½ MINUTES

Creamy mocha mousse tastes just about perfect nestled on a rich, chocolaty brownie shell. This tastes its very best if made at least six hours or even a day before serving and kept refrigerated until it is time to decorate with the coffee liqueur-spiked whipped cream.

1 BROWNIE PIE (SEE BROWNIE SUNDAE PIE (PAGE 180), COOLED

Mocha mousse:

12 OUNCES SEMISWEET CHOCOLATE, COARSELY CHOPPED

1 TEASPOON INSTANT COFFEE GRANULES

½ CUP MILK

3 TABLESPOONS GRANULATED SUGAR

PINCH OF SALT

2 TABLESPOONS VEGETABLE OIL

3 TABLESPOONS COFFEE-FLAVORED LIQUEUR SUCH AS KAHLUA OR TÍA MARIA

5 TEASPOONS VANILLA EXTRACT

1½ CUPS HEAVY CREAM

(INGREDIENTS CONTINUED)

Decoration:

1 CUP HEAVY CREAM
1 TABLESPOON GRANULATED SUGAR
½ TEASPOON VANILLA EXTRACT
1 TABLESPOON COFFEE-FLAVORED
LIQUEUR SUCH AS KAHLUA OR TÍA
MARIA

CHOCOLATE CURLS OR SHAVINGS (PAGE 26)
CHOCOLATE COFFEE BEANS

1   TO MAKE THE MOCHA MOUSSE: Put the chocolate and instant coffee in a food processor fitted with the metal chopping blade. Process for 20 to 30 seconds, until finely ground.

2   Combine the milk, sugar, and salt in a 1-quart microwave-safe glass measuring cup. Cover with waxed paper and microwave on HIGH (100 percent) power for 2 to 3½ minutes, until the mixture comes to a boil. Stir with a wooden spoon until the sugar is completely dissolved.

3   With the food processor running, pour the hot milk mixture through the feed tube. Process for 15 to 30 seconds, until the chocolate is melted and the mixture is smooth. Scrape down the sides of the bowl with a rubber spatula. Add the oil, liqueur, and vanilla extract. Process for 10 to 20 seconds, until creamy. Scrape the mixture into a 2½-quart bowl and let it cool for 5 to 10 minutes, until tepid.

4   Pour the cream into a chilled 3-quart bowl. Using a hand-held electric mixer set at high speed, whip just until soft mounds start to form. Do not overwhip.

5   Using a wire whisk, gently stir one-fourth of the cream into the chocolate mixture just until blended. Using a rubber spatula, scrape this mixture back into the bowl of whipped cream and fold the two mixtures together until combined.

6   Spoon the mousse onto the Brownie Pie. Using a small offset (crooked) metal cake spatula or the back of a spoon, smooth the mousse so that it mounds slightly in the center. Cover the surface of the mousse with plastic wrap and refrigerate for at least 6 hours or overnight. The pie may be frozen at this stage for up to two weeks.

7   TO MAKE THE DECORATION: Put the cream, sugar, and vanilla extract in a chilled 3-quart bowl. Using a hand-held electric mixer set at high speed, whip until soft peaks start to form. Add the coffee-flavored liqueur and continue beating until stiff peaks start to form.

8   Reserve 1 cup of the whipped cream to pipe a border around the top of the pie. Using the back of a spoon, spread the remaining whipped cream evenly over the mousse filling.

9   Fit a pastry bag with a closed star tip (such as Ateco #5) and fill with the reserved whipped cream. Pipe 10 rosettes around the edge of the pie. Top each rosette with a chocolate coffee bean. Scoop up some of the chocolate curls with a spoon and sprinkle them on top of the pie within the piped border. Keep the pie refrigerated until ready to serve.

Caramel Satin Cream Pie

makes one 10-inch pie; serves 10

preparation time: ABOUT 45 MINUTES PLUS TIME TO MAKE THE PECAN GRAHAM CRACKER PIE
CRUST PLUS 2 TO 3 HOURS CHILLING

microwave time: 14 MINUTES 30 SECONDS TO 20 MINUTES

When she wanted something really special to serve her husband David, who has a fondness for caramel desserts, Adrienne created this silky, smooth pie filling for the Pecan Graham Cracker Pie Crust. The buttery crust marries perfectly with the filling, resulting in a sleek, elegant dessert.

1   PECAN GRAHAM CRACKER PIE CRUST
    (PAGE 161), COOLED

Caramel satin cream filling:

2 TABLESPOONS DARK RUM

1 TABLESPOON WATER

1 TABLESPOON VANILLA EXTRACT

2¾ TEASPOONS UNFLAVORED GELATIN

1 CUP PLUS 1 TABLESPOON
    GRANULATED SUGAR (USED IN TWO
    MEASUREMENTS)

¼ CUP WATER

¼ TEASPOON LEMON JUICE

1½ CUPS HEAVY CREAM, USED IN TWO
    MEASUREMENTS

5 LARGE EGG YOLKS

⅛ TEASPOON SALT

1½ CUPS MILK

(INGREDIENTS CONTINUED)

Toasted pecans and whipped cream garnish:

⅓ CUP HEAVY CREAM   10 TOASTED PECAN HALVES

1   TO MAKE THE CARAMEL SATIN CREAM FILLING: Put the rum, water, and vanilla in a small cup. Sprinkle the gelatin over the top of the liquid and let the mixture stand for at least 5 minutes.

2   Combine 1 cup of sugar with the water and lemon juice in a high-sided 1½-quart microwave-safe glass ceramic casserole. Cover with waxed paper and microwave on HIGH (100 percent) power for 2 minutes. Stir with a wooden spoon to dissolve any remaining sugar crystals. Cover again and continue to microwave on HIGH (100 percent) power for 2 minutes, until the syrup comes to a rapid boil.

3   Remove the waxed paper and continue to microwave on HIGH (100 percent) power for 3 to 5 minutes, without stirring, until the syrup turns to a dark amber caramel. During microwaving, watch the syrup closely. When the syrup starts to change color, swirl the casserole a couple of times so that the caramel browns evenly. Do not let the caramel burn.

4   Put the casserole on a flat, heatproof work surface. Slowly pour ¾ cup of cream into the hot caramel, being very careful it does not splash. Stir with a long-handled wooden spoon until blended.

5   Cover the casserole with waxed paper and microwave on HIGH (100 percent) power for 30 to 60 seconds, until the caramel cream is steaming hot. Stir until the caramel is completely melted into the cream.

6   Combine the egg yolks, the remaining tablespoon of sugar, and the salt in a 1-quart microwave-safe glass measuring cup. Stir vigorously with a small wire whisk until thoroughly blended. Stir in the milk. While continuing to stir, ladle the hot caramel cream into the egg yolk/milk mixture

7   Microwave uncovered on MEDIUM-HIGH (70 percent) power for 2 minutes. Whisk vigorously.

8   Continue to microwave uncovered on MEDIUM-HIGH (70 percent) power for 5 to 8 minutes, whisking vigorously every 60 seconds, until the custard thickens slightly. Take care that the custard does not get so hot it curdles. Test for doneness by coating the back of a metal spoon with some of the custard. It is done when you can run your finger down the back of the coated spoon and the path remains in the custard. The custard will register 175°F on an instant-read thermometer.

9   Add the softened gelatin mixture to the hot caramel custard and stir until the gelatin is completely dissolved. Strain the custard into a 2½-quart non-corrosive metal bowl.

10 Set the bowl over a larger bowl containing ice and ice water for 5 to 10 minutes, stirring frequently, until the custard is cold and starts to thicken. Remove the bowl from the larger bowl holding the ice water.

11 Chill a 2½-quart bowl. Whip the remaining ¾ cup cream in the bowl using a hand-held electric mixer or whisk until soft peaks start to form. Using a rubber spatula, fold the cream into the cooled caramel custard.

12 Scrape the filling into the prepared pie crust. Refrigerate the pie for 2 to 3 hours until set.

13 TO PREPARE THE TOASTED PECANS AND WHIPPED CREAM GARNISH: Put the pecan halves in a 6-ounce microwave-safe custard cup. Microwave, uncovered, on HIGH (100 percent) power for 2 minutes. Stir the nuts. Continue to microwave on HIGH (100 percent) power for 2 to 4 minutes, stirring every 60 seconds, until the nuts are lightly toasted and fragrant. Transfer the nuts to a plate to cool.

14 Chill a 2½-quart bowl. Whip the cream in the bowl using a hand-held electric mixer or whisk until stiff peaks start to form.

15 Fill a pastry bag with a closed star tip (such as Ateco #5) and fill with the whipped cream. Pipe 10 swirled rosettes around the top edge of the pie. Top each rosette with a toasted pecan half. Refrigerate the pie until ready to serve.

Brownie Sundae Pie

makes one 10-inch pie; serves 8 to 10

preparation time: ABOUT 15 MINUTES PLUS CHILLING AND TIME TO MAKE THE QUICK HOT
FUDGE SAUCE OR THE BITTERSWEET CHOCOLATE SAUCE

microwave time: 9 TO 13½ MINUTES PLUS STANDING

*T*his pie is made to order for fans of brownies à la mode. *We make a rich, fudgy brownie, bake it in a pie plate, and then serve it in wedges topped with ice cream and chocolate sauce. So simple it's brilliant. For easy slicing chill the brownie pie in the freezer for about 20 minutes.*

Brownie pie:

½ CUP PLUS 1 TABLESPOON SIFTED
ALL-PURPOSE FLOUR

½ TEASPOON DOUBLE-ACTING BAKING
POWDER

¼ TEASPOON BAKING SODA

⅛ TEASPOON SALT

3 OUNCES UNSWEETENED CHOCOLATE

½ CUP PACKED LIGHT BROWN SUGAR

⅓ CUP WATER

⅓ CUP GRANULATED SUGAR

⅓ CUP SOUR CREAM, CHILLED (SPOONED
INTO A MEASURING CUP AND LEVELED
WITH THE EDGE OF A KITCHEN KNIFE)

¼ CUP VEGETABLE OIL

2 TABLESPOONS LIGHT CORN SYRUP

2 TEASPOONS VANILLA EXTRACT

1 JUMBO EGG, CHILLED

¼ CUP FINELY CHOPPED WALNUTS

Assembly:

2 PINTS GOOD-QUALITY VANILLA OR
COFFEE ICE CREAM

QUICK HOT FUDGE SAUCE (PAGE 289) OR
BITTERSWEET CHOCOLATE SAUCE (PAGE
290)

1   TO MAKE THE BROWNIE PIE: Put the flour, baking powder, baking soda, and salt into a 1½-quart bowl. Using a wire whisk, complete 12 to 15 strokes to ensure that the ingredients are thoroughly blended.

2   Put the chocolate, brown sugar, and water in a 2½-quart microwave-safe bowl. Cover with waxed paper and microwave on MEDIUM-HIGH (70 percent) for 2 to 3½ minutes, until the mixture is steaming hot. Do not let it boil. Let the

mixture stand for 1 minute. Whisk until the chocolate is completely melted. Add the granulated sugar, sour cream, oil, corn syrup, and vanilla extract. Stir until blended. Add the egg and whisk vigorously for 30 seconds, until the mixture is creamy. Stir in the flour mixture and walnuts until blended.

3   Lightly oil the bottom of a 10-inch microwave-safe glass pie plate. Scrape the batter into the plate and spread evenly with the back of a spoon.

4   Put the pie on an inverted 9-inch microwave-safe glass pie plate and microwave, uncovered, on MEDIUM (50 percent) power for 5 minutes. If you do not have a turntable, rotate the pie a half turn every 2½ minutes.

5   Continue to microwave on HIGH (100 percent) power for 2 to 5 minutes. Test for doneness after 2 minutes by inserting a wooden toothpick into the brownie about 3 inches from the edge; it should come out with a few moist crumbs clinging to it. Any small wet patches on the surface will disappear as the brownie cools. Put the pie plate on a flat heatproof surface, cover with a clean kitchen towel, and let it stand for 15 minutes. Put the pie in the freezer for 20 minutes, until chilled, before cutting.

6   To ASSEMBLE: Cut the pie into wedges and top with a scoop of ice cream and hot fudge or chocolate sauce.

English Toffee Ice Cream Pie

makes one 9-inch pie; serves 10

preparation time: ABOUT 30 MINUTES PLUS 5 MINUTES COOLING AND AT LEAST 6 HOURS FREEZING AND TIME TO MAKE THE SATINY CHOCOLATE SAUCE

microwave time: 8½ TO 12 MINUTES

This recipe uses everyday ingredients—milk chocolate, crisped rice cereal, store-bought coffee ice cream, and toffee candy bars—with spectacular results. Without the garnish the pie can be assembled and frozen for as long as two weeks.

Milk chocolate pie shell:

⅓ CUP PECAN HALVES

10 OUNCES MILK CHOCOLATE CHIPS
    (ABOUT 1¾ CUPS)

½ CUP CRISPED RICE CEREAL

Ice cream filling:

½ CUP FINELY CHOPPED SKOR OR HEATH
    BARS

½ CUP PECAN HALVES

2 PINTS HIGH-QUALITY STORE-BOUGHT
    COFFEE ICE CREAM

2 TABLESPOONS DARK RUM (OPTIONAL)

Decoration:

⅓ CUP HEAVY CREAM

1 TEASPOON GRANULATED SUGAR

⅛ TEASPOON VANILLA EXTRACT

½ CUP COARSELY CHOPPED SKOR OR
    HEATH BARS

8 TO 10 WHOLE TOASTED PECANS

SATINY CHOCOLATE SAUCE (PAGE 288)

---

kitchen note:

Since toasted pecans are used in the pie shell, ice cream, and garnish, save time by toasting the total amount at one time before you start. Then, when the recipe calls for chopped pecans, chop those that you need.

1 TO PREPARE THE PECANS: Measure all the pecans needed for the whole recipe. Put them in a 9-inch microwave-safe glass pie plate and spread them into a single layer. Microwave on HIGH (100 percent) power for 2 minutes. Stir with a wooden spoon. Continue to microwave on HIGH (100 percent) power for 4 to 6 minutes, until the nuts are lightly toasted and fragrant. Transfer the nuts to a plate to cool completely. Chop the pecans when cool.

2 TO MAKE THE MILK CHOCOLATE PIE SHELL: Line a 9-inch glass pie plate with aluminum foil, leaving a 2-inch overhang around the edge. Tuck the overhang under the plate.

3 Put the chocolate chips in a 1½-quart microwave-safe bowl. Microwave, uncovered, on MEDIUM (50 percent) power for 2½ to 5 minutes, until the chocolate is shiny. Stir with a rubber spatula until smooth. Let the chocolate cool for 5 minutes. Stir in ⅓ cup chopped pecans and the crisped rice cereal.

4 Scrape the chocolate mixture into the prepared pie plate. Using the back of a spoon, spread it in a thin, even layer over the bottom, up the sides, and onto the rim of the pie plate. Freeze the chocolate shell for 20 to 30 minutes, until firm.

5   Remove the pie shell from the freezer. Holding on to the foil overhang, lift the chocolate shell from the pie plate. Invert the shell and carefully peel off the foil. Put the shell back into the pie plate and return it to the freezer.

6   To make the ice cream filling: Put the chopped toffee candy bars and the remaining ½ cup of chopped pecans in a 1-quart bowl and stir to combine. Set aside.

7   Remove the lids and foil, if any, from the top of the ice cream containers. Microwave the ice cream, 1 pint at a time, on medium (50 percent) power for 10 seconds at a time, until it starts to soften. Do not allow the ice cream to melt.

8   Using a rubber spatula, scrape the ice cream into a 2½-quart bowl. Quickly stir in the rum until blended.

9   Remove the pie shell from the freezer and, working swiftly, spread half the ice cream in it. Sprinkle the toffee-pecan mixture in an even layer over the ice cream. Using the back of a spoon, spread the remaining ice cream on top in an even layer. Cover the pie with plastic wrap and freeze for at least 6 hours or overnight. The pie can be frozen at this stage, well wrapped, for up to two weeks.

10   To make the decoration: Combine the cream, sugar, and vanilla extract in a chilled 2½-quart bowl. Using a hand-held electric mixer set at high speed, whip the cream until stiff peaks start to form.

11   Sprinkle the top of the pie with chopped toffee candy bars. Fit a pastry bag with a closed star tip (such as Ateco #5) and fill it with the whipped cream. Pipe 10 swirled rosettes around the edge of the pie. Top each rosette with a pecan half. Freeze the pie while preparing the chocolate sauce.

12   Flavor the Satiny Chocolate Sauce with rum, if desired. Serve the pie with the warm sauce. Use a hot, sharp knife to cut the pie into wedges. Rinse the knife under hot water and wipe the blade dry before cutting each wedge.

Strawberry Ice Cream Pie

makes one 9-inch pie; serves 8 to 10

preparation time: ABOUT 10 MINUTES PLUS AT LEAST 6 HOURS FREEZING AND TIME TO MAKE THE CHOCOLATE WAFER PIE CRUST AND THE STRAWBERRY SAUCE

microwave time: 20 TO 60 SECONDS

Adding a splash of orange-flavored liqueur to store-bought strawberry ice cream and to the whipped cream garnish makes all the difference in this splendid dessert. The combination of strawberries and chocolate is always a big hit, too. The undecorated pie can be assembled two weeks ahead of time.

2 PINTS HIGH-QUALITY, STORE-BOUGHT STRAWBERRY ICE CREAM

4 TABLESPOONS ORANGE-FLAVORED LIQUEUR SUCH AS GRAND MARNIER, COINTREAU, OR TRIPLE SEC (USED IN TWO MEASUREMENTS)

1 CHOCOLATE WAFER PIE CRUST (PAGE 157), CHILLED

½ CUP HEAVY CREAM

2 TEASPOONS GRANULATED SUGAR

¼ TEASPOON VANILLA EXTRACT

STRAWBERRY SAUCE (PAGE 281), CHILLED

FRESH STRAWBERRIES FOR GARNISH

1   Remove the lid and foil, if any, from the top of the ice cream containers. Microwave the ice cream, 1 pint at a time, on MEDIUM (50 percent) power for 10 seconds at a time, until it starts to soften. Do not let the ice cream melt.

2   Using a rubber spatula, scrape the ice cream into a 2½-quart bowl. Quickly stir in 3 tablespoons of liqueur until blended.

3   Scrape the ice cream into the chocolate wafer crust and, working swiftly, spread it evenly with the back of a spoon. Cover the top of the pie with plastic wrap and freeze for at least 6 hours or overnight. The pie can be frozen at this stage, well wrapped, for up to two weeks.

4   Combine the cream, sugar, and vanilla extract in a chilled 2½-quart bowl. Using a hand-held electric mixer at high speed, whip the cream until soft peaks start to form. Add the remaining tablespoon of liqueur and continue to beat until stiff peaks start to form.

5   Fit a pastry bag with a closed star tip (such as Ateco #4) and fill with the whipped cream. Pipe a decorative border around the edge of the pie. Serve the pie with the Strawberry Sauce, garnished with fresh strawberries.

Chocolate Mint Oreo Ice Cream Pie

makes one 9-inch pie; serves 8 to 10

preparation time: ABOUT 30 MINUTES PLUS AT LEAST 6 HOURS FREEZING

microwave time: 5 TO 10 MINUTES

*A*drienne's husband David requests this pie every year for his birthday, even though he is married to a professional cook and could have almost any dessert imaginable. It is inspired by a pie David's childhood babysitter and then his mother made for birthdays and other special occasions. Over the years it has changed a little: first when David's sister Jean, making the pie as a birthday surprise, substituted Ben and Jerry's Mint with Oreo Cookie Ice Cream; and then when Adrienne concocted her own version of the Ben and Jerry's ice cream by using plain vanilla ice cream enhanced with Oreos and mint extract.

We discovered it was a natural for the microwave oven. Try this latest incarnation with its crisp, crunchy crust, delicious mint and cookie ice cream filling, and sweetened billowy topping garnished with chocolate swirls; it will probably become a tradition in your family, too.

Crispy chocolate pie shell:

8 OUNCES SEMISWEET CHOCOLATE, COARSELY CHOPPED

4 TABLESPOONS UNSALTED BUTTER, CUT INTO TABLESPOONS

1 CUP CRISPED RICE CEREAL

Mint Oreo ice cream:

2 PINTS HIGH-QUALITY VANILLA ICE CREAM

1¼ TEASPOONS PEPPERMINT EXTRACT

1⅔ COARSELY CHOPPED OREO COOKIES (ABOUT 12 COOKIES)

Whipped cream topping:

1 CUP HEAVY CREAM

1 TABLESPOON GRANULATED SUGAR

¼ TEASPOON VANILLA EXTRACT

⅛ TEASPOON PEPPERMINT EXTRACT

Fudge drizzle:

2 OUNCES SEMISWEET CHOCOLATE, COARSELY CHOPPED

1 TABLESPOON LIGHT CORN SYRUP

1 TABLESPOON HEAVY CREAM

1 TEASPOON UNSALTED BUTTER

½ TEASPOON VANILLA EXTRACT

1   To MAKE THE CRISPY CHOCOLATE PIE SHELL: Line a 9-inch glass pie plate with aluminum foil, leaving a 2-inch overhang around the edge of the plate. Tuck the overhang under the plate.

2   Combine the chocolate and butter in a 1½-quart microwave-safe bowl. Microwave, uncovered, on MEDIUM (50 percent) power for 2½ to 5 minutes, until the butter is half melted and the chocolate is shiny. Stir with a rubber spatula until smooth. Stir in the crisped rice.

3   Scrape the chocolate mixture into the prepared pie plate. Using the back of a spoon, spread the mixture in a thin, even layer over the bottom, up the sides, and onto the rim of the plate. Freeze the shell for 20 to 30 minutes, until firm.

4   Remove the pie shell from the freezer. Holding on to the aluminum foil overhang, lift the shell from the plate. Invert the shell and carefully peel off the aluminum foil. Put the shell back in the pie plate and return it to the freezer.

5   To PREPARE THE MINT OREO ICE CREAM: Remove the lid and foil, if any, from the top of the ice cream container. Microwave the ice cream, 1 pint at a time, on MEDIUM (50 percent) power for 10 seconds at a time, until it starts to soften. Do not allow the ice cream to melt.

6   Using a rubber spatula, scrape the ice cream into a 2½-quart bowl. Quickly stir in the peppermint extract until blended. Stir in the chopped Oreo cookies.

7   Remove the pie shell from the freezer and, working swiftly, spread the ice cream in it. Use the back of a spoon to spread the ice cream evenly. Cover the pie with plastic wrap and freeze for at least 6 hours or overnight. The pie can be frozen at this stage, well wrapped, for up to two weeks.

8   To PREPARE THE WHIPPED CREAM TOPPING: Combine the cream, sugar, and vanilla and peppermint extracts in a chilled 3-quart bowl. Using a hand-held electric mixer set at high speed, whip the cream until stiff peaks start to form when the beaters are lifted.

9   If desired, reserve 1 cup of the whipped cream for piping a border on the pie and keep it refrigerated until ready to use. Spoon the remaining whipped cream over the filling and spread it in an even layer with the back of a spoon. Put the pie in the freezer while preparing the fudge drizzle.

10   To MAKE THE FUDGE DRIZZLE: Combine the chocolate, corn syrup, cream, and butter in a 1-cup microwave-safe glass measuring cup. Stir with a wooden spoon until blended.

11   Cover the cup with waxed paper. Microwave on HIGH (100 percent) power for 1 to 3 minutes, until the mixture comes to a gentle boil. Whisk until smooth. Stir in the vanilla extract.

12   Using a fork or rubber spatula, drizzle the fudge over the top of the

whipped cream in a random spatter and drizzle design. There will be some fudge left over.

13   Fit a pastry bag with a closed star tip (such as Ateco #5) and fill with the reserved whipped cream, if desired. Pipe a decorative border around the edge of the pie. Freeze until ready to serve.

CHAPTER SEVEN

Ice Cream, Sorbet, and Frozen Yogurt

Deep Dark Chocolate Ice Cream with Chocolate
  Flakes
Caramel Ice Cream
Mocha Toffee Chip Ice Cream
Cinnamon Spice Ice Cream
Ginger Pecan Ice Cream
Blueberries 'n' Cream Ice Cream Bombe
Plum Swirl Ice Cream Terrine with Chocolate
  Sauce
Peach Melba Ice Cream Sundaes
Caribbean Tropical Fruit Sundaes
Blueberry Lime Sorbet
Strawberry Sorbet
Raspberry Sorbet
Nectarine Frozen Yogurt
Fresh Figs and Lemon Yogurt Ice

There is nothing like a bowl of ice cream. Even on the chilliest winter day, the smooth creaminess of the icy sweet is splendidly satisfying. And in the summertime, ice cream and sorbets are essential!

Yes, you say, everyone likes ice cream, but what is a chapter on frozen confections doing in a book on *cooking* in the microwave oven? That is a good question to which we have an equally good answer.

First of all, many frozen desserts are made from cooked custard or syrup bases. Second, we make enticing fillings and stir-ins designed to transform plain yogurts and ice creams into frozen delights. Caramel Ice Cream, for example, is one of our favorites, and making caramel in the microwave oven is much less bother than on top of the stove. And finally, we use the microwave oven as a handy kitchen tool to soften store-bought ice cream so that we can stir any number of wonderful flavorings into it to create something brand new.

Convinced? Take a look at the following recipes and start making room in the freezer for these outrageous frozen desserts.

Ice Cream, Sorbet, and Yogurt Tips

For especially creamy ice cream, chill the custard base well before freezing.
Make room in the freezer for the ice cream maker canister or other container before you start making the dessert. In some recipes, assembled, single-serving sundaes are stored in the freezer. They take up lots of room.
We developed and tested these desserts in both a countertop electric ice cream maker that uses Freon for freezing and in a more modest maker that relies on the traditional combination of salt and ice.
When we call for store-bought ice cream, we hope you will buy the best brand

available. These high-quality products have far less air incorporated in them than others, and taste creamier and richer, too. They actually feel *heavier (ice cream is packed by volume, not weight). And yes, they generally cost a little more.*

*Softening ice cream in the microwave oven is more efficient than letting it soften on the counter or in the refrigerator. It gives you more control and less mess.

*Pack frozen ice cream or sorbet in a 1-quart microwave-safe container, then freeze it for a few hours or overnight. This will make it firmer and more flavorful than if eaten right away. The ice cream or sorbet can be softened in the container, if necessary.

*Frozen yogurt made with regular plain yogurt is richer than that made with low-fat yogurt.

Deep Dark Chocolate Ice Cream with Chocolate Flakes

makes about 1 quart

preparation time: ABOUT 30 MINUTES PLUS 1 TO 2 HOURS CHILLING AND TIME IN THE ICE CREAM MAKER

microwave time: 9 TO 15 MINUTES

Adrienne—*who made truffles for Bloomingdale's and is food editor of* Chocolatier *magazine—thought she had seen (or tasted) it all. But she went wild for this chocolate ice cream. ''I didn't share it with anyone but David,'' she gleefully admitted. When Mary tested it, she and daughter Laura became fast fans, too. So take it from a couple of chocolate hounds—this is an amazingly rich and creamy ice cream.*

It is worth going to the trouble of making thin chocolate flakes rather than simply chopping chocolate to add to the ice cream. The flakes add a delightful chocolaty crunch without any of the waxiness of frozen chunks of chocolate.

5 LARGE EGG YOLKS

½ CUP GRANULATED SUGAR

⅛ TEASPOON SALT

1½ CUPS HEAVY CREAM

¾ CUP MILK

8 OUNCES SEMISWEET CHOCOLATE, COARSELY CHOPPED (USED IN TWO MEASUREMENTS)

4 TEASPOONS VANILLA EXTRACT

1 Combine the egg yolks, sugar, and salt in a 1-quart microwave-safe measuring cup. Whisk vigorously with a small wire whisk until thoroughly blended. Stir in the cream and milk.

2 Microwave, uncovered, on MEDIUM-HIGH (70 percent) power for 2 minutes. Take the measuring cup from the microwave and whisk vigorously.

3 Continue to microwave, uncovered, on MEDIUM-HIGH (70 percent) power for 5 to 8 minutes, whisking vigorously every 60 seconds, until the custard thickens slightly. Take care that the custard does not get so hot it curdles. Test for doneness by coating the back of a metal spoon with some of the custard; it is done when you can run your finger down the back of the coated spoon and the path remains in the custard. The custard will register 175°F. on an instant-read thermometer.

4 As soon as the custard is ready, add 6 ounces of the coarsely chopped chocolate to it; reserve the last 2 ounces for the chocolate flakes. Let the custard stand for 30 seconds and then whisk until smooth. Strain the chocolate custard into a 2½-quart noncorrosive metal bowl.

5 Set the bowl over a larger bowl containing ice and ice water for 5 to 10 minutes, stirring frequently, until the custard is cool. Remove the bowl from the larger bowl holding the ice water and stir in the vanilla extract.

6 Cover the surface of the custard with plastic wrap and refrigerate for no longer than 1 to 2 hours, stirring occasionally, until very cold and thick.

7 Scrape the custard into an ice cream maker and freeze according to the manufacturer's instructions. While the ice cream freezes, make the chocolate flakes.

8 Put the reserved 2 ounces of coarsely chopped chocolate in a 6-ounce microwave-safe custard cup and cover with waxed paper. Microwave on MEDIUM (50 percent) power for 2 to 5 minutes, until the chocolate looks shiny. Stir until smooth.

9 Cover a flat metal baking sheet with waxed paper. Dip the tip of your finger into the melted chocolate and affix the corners of the waxed paper to the

> **kitchen note:**
>
> *Microwave the custard base on MEDIUM-HIGH (70 percent) power to keep it from becoming too hot, and stir it at regular intervals. It could curdle otherwise.*

baking sheet with small dabs of chocolate. Scrape the chocolate onto the waxed paper and, using an offset (crooked) metal cake spatula, spread it into an 11-by-6-inch rectangle about $\frac{1}{16}$ inch thick. Refrigerate for 10 to 15 minutes, until the chocolate is firm.

10   Lift the waxed paper from the baking sheet and gently invert the chocolate rectangle on the counter. Peel the waxed paper off the chocolate rectangle. Lay the waxed paper back on the baking sheet and then set the chocolate rectangle on it. This will prevent the chocolate from melting while it is being cut. With a large, sharp knife, quickly cut the rectangle into $\frac{1}{2}$-inch-wide strips. Cut each strip into $\frac{1}{2}$-inch squares, and then finally cut each square into $\frac{1}{4}$-inch flakes. If the chocolate starts to soften during this process, refrigerate it on the baking sheet for 2 to 3 minutes, until it hardens. Scrape the chocolate flakes into a small bowl and refrigerate them until it is time to add them to the ice cream.

11   Just before the ice cream finishes freezing, add the chocolate flakes. Continue churning until the flakes are incorporated and the ice cream machine has completed its job. The ice cream is ready to eat or, if you prefer, may be packed into a 1-quart microwave-safe container and frozen for a few hours or overnight. This will make it firmer and more flavorful than if eaten right away. The ice cream may be softened, if necessary, in the container.

Caramel Ice Cream

makes about 1 quart

preparation time: ABOUT 20 MINUTES PLUS 1 TO 2 HOURS CHILLING AND TIME IN THE ICE
CREAM MAKER

microwave time: 10 TO 20 MINUTES

With a few precautions, caramel works wonderfully in the microwave oven. When the creamy mixture is stirred into a rich, custard-based ice cream, the results are superb. Try some of this magnificent ice cream with still-warm Apple and Pear Crumble (page 149), or Pumpkin Gingerbread (page 118), or simply drizzled with Satiny Chocolate Sauce (page 288).

1 CUP PLUS 1 TABLESPOON GRANULATED SUGAR (EACH MEASUREMENT USED SEPARATELY)

3 TABLESPOONS WATER

1/4 TEASPOON LEMON JUICE

1 1/2 CUPS HEAVY CREAM

5 LARGE EGG YOLKS

1/8 TEASPOON SALT

1 1/2 CUPS MILK

4 TEASPOONS VANILLA EXTRACT

kitchen note:

Caramel forms quickly in the microwave. During the last minute of cooking, watch it carefully; burnt caramel is unappetizingly bitter. We cannot overemphasize the importance of using a high-sided 1 1/2-quart microwave-safe glass ceramic casserole for the caramel. Microwave-safe glass casseroles or measuring cups are not recommended by their manufacturers or anyone else because they may crack when holding the hot caramel.

1   Combine 1 cup of sugar with the water and lemon juice in a high-sided 1 1/2-quart microwave-safe *glass ceramic* casserole. Cover with waxed paper and microwave on HIGH (100 percent) power for 2 minutes. Stir with a wooden spoon to dissolve any remaining sugar crystals. Cover again and continue to microwave on HIGH (100 percent) power for 2 minutes.

2   Remove the waxed paper and continue to microwave on HIGH (100 percent) power for 3 to 5 minutes, without stirring, until the syrup turns into a dark amber caramel. During microwaving, watch the syrup closely. When it starts to change color, swirl the casserole a couple of times so that the caramel browns evenly. Do not let the caramel burn.

3   Put the casserole on a flat heatproof surface. Slowly pour 1 cup of cream into the caramel, being very careful it does not splash. Stir with a long-handled wooden spoon until blended.

4 Cover the casserole with waxed paper and microwave on HIGH (100 percent) power for 30 to 60 seconds, until the caramel cream is steaming hot. Stir until the caramel is completely melted into the cream.

5 Combine the egg yolks, the remaining tablespoon of sugar, and the salt in a 1-quart microwave-safe glass measuring cup. Stir vigorously with a small wire whisk until thoroughly blended. Stir in the remaining ½ cup of cream and the milk. Stir in the hot caramel cream.

6 Microwave, uncovered, on MEDIUM-HIGH (70 percent) power for 2 minutes. Whisk vigorously.

7 Continue to microwave, uncovered, on MEDIUM-HIGH (70 percent) power for 5 to 8 minutes, whisking vigorously every 60 seconds, until the custard thickens slightly. Take care that the custard does not get so hot it curdles. Test for doneness by coating the back of a metal spoon with some of the custard; it is done when you can run your finger down the back of the coated spoon and the path remains in the custard. The custard will register 175°F. on an instant-read thermometer.

8 Strain the custard into a 2½-quart noncorrosive metal bowl.

9 Set the bowl over a larger bowl containing ice and ice water for 5 to 10 minutes, stirring frequently, until the custard is cool. Remove the bowl from the larger bowl holding the ice water and stir in the vanilla extract.

10 Cover the surface of the custard with plastic wrap and refrigerate for 1 to 2 hours, until very cold and thick. The custard may be prepared up to one day in advance.

11 Scrape the custard into an ice cream maker and freeze according to the manufacturer's instructions.

12 The ice cream is ready to eat, or if you prefer, it may be packed into a 1-quart microwave-safe container and frozen for a few hours or overnight. This will make it firmer and more flavorful than if eaten right away. The ice cream may be softened, if necessary, in the container.

Mocha Toffee Chip Ice Cream

makes about 1 quart

preparation time: ABOUT 15 MINUTES PLUS 1 TO 2 HOURS CHILLING AND TIME IN THE ICE
CREAM MAKER

microwave time: 9 TO 12 MINUTES

*A*dding *chopped-up pieces of cookies or candy to store-bought ice cream is nothing new; even manufacturers now sell a few flavors with these items already incorporated. Our contribution has a delicious difference: We first* make *a rich, velvety mocha ice cream and then toss in a handful of chopped-up toffee candy bars. This incredible ice cream is even better served with Quick Hot Fudge Sauce (page 289) or Satiny Chocolate Sauce (page 288).*

5 LARGE EGG YOLKS	2 TABLESPOONS INSTANT COFFEE GRANULES
½ CUP GRANULATED SUGAR	4 TEASPOONS VANILLA EXTRACT
⅛ TEASPOON SALT	½ CUP FINELY CHOPPED SKOR OR HEATH BARS
2 CUPS HEAVY CREAM	
1 CUP MILK	

1   Combine the egg yolks, sugar, and salt in a 1-quart microwave-safe measuring cup. Whisk vigorously with a small wire whisk until thoroughly blended. Stir in the cream and milk.

2   Microwave, uncovered, on MEDIUM-HIGH (70 percent) power for 3 minutes. Take the measuring cup from the microwave and whisk vigorously.

3   Continue to microwave, uncovered, on MEDIUM-HIGH (70 percent) power for 6 to 9 minutes, whisking vigorously every 60 seconds, until the custard thickens slightly. Take care that the custard does not get so hot it curdles. Test for doneness by coating the back of a metal spoon with some of the custard; it is done when you can run your finger down the back of the coated spoon and the path remains in the custard. The custard will register 175°F. on an instant-read thermometer.

4   As soon as the custard is ready, add the instant coffee granules and stir to dissolve them. Strain the custard into a 2½-quart noncorrosive metal bowl.

5   Set the bowl over a larger bowl containing ice and ice water for 5 to 10 minutes, stirring frequently, until the custard is cool. Remove the bowl from the larger bowl holding the ice water and stir in the vanilla extract.

6 Cover the surface of the custard with plastic wrap and refrigerate for 1 to 2 hours, until very cold and thick. The custard may be prepared up to one day in advance.

7 Scrape the custard into an ice cream maker and freeze according to the manufacturer's instructions.

8 Just before the ice cream finishes freezing, add the chopped candy bars. Continue churning until the pieces are incorporated and the ice cream machine has completed its task. The ice cream is ready to eat, but if you prefer, it may be packed into a 1-quart microwave-safe container and frozen for a few hours or overnight. This will make it firmer and more flavorful than if eaten right away. The ice cream may be softened, if necessary, in the container.

Cinnamon Spice Ice Cream

makes about 1 pint

preparation time: ABOUT 5 MINUTES PLUS 3 HOURS FREEZING

microwave time: 20 TO 60 SECONDS

In the recipe for Mocha Toffee Chip Ice Cream on page 197 we make the ice cream and add chopped candy bars to it. This one is easier. We buy the ice cream and flavor it with a heady mixture of spices and rum. You could easily double our recipe to make a quart, which is a good idea since the final ice cream is really good.

Keep in mind that the longer the ice cream sits in the freezer, the better its flavor will be. Freeze it for at least 2 hours (overnight is better). Serve it with Apple and Pear Crumble (page 149), French Apple Cake (page 108), or Rum-Raisin Stuffed Apples (page 148). Or eat it by itself.

Unbelievable Microwave Desserts

1 PINT HIGH-QUALITY VANILLA ICE
  CREAM
1 TEASPOON GROUND CINNAMON
⅛ TEASPOON GROUND CLOVES

⅛ TEASPOON FRESHLY GRATED
  NUTMEG
1 TABLESPOON DARK RUM OR 2
  TEASPOONS APPLE JUICE

1   Remove the lid and foil seal, if any, from the pint of ice cream. Microwave it on MEDIUM (50 percent) power for 10 seconds at a time until the ice cream starts to soften. Do not let the ice cream melt.

2   Put the cinnamon, cloves, and nutmeg in a 6-ounce custard cup. Stir in 1 teaspoon of the rum to make a smooth paste. Stir in the rest of the rum.

3   Use a rubber spatula to scrape the softened ice cream into a 2½-quart bowl. Add the spice mixture and quickly stir it into the ice cream. Repack the ice cream in the container, cover, and freeze for at least 2 hours or until serving.

kitchen note:

In this recipe and others where we add ingredients to store-bought ice cream, use the microwave oven for softening the ice cream. Never microwave the pint of ice cream for more than 10 seconds at a time, and check at each interval to ensure slow and even softening. Remember that ice cream continues to soften even after it is taken from the microwave oven.

Ginger Pecan Ice Cream

makes about 1 pint

preparation time: ABOUT 10 MINUTES PLUS 2 HOURS FREEZING

microwave time: 2 TO 6 MINUTES

*T*his *ice cream is made simply by adding a little gingery milk to microwave-softened ice cream and letting it infuse the ice cream for two or more hours. The result is a mellow confection that deliciously accentuates the flavor of Pumpkin Gingerbread (page 118) or Apple and Pear Crumble (page 149). It tastes good on its own, too.*

¼ CUP PECAN HALVES

3 TABLESPOONS CRYSTALLIZED GINGER

1 PINT HIGH-QUALITY VANILLA ICE CREAM

¼ TEASPOON GROUND GINGER

1 TEASPOON MILK

kitchen note:

Don't be tempted to substitute fresh ginger for the candied type here. Candied ginger has its own special flavor and texture. We also toast the pecans to bring out their buttery essence.

1   Spread the pecans in a 9-inch microwave-safe glass pie plate. Microwave, uncovered, on HIGH (100 percent) power for 2 to 5 minutes, stirring every 60 seconds, until the nuts are lightly toasted and fragrant. Spread the nuts on a plate to cool. Coarsely chop the nuts and set aside.

2   Soak the crystallized ginger in warm water for a minute or two to remove the sugar coating. Rinse and drain well. Pat the ginger dry with a paper towel and then finely chop it. Set aside.

3   Remove the lid and foil seal, if any, from the pint of ice cream. Microwave it on MEDIUM (50 percent) power for 10 seconds at a time until the ice cream starts to soften. Do not let the ice cream melt.

4   Put the ground ginger in a 6-ounce custard cup and stir in the milk until blended.

5   Use a rubber spatula to scrape the softened ice cream into a 2½-quart bowl. Add the ginger-milk mixture, chopped crystallized ginger, and chopped pecans, and quickly stir them into the ice cream. Repack the ice cream in the container, cover, and freeze for at least 2 hours or until serving.

Blueberries 'n' Cream Ice Cream Bombe

serves 12

preparation time: ABOUT 15 MINUTES PLUS 9 HOURS FREEZING

microwave time: 10 TO 14 MINUTES PLUS 10 MINUTES STANDING

This bombe takes some time to prepare, but most of it is freezer time, which means you can be out of the kitchen attending to other business. Once you have made the sorbet, you can dress it up by freezing it inside a mound of store-bought ice cream (we suggest buying the creamiest, richest brand in the market). Our easy method turns two everyday frozen confections into a tantalizingly delicious dessert that is perfect for making ahead of time.

5 PINTS HIGH-QUALITY VANILLA
   ICE CREAM
BLUEBERRY LIME SORBET
   (PAGE 209)

MELBA SAUCE (PAGE 282),
   CHILLED
FRESH BERRIES FOR GARNISH

1   Put a 2½-quart metal bowl in the freezer for 10 minutes to chill.

2   Remove the lids and foil seals, if any, from 4 pints of ice cream. Keep the fifth pint covered but on the kitchen counter. Microwave each pint on MEDIUM (50 percent) power for 10 seconds at a time until it starts to soften. Do not let the ice cream melt.

3   As each pint softens, scrape it into the chilled bowl. When all 4 pints are in the bowl, spread the ice cream over the bottom and up the sides of the bowl with a rubber spatula, leaving a hollow in the center large enough to hold the sorbet.

4   Scrape the frozen blueberry lime sorbet into the hollow left in the ice cream. Spread it evenly.

5   Remove the lid and foil seal, if any, from the last pint of ice cream. Microwave it on MEDIUM (50 percent) power for 10 seconds at a time, until it starts to soften. Do not let it melt.

6   Use a rubber spatula to spread the last pint of softened ice cream over the top of the blueberry ice and to the edge of the

kitchen notes:

In this recipe we use the method described on page 24 for softening ice cream. High-quality ice cream, which has a minimum of air incorporated in it, tends to freeze very hard. The microwave oven quickly softens it without melting it.

Also remember to clear an area of the freezer large enough to hold the bowl before making the bombe.

bowl. Spread it evenly and then cover the bowl with plastic wrap.

7 Freeze the bombe for at least 8 hours or overnight. You may keep the bombe frozen for as long as two weeks.

8 At least an hour or so before serving, take the bombe from the freezer and remove the plastic wrap. Set a large bowl in the sink and fill it with cool tap water. Immerse the bowl containing the bombe in the water, submerging it about three-fourths of the way up the sides. Be careful that no water gets in the ice cream. Let the bombe sit in the water for 1 to 3 minutes, or until the ice cream begins to loosen from the sides of the bowl. Lift the bowl from the water and dry the outside of the bowl with a kitchen towel.

9 Working quickly, lay a 9-inch round cardboard or a serving plate over the top of the bowl and invert the bowl so that the bombe is released. Cover the bombe with plastic wrap and freeze for at least 1 hour.

10 To serve the bombe, cut it into wedges with a long, sharp knife. Wipe the blade clean between slices. Serve the wedges on large dessert plates with Melba Sauce and garnished with fresh berries.

variations

Strawberries 'n' Cream Ice Cream Bombe

Substitute the Strawberry Sorbet on page 210 for the Blueberry Lime Sorbet, and Strawberry Sauce on page 281 for the Melba Sauce.

Raspberries 'n' Cream Ice Cream Bombe

Substitute the Raspberry Sorbet on page 212 for the Blueberry Lime Sorbet.

Plum Swirl Ice Cream Terrine with Chocolate Sauce

serves 10

preparation time: ABOUT 25 MINUTES PLUS 1 TO 2 HOURS CHILLING AND 8 HOURS FREEZING

microwave time: 16½ TO 25½ MINUTES PLUS 30 SECONDS STANDING

As with the Blueberries 'n' Cream Ice Cream Bombe above, we rely on store-bought ice cream for the base of this dessert. Softening the ice cream in the microwave oven makes it easy to work with, and swirling it with a sweet plum compote makes it colorful and extra tasty.

Plum swirl:

1 SMALL ORANGE

1 POUND LARGE, RIPE PURPLE OR BLACK PLUMS (ABOUT 4 PLUMS)

½ CUP GRANULATED SUGAR

Assembly:

4 PINTS HIGH-QUALITY VANILLA ICE CREAM

SATINY CHOCOLATE SAUCE (PAGE 288), FLAVORED WITH ORANGE-FLAVORED LIQUEUR SUCH AS GRAND MARNIER, COINTREAU, OR TRIPLE SEC

1   TO MAKE THE PLUM SWIRL: Using a swivel vegetable peeler, peel off 6 strips of orange zest, each about ¾ inch by 2½ inches wide. Be careful not to include any bitter white pith. Chop the zest finely with a sharp knife. You will need 1 tablespoon of finely chopped zest.

2   Cut the plums into quarters and remove the pits. Reserve 2 pits and discard the others. With a large, sharp knife, crack the reserved pits in half and remove the kernels. Finely chop the kernels and set them aside. Cut each plum quarter into 8 pieces.

3   In a 2-quart microwave-safe glass measuring cup, combine the plums, sugar, chopped kernels, and orange zest. Cover with waxed paper and microwave on HIGH (100 percent) power for 5 to 7 minutes, until the mixture starts to boil. Stir once after 2 to 3 minutes.

(CONTINUED)

4   Remove the waxed paper and continue to microwave on HIGH (100 percent) power for 8 to 12 minutes, stirring once, until the chunks of fruit are translucent and the mixture has reduced to 1½ cups. Transfer the mixture to a bowl and refrigerate for 1 to 2 hours, until cold.

5   To ASSEMBLE: Put an 8½-by-4½-by-2-inch glass loaf pan in the freezer for 10 minutes to chill.

6   Remove the lids and foil seals, if any, from the pints of ice cream. Microwave each pint separately on MEDIUM (50 percent) power for 10 seconds at a time, until it starts to soften. Do not let the ice cream melt.

7   Scoop about 2½ cups of softened ice cream into the chilled loaf pan. Using the back of a spoon, quickly spread it over the bottom of the pan. Spoon half of the chilled plum swirl over the ice cream and then spread another 2½ cups of ice cream over it. Top with the rest of the plum swirl and finally with the remaining ice cream.

8   Position the loaf pan so that it is sitting horizontally in front of you. Insert a table knife into the ice cream at the upper left corner. The tip of the knife should be pointed down but not quite touching the bottom of the pan. Lift the knife up and gently fold the ice cream and plum swirl together to form a swirled pattern. Repeat this folding and swirling process 4 or 5 more times, covering the length of the pan.

9   Lift out the knife and once again position it in the upper left corner. This time draw it in a zigzag pattern across the length of the loaf pan. Smooth the top with a spatula.

10   Wrap the loaf pan with plastic wrap and freeze for at least 8 hours or overnight.

11   At least 1 hour or so before serving, take the loaf pan from the freezer and remove the plastic wrap. Set a large bowl in the sink and fill it with cool tap water. Immerse the loaf pan in the water, submerging it about three-fourths of the way up the sides. Be careful that no water gets in the ice cream. Let the pan sit in the water for 1 to 3 minutes, or until the ice cream begins to loosen from the sides. Lift the loaf pan from the water and dry the outside of it with a kitchen towel.

12   Working quickly, lay a small cutting board over the top of the loaf pan and invert it so that the terrine released from the pan. Cover the terrine with plastic wrap and freeze for at least 1 hour, until firm.

13   Make the chocolate sauce flavored with the liqueur. Let the sauce cool until tepid.

14   Spoon the sauce onto 10 dessert plates. Remove the plastic wrap from the terrine and cut it into 10 slices. Wipe the blade of the knife clean between slices. Lay the slices in the center of the plates and serve immediately.

Peach Melba Ice Cream Sundaes

serves 6

preparation time: ABOUT 20 MINUTES INCLUDING ASSEMBLY

microwave time: 10 TO 12 MINUTES

*E*scoffier named his creation of peaches, ice cream, and raspberry sauce after the famous opera singer, Nellie Melba—the same soprano for whom he named the thin slices of toast. As the story goes, Dame Melba always requested peaches and ice cream when she dined at the Ritz-Carlton in London (and elsewhere); one evening the renowned chef decided to amuse and delight her by adding the sauce. Evidently the rest is history.

Surely neither the diva nor the chef imagined that a contraption called the microwave oven would aid in making the dessert, but we use it to make the sauce, to boil water (which facilitates peeling the peaches), and finally, to soften the ice cream. For a real show-stopping dessert, try this sundae with Vanilla-Scented Peaches (page 136) or Brandied Peaches (page 137).

6 CUPS HOT TAP WATER

6 LARGE, FIRM, RIPE PEACHES (ABOUT 2 POUNDS)

3 TABLESPOONS GRANULATED SUGAR

2 TABLESPOONS KIRSCH OR ORANGE-FLAVORED LIQUEUR SUCH AS GRAND MARNIER, COINTREAU, OR TRIPLE SEC

1 CUP HEAVY CREAM

¼ TEASPOON VANILLA EXTRACT

3 PINTS HIGH-QUALITY VANILLA ICE CREAM

¾ CUP FRESH RASPBERRIES

MELBA SAUCE (PAGE 282), FLAVORED WITH KIRSCH OR ORANGE-FLAVORED LIQUEUR SUCH AS GRAND MARNIER, COINTREAU, OR TRIPLE SEC, CHILLED

1   Put six 10-ounce pilsner glasses in the freezer to chill.

2   Put the hot tap water in a 3-quart microwave-safe casserole. Cover and microwave on HIGH (100 percent) power for 10 to 12 minutes, until the water boils.

3   Remove the casserole to a heatproof surface. Add the peaches and let them stand for 1 minute.

4   Using a slotted spoon, remove the peaches from the hot water and drain them on a clean kitchen towel. While the peaches are still hot, remove the skins

using a small, sharp knife. Be careful not to nick the peach flesh. If the skins do not peel easily, put the peaches back in the hot water one at a time for about 15 seconds before trying again.

5   Cut each peach into 12 slices. Discard the pits. Put the slices into a 1½-quart glass or ceramic bowl. Toss the slices with 2 tablespoons of sugar and 1 tablespoon of kirsch or orange-flavored liqueur. Cover and refrigerate for no more than 30 minutes, until ready to assemble the sundaes.

6   Put the cream in a chilled 3-quart bowl. Add the remaining tablespoon of sugar, the remaining tablespoon of kirsch or liqueur, and the vanilla extract. Using a hand-held electric mixer set at high speed, whip until stiff peaks start to form. Refrigerate the bowl of cream.

7   Remove the lids and foil seals, if any, from the pints of ice cream. Micro-wave each pint separately on MEDIUM (50 percent) power for 10 seconds at a time, until it starts to soften. Do not let the ice cream melt.

8   Reserve 12 peach slices and 6 raspberries for garnish. Layer the remaining peach slices and raspberries with 3 small scoops of vanilla ice cream and spoon-fuls of the cold Melba Sauce in the chilled pilsner glasses.

9   Top the sundaes with generous spoonfuls of whipped cream. Alternatively, fill a pastry bag with a closed star tip (such as Ateco #6) with the whipped cream and pipe a large mound of cream on top of each sundae. Garnish each sundae with 2 peach slices and a raspberry. Serve immediately.

Caribbean Tropical Fruit Sundaes

serves 8

preparation time: ABOUT 30 MINUTES INCLUDING ASSEMBLY, PLUS TIME IN THE ICE CREAM MAKER

microwave time: 3 MINUTES AND 15 SECONDS TO 7 MINUTES AND 15 SECONDS PLUS 10 MINUTES STANDING

*W*e like to use the lush-tasting tropical fruit that is so easy to find in the supermarket much of the year. Pineapples and bananas have long been staples, but now we can buy papayas and mangoes, too. We created this sundae to showcase these fruits.

    The slightly more expensive pineapples that have been air-shipped from Hawaii are the best tasting and freshest. These have been picked mere days before they reach the store, while other pineapples are trucked overland after shipping and may not be as succulent. Hawaiian papayas are the fruit of choice, too, although papayas from the Caribbean islands and Central America are also wonderful. Choose fruits that yield slightly to the touch—rather like an avocado. A few blemishes make no difference.

Coconut lime ice cream:

2 LARGE LIMES

1 15-OUNCE CAN SWEETENED CREAM OF COCONUT SUCH AS COCO LOPEZ

1¼ CUPS MILK

1½ CUPS HEAVY CREAM

½ TEASPOON VANILLA EXTRACT

Tropical fruit sauce:

¼ CUP GRANULATED SUGAR

2 TABLESPOONS FRESH LIME JUICE

1 CUP ½-INCH-DICED BANANAS

1 CUP ½-INCH-DICED PAPAYA

1 CUP ½-INCH DICED FRESH PINEAPPLE

3 TABLESPOONS DARK RUM

Assembly:

¼ CUP TOASTED SWEETENED FLAKED COCONUT (SEE KITCHEN NOTE BELOW)

½ PAPAYA, PEELED, HALVED, SEEDED, AND CUT INTO 8 SPEARS, EACH ABOUT ¼ INCH THICK

16 FRESH PINEAPPLE LEAVES

ICE CREAM, SORBET, and FROZEN YOGURT

kitchen note:

To toast the coconut, spread it in a 9-inch microwave-safe glass pie plate. Microwave, uncovered, on HIGH (100 percent) power for 1 minute. Stir with a flat-edged wooden spoon and continue to microwave on HIGH for 4 to 7 minutes, stirring every 30 seconds, until the coconut turns golden.

Be sure you have room in the freezer to put each assembled sundae as you make it.

1   To MAKE THE COCONUT LIME ICE CREAM: Using a swivel vegetable peeler, peel off strips of lime zest, being careful not to include any bitter white pith. Finely chop the zest with a large, sharp knife. You will need 4 teaspoons of finely chopped zest. Reserve the limes to use for squeezing the juice for the fruit sauce.

2   In a 1-quart microwave-safe glass measuring cup, combine the cream of coconut and lime zest. Cover the measuring cup with waxed paper and microwave on HIGH (100 percent) power for 3 to 5 minutes, until the cream of coconut starts to boil. Let the mixture stand for 10 minutes.

3   Strain the mixture through a fine-meshed sieve into a 3-quart noncorrosive metal bowl. Whisk in the milk.

4   Set the bowl over a larger bowl containing ice and ice water. Stir frequently for 5 to 10 minutes, until the mixture is cold. Remove the bowl from the bowl holding the ice water and stir in the cream and vanilla extract.

5   Transfer the mixture to an ice cream maker and freeze according to the manufacturer's instructions. The ice cream is ready to eat, or if you prefer, it may be packed into a microwave-safe container and frozen for a few hours or overnight. This will make it firmer than if eaten right away.

6   To MAKE THE TROPICAL FRUIT SAUCE: Combine the sugar and lime juice in a 1-cup microwave-safe glass measuring cup. Cover with waxed paper and microwave on HIGH (100 percent) power for 45 seconds. Stir with a wooden spoon to dissolve any remaining sugar crystals.

7   Cover again and microwave on HIGH (100 percent) power for 30 seconds to 1½ minutes, or until the syrup comes to a boil. Let the syrup cool completely before proceeding with the recipe. The syrup may be kept chilled for an hour or so before mixing with the fruit and assembling the sundaes.

8   Combine the fruit, cooled syrup, and rum in a 1½-quart bowl. Stir gently to mix well.

9   To ASSEMBLE: Spoon about 2 tablespoons of the fruit sauce into the bottom of a chilled parfait or stemmed wineglass. Place a scoop of coconut lime ice cream on top of the sauce and then spoon another 2 tablespoons of sauce over it. Sprinkle with toasted coconut and garnish with a papaya spear and 2 pineapple leaves. After you assemble each sundae, put it in the freezer and then assemble the next one.

Blueberry Lime Sorbet

makes about 1 quart

preparation time: ABOUT 10 MINUTES PLUS 2 TO 3 HOURS CHILLING AND TIME IN THE ICE CREAM MAKER

microwave time: 7 TO 10 MINUTES PLUS 10 MINUTES STANDING

*Y*ou *may already have noticed that we are quite fond of the combination of blueberries and lime. The Blueberry Tart on page 168 is made with a lime-infused pastry cream, and the Blueberry Sauce on page 280 is lightly perfumed with lemon or lime juice. The tang of lime or lemon accents the sweetness of the berries as few other ingredients can, and this sweet, full-flavored sorbet is a little different from most others, with just enough "zip" to send you back for seconds. Be sure to select tart, flavorful blueberries.*

1 LARGE LIME	¼ CUP FRESH LIME JUICE
4 CUPS FRESH BLUEBERRIES	LIME SLICES, CUT INTO QUARTERS, FOR
1 CUP GRANULATED SUGAR	GARNISH
⅓ CUP WATER	BLUEBERRY SAUCE (PAGE 280) (OPTIONAL)

> **kitchen note:**
>
> *First peel off the zest, then squeeze the same lime for its juice.*

1   Using a swivel vegetable peeler, peel off several strips of lime zest, being careful not to include any bitter white pith. Finely chop the zest with a sharp knife. You will need 2 teaspoons of finely chopped zest.

2   Combine the blueberries, sugar, water, and chopped lime zest in a 2-quart microwave-safe measuring cup. Stir with a wooden spoon until blended. Cover with waxed paper and microwave on HIGH (100 percent) power for 4 minutes. Stir to dissolve any remaining sugar crystals.

3   Cover the cup again and microwave on HIGH (100 percent) power for 3 to 6 minutes, until the mixture comes to a boil and the berries are soft. Let the mixture stand, covered, for 10 minutes.

4   Press the mixture through a fine sieve into a noncorrosive bowl. Measure 2¾ cups of blueberry puree. Discard the skins and seeds. Stir in the lime juice. Cover and refrigerate for 2 to 3 hours, until the mixture is very cold. The sorbet mixture may be kept refrigerated for up to two days before freezing in an ice cream machine.

5   Pour the cold blueberry mixture into an ice cream maker and freeze according to the manufacturer's instructions. The sorbet ice is ready to eat, or if you prefer, it may be packed into a microwave-safe container and frozen for a few hours or overnight. This will make it firmer and more flavorful than if eaten right away. The sorbet may be softened, if necessary, in the container. Serve the sorbet in stemmed glasses. If desired, spoon some blueberry sauce into the bottom of each glass and top with a scoop of sorbet. Garnish with the quartered lime slices.

Strawberry Sorbet

makes about 1 quart

preparation time: ABOUT 10 MINUTES PLUS 2 TO 3 HOURS CHILLING AND TIME IN THE ICE
CREAM MAKER

microwave time: 9 TO 12 MINUTES

These next two desserts, frosty strawberry and raspberry sorbets, are classics that taste lusciously of the berries while melting smoothly on the tongue. We make both with frozen berries, the kind you can always find in the supermarket. The base is so easy to make you will be able to enjoy these all year long.

1 20-OUNCE BAG UNSWEETENED FROZEN
   STRAWBERRIES (ABOUT 4 CUPS)
1 CUP GRANULATED SUGAR

¼ CUP WATER
3 TABLESPOONS FRESH LEMON JUICE

1   Combine the strawberries, sugar, and water in a 2-quart microwave-safe measuring cup. Stir with a wooden spoon until blended. Cover with waxed paper and microwave on HIGH (100 percent) power for 6 minutes. Stir to dissolve any remaining sugar crystals.

2   Cover the cup again and microwave on HIGH (100 percent) power for 3 to 6 minutes, until the mixture is steaming hot and the berries are very soft. Do not let the mixture boil.

3   Press the mixture through a fine sieve into a noncorrosive bowl. Measure 2¾ cups of strawberry juice. Discard the pulp. Stir in the lemon juice. Cover and refrigerate for 2 to 3 hours, until the mixture is very cold. The sorbet mixture may be kept refrigerated for up to two days before freezing in an ice cream maker.

4   Pour the cold strawberry mixture into an ice cream maker and freeze according to the manufacturer's instructions. The sorbet ice is ready to eat, or if you prefer, it may be packed into a microwave-safe container and frozen for a few hours or overnight. This will make it firmer and more flavorful than if eaten right away. The sorbet may be softened, if necessary, in the container. Serve the sorbet in stemmed glasses.

Raspberry Sorbet

makes about 1 quart

preparation time: ABOUT 10 MINUTES PLUS 2 TO 3 HOURS CHILLING AND TIME IN THE ICE
CREAM MAKER

microwave time: 9 TO 11 MINUTES

Like the Strawberry Sorbet, this is a classic—a sorbet you will serve over and over again, with cake, brownies, fresh fruit, and berries, or simply by itself as a refreshing light dessert. Be sure to buy unsweetened berries.

2 12-OUNCE BAGS UNSWEETENED
FROZEN RASPBERRIES (ABOUT 6
CUPS)

1½ CUPS GRANULATED SUGAR
1 CUP WATER
¼ CUP FRESH LEMON JUICE

1   Combine the raspberries, sugar, and water in a 2-quart microwave-safe measuring cup. Stir with a wooden spoon until blended. Cover with waxed paper and microwave on HIGH (100 percent) power for 5 minutes. Stir to dissolve any remaining sugar crystals.

2   Cover the cup again and microwave on HIGH (100 percent) power for 4 to 7 minutes, until the mixture is steaming hot and the berries are very soft. Do not let the mixture boil.

3   Press the mixture through a fine sieve into a noncorrosive bowl. Measure 3⅓ cups of the raspberry juice. Discard the seeds. Stir in the lemon juice. Cover and refrigerate for 2 to 3 hours, until the mixture is very cold. The sorbet mixture may be kept refrigerated for up to 2 days before freezing in an ice cream maker.

4   Pour the cold raspberry mixture into an ice cream maker and freeze according to the manufacturer's instructions. The sorbet ice is ready to eat, or if you prefer, it may be packed into a microwave-safe container and frozen for a few hours or overnight. This will make it firmer and more flavorful than if eaten right away. The sorbet may be softened, if necessary, in the container. Serve the sorbet in stemmed glasses.

Nectarine Frozen Yogurt

makes about 1 quart

preparation time: ABOUT 10 MINUTES PLUS 5 TO 10 MINUTES CHILLING AND TIME IN THE ICE CREAM MAKER

microwave time: 30 SECONDS TO 1½ MINUTES

Please don't turn the page just because you cannot find nectarines in the market. They may be out of season (after all, their season is a relatively short summer one), but you can make an equally good frozen yogurt with nearly any ripe fruit or melon. Try this with strawberries, peaches, cantaloupe, mango, or pineapple. Or combine any of these.

Measure the fruit by volume rather than by weight: We call for 2 cups of peeled and coarsely chopped nectarines, so if you decide to use pineapple, for example, coarsely chop the fruit and pile it into a 2-cup measure. Speaking of substitutions, you can use regular plain yogurt rather than low-fat. It will produce a richer tasting and creamier frozen product.

¼ CUP PLUS 3 TABLESPOONS COLD WATER (EACH MEASUREMENT USED SEPARATELY)

2 TEASPOONS UNFLAVORED GELATIN

2 CUPS PEELED AND COARSELY CHOPPED NECTARINES, CHILLED

¾ CUP PLUS 2 TABLESPOONS GRANULATED SUGAR (USED IN TWO MEASUREMENTS)

2½ CUPS PLAIN REGULAR OR LOW-FAT YOGURT, CHILLED (SPOONED INTO A MEASURING CUP AND LEVELED WITH THE EDGE OF A KITCHEN KNIFE)

½ TEASPOON VANILLA EXTRACT

1   Put 3 tablespoons of water in a 6-ounce custard cup. Sprinkle the gelatin over the water and let it soften for at least 5 minutes.

2   Combine the nectarines and ¼ cup plus 2 tablespoons of sugar in a food processor fitted with a metal chopping blade. Process for 15 to 25 seconds, until pureed.

3   Scrape the puree into a 2½-quart noncorrosive metal bowl.

4   Combine the remaining ¼ cup of water and the remaining ½ cup of sugar in a 2-cup microwave-safe glass measuring cup. Cover with waxed paper and

microwave on HIGH (100 percent) power for 1 minute. Stir with a wooden spoon to dissolve any remaining sugar crystals.

5   Cover again and microwave on HIGH (100 percent) power for 30 seconds to 1½ minutes, until the syrup comes to a boil.

6   Take the measuring cup from the microwave and add the softened gelatin. Stir with a wooden spoon until completely dissolved.

7   Add the syrup to the puree and stir gently to combine. Set the bowl over a larger one containing ice water and stir frequently for 5 to 10 minutes, until the mixture is cold.

8   Remove the bowl from the bowl holding the ice water and whisk in the yogurt and vanilla extract. When well mixed, transfer the mixture to an ice cream maker and freeze according to the manufacturer's instructions. The yogurt ice is ready to eat, or if you prefer, it may be packed into a microwave-safe container and frozen for a few hours or overnight. This will make it firmer and more flavorful than if eaten right away. The frozen yogurt may be softened, if necessary, in the container.

Fresh Figs and Lemon Yogurt Ice

serves 8

preparation time: ABOUT 20 MINUTES PLUS 5 TO 10 MINUTES CHILLING AND TIME IN THE ICE
CREAM MAKER

microwave time: 2 TO 4 MINUTES PLUS 5 MINUTES STANDING

T*he refreshing taste of lemony, icy yogurt complements the jammy sweetness of soft, ripe figs. Although you can opt to serve the yogurt by itself, do try it with the figs for a special taste and texture experience.*

¼ CUP PLUS 3 TABLESPOONS
COLD WATER (EACH MEASURE-
MENT USED SEPARATELY)
2 TEASPOONS UNFLAVORED
GELATIN
¾ CUP GRANULATED SUGAR
2 TABLESPOONS FRESH LEMON
JUICE
1½ TEASPOONS FINELY GRATED
LEMON ZEST

3 CUPS REGULAR OR LOW-FAT
PLAIN YOGURT, CHILLED
(SPOONED INTO A MEASURING
CUP AND LEVELED WITH THE
EDGE OF A KITCHEN KNIFE)
½ TEASPOON VANILLA EXTRACT
8 LARGE RIPE PURPLE OR GREEN
FIGS FOR GARNISH

1   Put 3 tablespoons of water in a 6-ounce custard cup. Sprinkle the gelatin over the water and let it soften for 5 to 10 minutes.

2   In a 2-cup microwave-safe glass measuring cup, combine the remaining ¼ cup of water, sugar, lemon juice, and lemon zest. Cover the cup with waxed paper and microwave on HIGH (100 percent) power for 1 minute. Stir with a wooden spoon to dissolve any remaining sugar crystals.

3   Cover again and microwave on HIGH (100 percent) power for 30 seconds to 1½ minutes, until the syrup comes to a boil. Let the mixture stand for 5 minutes.

4   Still covered, microwave on HIGH (100 percent) power for 30 seconds to 1½ minutes, until the syrup comes to a boil again. Add the softened gelatin and stir with a wooden spoon until completely dissolved.

5   Pour the syrup into a 2½-quart noncorrosive metal bowl. Set the bowl over a larger one containing ice water. Stir frequently for 5 to 10 minutes, or until the mixture is cold and starts to thicken slightly.

> **kitchen note:**
>
> *After several hours or overnight in the freezer, the yogurt ice may be too hard to scoop neatly and easily. If it has been packed in a microwave-safe container, soften it, uncovered, by microwaving it on MEDIUM (50 percent) power for 10 seconds at a time until it is soft enough to scoop. Do not let it get too soft.*

6   Remove the bowl from the bowl holding the ice water and whisk in the yogurt and vanilla extract. When well mixed, transfer the mixture to an ice cream maker and freeze according to the manufacturer's instructions. The yogurt ice is ready to eat, or if you prefer, it may be packed into a microwave-safe container and frozen for a few hours or overnight. This will make it firmer and more flavorful than if eaten right away. The yogurt ice may be softened, if necessary, in the container.

7   When you are ready to serve, cut each fig into 5 thin slices. Put a scoop of frozen yogurt ice in the center of a dessert plate and arrange 5 slices, stem ends pointing outward, evenly around the yogurt. Serve immediately.

ICE CREAM, SORBET, and FROZEN YOGURT

CHAPTER EIGHT

Muffins and Coffee Cakes

Buttermilk Bran Muffins

Whole Wheat Banana Nut Muffins

Banana Cranberry Muffins

Autumn Spice Muffins

Holiday Muffins

Zucchini Lemon Spice Muffins

Lemon Blueberry Muffins

Chunky Apple Muffins

Cinnamon Swirl Coffee Cake

Blueberry Orange Tea Cake

Pumpkin Ginger Tea Ring

Cranberry Streusel Coffee Cake

Walnut Fudge Brownies

One of the most gratifying discoveries we made while developing recipes for this book was that it is possible to "bake" warm, crumbly muffins, coffee cakes, and tea cakes in the microwave oven in a matter of minutes. The muffins are, by design, smaller than more conventional ones—just take a look at the size of microwave-safe muffin pans—but that is no deterrent. In fact, it's a benefit: One small muffin—especially when it tastes as good as our Lemon Blueberry, Autumn Spice, Buttermilk Bran, or Chunky Apple—is eminently satisfying. The coffee cakes are equally delicious. Bake one the next time you invite guests over for brunch or afternoon tea, or make one for a club or committee meeting. No one will believe it came out of a microwave oven.

Many of our muffins and coffee cakes are chock-full of luscious fruits and berries, which make them moist but also make them possible. The water and sugar in the fruit attract microwaves and contribute to successful cooking. The fruit also contributes to the final texture, not to mention flavor. We rely mostly on oil, butter, yogurt, sour cream, and milk for much needed fat and moisture, all of which attract microwaves and contribute to the overall goodness of these baked goods.

Finally, in the category of "last but not least," we have included a recipe for Walnut Fudge Brownies on page 245. It is one of Adrienne's original microwave recipes, updated and refined so that it is even better than it was a year ago. We were not sure in which chapter it belonged, but brownies taste awfully good with a cup of coffee or tea and are always welcome at meetings or as snacks. Makes sense, doesn't it?

Muffin Tips

*When you are making microwave muffin batters, the ingredients need to be at room temperature, as they do for conventional batters.

*In recipes calling for softened butter, we explain how to soften it in the microwave.

*Inaccurate measuring can affect the outcome of the recipe. For instance, too much flour results in a dry muffin or coffee cake. We instruct you to sift the flour and then measure. This ensures accuracy of measurement.

*Another way to ensure accuracy is to be sure to use the kind of measuring cup designed for dry ingredients—the kind that allow you to level the ingredients with the sweep of a knife, thereby ensuring accuracy.

*In many recipes we call for sifted whole-wheat flour. Be sure to use a fine-meshed sieve. This is important for two reasons: first it aerates the flour, and second it removes coarse bran so that the muffins have a fine, light texture.

*We suggest using Jack Frost or Town House Fine Granulated sugar, which has finer grains than other brands. Other brands work well but should be sifted first. Do not use superfine sugar.

*To save time, measure the ingredients ahead of time (perhaps the night before or in the morning before work) and combine them just before baking. But please, do not mix them together any sooner. The liquid ingredients will activate the leavener (baking powder and/or soda), something that should not happen until shortly before baking.

*Muffin batter needs to stand for 5 minutes for the same reason cupcake batter does: to give the leaveners time to begin working, since the actual cooking time is so short. Do not let the batter stand for any longer than specified before baking, otherwise the muffins may overflow the cups during baking or lose their lightness.

*When filling the lined muffin cups, distribute the batter evenly so that the muffins will bake evenly. We have found that muffins cook most evenly in microwave ovens with turntables. If you do not have a turntable, be sure to rotate the pan as described in the recipe.

*Bake the muffins for the minimal amount of time suggested in the recipe and then test each one for doneness. If they are not ready, return them to the microwave for 10 seconds and test again. Remove any muffins that test done and continue cooking the remaining muffins until they all are done. Remember that small wet patches will dry upon standing. This care is necessary to keep the muffins from overcooking. Overcooked muffins will be dry and hard.

*We always line the muffin cups with two paper liners. Since we try very hard not to be wasteful, you can be sure this is for a good reason. The outside liner absorbs moisture from the muffin, while the inside liner holds the batter in place. This helps the batter cook more evenly and quickly.

*The outside paper liner must be removed before the muffins are left to cool on wire racks, otherwise the cooling muffin might reabsorb some of the moisture, which results in a hard, tough muffin. Remove the outside liners as soon as the muffins are taken from the microwave oven.

*Wipe the muffin pan with a kitchen or paper towel to remove excess moisture before baking the second batch.

*If you want large muffins, bake the batter in 6-ounce custard cups lined with two paper liners. Fill them half to three-quarters full with batter. Arrange no more than 6 custard cups in a circle in the microwave and increase the cooking time a little—test for doneness according to the recipe. The larger custard cups will mean the batter will yield fewer muffins.

*Muffins baked in the microwave oven do not form a crust, as they do in a conventional oven. This means the muffins expand to their full volume and are especially light and moist. It also means that without the protective crust, they can dry out quickly after baking. As soon as they cool, put the muffins in an airtight container or wrap them individually in waxed paper and plastic for freezing.

*Defrost individually wrapped muffins still in their wrapper by microwaving on MEDIUM-LOW (30 percent) power for 30 to 60 seconds.

Buttermilk Bran Muffins

makes 18 muffins

preparation time: ABOUT 15 MINUTES PLUS 5 MINUTES SOAKING AND 5 MINUTES STANDING

microwave time: 4½ TO 8 MINUTES

*W*hen Adrienne first developed this recipe, the muffins were delicious. But not quite satisfied, she refined it, adding molasses and a touch more sugar and reworking the mixing method—small alterations, perhaps, but ones that make a marked difference to the taste and texture of the muffin. The result? Especially light and moist muffins with a definitive but not overwhelming taste of bran. Keep a bowl of this chilled batter in the refrigerator so that you can have a freshly baked bran muffin any time of day—in minutes.

kitchen note:

It is important to sift the whole wheat flour for these muffins with a fine-meshed sieve. Aerating the flour this way and sifting out the coarse bran contribute greatly to the overall texture and flavor of the muffins.

Chilling the batter helps develop flavor; do not skip this step unless you are pressed for time.

2 CUPS BRAN FLAKE CEREAL
1⅓ CUPS BUTTERMILK
⅓ CUP PLUS 2 TABLESPOONS CANOLA OR SAFFLOWER OIL
2 LARGE EGG WHITES
3 TABLESPOONS MOLASSES
1 TABLESPOON VANILLA EXTRACT
1⅔ CUPS SIFTED WHOLE WHEAT FLOUR

1¼ TEASPOONS DOUBLE-ACTING BAKING POWDER
1¼ TEASPOONS BAKING SODA
¼ TEASPOON SALT
⅓ CUP LIGHTLY PACKED DARK BROWN SUGAR
⅓ CUP CURRANTS

1   Combine the bran flakes and buttermilk in a 2½-quart bowl. Stir until the flakes are moistened. Let the mixture soak for 5 minutes. Add the oil, egg whites, molasses, and vanilla extract. Stir vigorously with a wooden spoon for 45 seconds, until the mixture is creamy.

2   Combine the flour, baking powder, baking soda, and salt in a second 2½-quart bowl. Press the brown sugar through a coarse sieve over the flour mixture. Use a wire whisk and complete 12 to 15 strokes to ensure that the ingredients are thoroughly blended.

3   Make a well in the center of the flour mixture and spoon the bran mixture and currants into it. Using a rubber spatula, fold the bran mixture and the currants into the flour just until moistened and with no pockets of flour in the batter. Let the batter stand for 5 minutes or cover its surface with plastic wrap and refrigerate for at least 2 hours (but it can be refrigerated up to five days).

4   Line each cup of a 6-cup microwave-safe muffin pan or cupcake pan with 2 paper baking cups. Fill the cups three-fourths full of batter. Microwave on HIGH (100 percent) power for 2¼ to 4 minutes, rotating the pan, if you do not have a turntable, a half turn after 1 minute. Test for doneness after 2¼ minutes by inserting a wooden toothpick in the center of each muffin; it should come out clean. Any small wet patches will dry while standing. If not done, check the muffins at 10-second intervals.

5   Immediately remove the outside paper baking cup from each muffin and set the muffins on a wire rack to cool, leaving the inside paper baking cups in place.

6   Repeat the baking and cooling procedure with the rest of the batter. Serve the muffins warm or at room temperature. Leftover muffins can be stored in an airtight container for up to one day or individually wrapped and frozen.

Bran Muffin Baking Chart   (*for refrigerated bran muffin batter only*)

Fill muffin cups ¾ full of batter and microwave on HIGH (100 percent) power for the time specified:

1 muffin . . . 30 seconds to 1¼ minutes	4 muffins . . . 1½ to 2¾ minutes
2 muffins . . . 1 to 2 minutes	5 muffins . . . 1¾ to 3 minutes
3 muffins . . . 1¼ to 2¼ minutes	6 muffins . . . 3 to 4½ minutes

---

Whole Wheat Banana Nut Muffins

makes 12 muffins

preparation time: ABOUT 15 MINUTES PLUS 5 MINUTES STANDING

microwave time: 3½ TO 8 MINUTES

*T*wo *of our muffin recipes feature bananas for three very good reasons: First, they taste good; second, they are available all year round; and third, their moistness makes a valuable contribution to microwave muffin batter. Be sure the bananas are ripe, with brown speckles on their skins and creamy, unbruised fruit. Bananas ripen in just a few days if left at room temperature, so it should not be a problem to find a ripe one. But do not use overripe fruit. It will make the muffins heavy.*

2/3 CUP MASHED-UNTIL-LIQUEFIED RIPE BANANA (ABOUT 1 LARGE BANANA)

1/4 CUP CANOLA OR SAFFLOWER OIL

1 LARGE EGG WHITE, AT ROOM TEMPERATURE

2 TABLESPOONS LOW-FAT MILK

2 TEASPOONS VANILLA EXTRACT

2/3 CUP SIFTED ALL-PURPOSE FLOUR

1/2 CUP SIFTED WHOLE WHEAT FLOUR

1/4 CUP PLUS 2 TABLESPOONS FINELY CHOPPED PECANS (EACH MEASUREMENT USED SEPARATELY)

3/4 TEASPOON DOUBLE-ACTING BAKING POWDER

1/4 TEASPOON BAKING SODA

1/8 TEASPOON SALT

1/3 CUP PACKED LIGHT BROWN SUGAR

1   Combine the mashed banana, oil, egg white, milk, and vanilla extract in a 1-quart bowl. Whisk vigorously for 45 seconds, until the mixture is smooth and light in color.

2   Put the flours, 1/4 cup of pecans, baking powder, baking soda, and salt in a 2½-quart bowl. Press the sugar through a coarse sieve over the flour mixture. Use a wire whisk and complete 12 to 15 strokes to ensure that the ingredients are thoroughly blended.

3   Make a well in the center of the flour mixture and spoon the banana mixture into it. Using a rubber spatula, fold the dry and wet ingredients together just until the batter is moistened. Let the batter stand for 5 minutes.

4   Line each cup of a 6-cup microwave-safe muffin pan with 2 paper baking cups. Fill the cups half full of batter. Microwave on HIGH (100 percent) power for 1 minute and 45 seconds to 3½ minutes, rotating the pan, if you do not have a turntable, a half turn after 1 minute. Test for doneness after 1 minute and 45 seconds by inserting a wooden toothpick in the center of each muffin; it should come out clean. The tops of the muffins will no longer look wet. If not done, check the muffins at 10-second intervals.

5   Immediately remove the outside paper baking cup from each muffin and set the muffins on a wire rack to cool, leaving the inside paper baking cup in place.

6   Repeat the baking and cooling procedure with the rest of the batter. When the muffins are still warm, sprinkle them with the remaining 2 tablespoons of chopped pecans. Serve the muffins warm or at room temperature. You may store them for up to one day in an airtight container.

Banana Cranberry Muffins

makes 12 to 14 muffins

preparation time: ABOUT 10 MINUTES PLUS 5 MINUTES STANDING

microwave time: 4 TO 8½ MINUTES

*O*ur second muffin recipe using bananas adds zesty cranberries, which are sold fresh in the late fall and frozen the remainder of the year. It's a good idea to buy fresh berries in November or December and freeze them yourself so you can have these colorful and delicious muffins anytime. We find them especially tempting on a dreary February morning with a good cup of strong coffee.

⅔ CUP SIFTED WHOLE WHEAT FLOUR

¼ CUP SIFTED ALL-PURPOSE FLOUR

½ TEASPOON DOUBLE-ACTING BAKING POWDER

½ TEASPOON BAKING SODA

¼ TEASPOON SALT

½ CUP FINELY CHOPPED FRESH OR FROZEN CRANBERRIES

¼ CUP FINELY CHOPPED WALNUTS

½ CUP VEGETABLE OIL

½ CUP PACKED LIGHT BROWN SUGAR

1 LARGE EGG, AT ROOM TEMPERATURE

½ CUP MASHED-UNTIL-LIQUEFIED RIPE BANANA (ABOUT 1 MEDIUM BANANA)

2 TEASPOONS VANILLA EXTRACT

> **kitchen note:**
>
> *We use different amounts of mashed fruit in this and the preceding recipe, yet each measurement is reached by mashing one banana. Please note that in the Whole Wheat Banana Nut Muffins recipe the banana is specified as "large." In this recipe it is "medium." Because of the batter's bulk, this recipe may produce more than 12 muffins.*

1   Put the flours, baking powder, baking soda, and salt in a 1½-quart bowl. Use a wire whisk and complete 12 to 15 strokes to ensure that the ingredients are thoroughly blended. Stir in the cranberries and walnuts.

2   Using a hand-held electric mixer set at high speed, beat the oil, brown sugar, and egg in a 4-quart bowl for 2 minutes, until creamy and a beige color. Reduce the speed to low and beat in the banana and vanilla extract. Using a rubber spatula, fold in the flour mixture. Let the batter stand for 5 minutes.

3   Line each cup of a 6-cup microwave-safe muffin pan with 2 paper baking cups. Fill the cups two-thirds full of batter. Microwave on HIGH (100 percent) power for 1¾ to 3½ minutes, rotating the pan, if you do not have a turntable, a half turn after 1 minute. Test for doneness after 1¾ minutes by inserting a wooden toothpick in the center of each muffin; it should come out clean. The tops of the muffins will no longer look wet. If not done, check the muffins at 10-second intervals.

4 Immediately remove the outside paper baking cup from each muffin and set the muffins on a wire rack to cool, leaving the inside paper baking cup in place.

5 Repeat the baking and cooling procedure with the remaining batter. If the batter yields more than 12 muffins, cook the final 1 or 2 muffins for 30 seconds to 1½ minutes. Test these for doneness after 30 seconds. Serve the muffins warm or at room temperature. You may store them for up to one day in an airtight container.

Autumn Spice Muffins

makes 12 muffins

preparation time: ABOUT 15 MINUTES PLUS 5 MINUTES STANDING

microwave time: 4 TO 7 MINUTES

*R*un *your eye down the list of ingredients, and you will immediately see that these are cold weather muffins, using all those good spices and flavors that we associate with brisk fall days and cold, windy nights. These are wonderfully rich and moist, and would taste as good at suppertime with a bowl of thick hot soup as at lunchtime with sliced cold leftover ham.*

¾ CUP SIFTED ALL-PURPOSE FLOUR

¾ TEASPOON GROUND GINGER

¾ TEASPOON GROUND CINNAMON

¼ TEASPOON GROUND CLOVES

¼ TEASPOON FRESHLY GRATED NUTMEG

¼ TEASPOON DOUBLE-ACTING BAKING POWDER

¼ TEASPOON BAKING SODA

⅛ TEASPOON SALT

½ CUP FINELY CHOPPED WALNUTS

½ CUP CURRANTS

⅔ CUP PACKED LIGHT BROWN SUGAR

½ CUP VEGETABLE OIL

1 LARGE EGG, AT ROOM TEMPERATURE

¾ CUP CANNED UNSWEETENED PUMPKIN PUREE

2 TEASPOONS VANILLA EXTRACT

1 Put the flour, ginger, cinnamon, cloves, nutmeg, baking powder, baking soda, and salt in a 1½-quart bowl. Use a wire whisk and complete 12 to 15 strokes to ensure that the ingredients are thoroughly blended. Stir in the walnuts and currants.

2 Using a hand-held electric mixer set at high speed, beat the brown sugar, oil, and egg in a 4-quart bowl for 2 minutes, until creamy. Reduce the speed to low and beat in the pumpkin puree and vanilla extract. Using a rubber spatula, fold the flour mixture into the batter. Let the batter stand for 5 minutes.

3 Line each cup of a 6-cup microwave-safe muffin pan with 2 paper baking cups. Fill the cups two-thirds full of batter. Microwave on HIGH (100 percent) power for 2 to 3½ minutes, rotating the pan, if you do not have a turntable, a half turn after 1 minute. Test for doneness after 2 minutes by inserting a wooden toothpick in the center of each muffin; it should come out clean. The tops of the muffins will no longer look wet. If not done, check the muffins at 10-second intervals.

4 Immediately remove the outside paper baking cup from each muffin and set the muffins on a wire rack to cool, leaving the inside baking cups in place.

5 Repeat the baking and cooling procedure with the remaining batter. Serve the muffins warm or at room temperature. You may store them for up to one day in an airtight container.

> **kitchen note:**
>
> *The flavor of fresh nutmeg is incomparable. If you must use packaged nutmeg, be sure it is as fresh as possible. Old, rancid nutmeg tastes wretched.*

Holiday Muffins

makes 14 muffins

preparation time: ABOUT 15 MINUTES PLUS 5 MINUTES STANDING

microwave time: 4 MINUTES AND 45 SECONDS TO 8½ MINUTES

*E*ven if you do not particularly care for mincemeat (and neither of us loves it), we think you will be more than pleasantly surprised by these muffins. The mincemeat gives them a deliciously festive flavor. Consider serving them on Thanksgiving or Christmas morning, together with some Buttermilk Bran Muffins (page 222) or Banana Cranberry Muffins (page 225).

1 CUP PLUS 2 TABLESPOONS SIFTED WHOLE WHEAT FLOUR

¾ TEASPOON GROUND CINNAMON

¾ TEASPOON DOUBLE-ACTING BAKING POWDER

½ TEASPOON GROUND GINGER

¼ TEASPOON BAKING SODA

⅛ TEASPOON SALT

½ CUP VEGETABLE OIL

¼ CUP PACKED DARK BROWN SUGAR

1 LARGE EGG, AT ROOM TEMPERATURE

2 TEASPOONS VANILLA EXTRACT

¾ TEASPOON FINELY GRATED ORANGE ZEST

¾ CUP PREPARED MINCEMEAT

⅓ CUP BUTTERMILK OR ⅓ CUP PLUS 1 TABLESPOON PLAIN LOW-FAT YOGURT (SPOONED INTO A MEASURING CUP AND LEVELED WITH THE EDGE OF A KNIFE)

¼ CUP FINELY CHOPPED WALNUTS

---

kitchen note:

Be sure to use a fine-meshed sieve to sift the whole wheat flour so that the muffins will have a fine, light texture.

---

1   Put the flour, cinnamon, baking powder, ginger, baking soda, and salt in a 1½-quart bowl. Use a wire whisk and complete 12 to 15 strokes to ensure that the ingredients are thoroughly blended.

2   Using a hand-held electric mixer at high speed, beat the oil, brown sugar, egg, vanilla extract, and orange zest in a 4-quart bowl for 2 minutes, until creamy and a light brown color. Stir in the mincemeat and buttermilk with a rubber spatula. Stir in the walnuts. Add the flour mixture and stir until the batter is smooth. Let the batter stand for 5 minutes.

3   Line each cup of a 6-cup microwave-safe muffin or cupcake pan with 2 paper baking cups. Fill the cups two-thirds full with batter. Microwave on HIGH (100 percent) power for 2 to 3½ minutes, rotating the pan, if you do not have

a turntable, a half turn after 1 minute. Test for doneness after 2 minutes by inserting a wooden toothpick in the center of each muffin; it should come out clean. The muffin tops will no longer look wet. If not done, check the muffins at 10-second intervals.

4   Immediately remove the outer paper baking cup from each muffin. Set the muffins, still in the inner cups, on a wire rack to cool. Repeat the baking and cooling procedure twice more with the remaining muffin batter. Cook the last 2 muffins for 30 seconds to 1½ minutes, testing for doneness after 30 seconds. Serve the muffins warm or at room temperature. They may be stored for up to one day in an airtight container.

Zucchini Lemon Spice Muffins

makes 12 to 14 muffins

preparation time: ABOUT 15 MINUTES PLUS 5 MINUTES STANDING

microwave time: 4 TO 8½ MINUTES

Zucchini makes muffins moist and rich, and the lemon zest, acting in concert with the cinnamon, cloves, and nutmeg, provides a nice flavor balance. Try these on one of those crisp fall afternoons with a tall glass of milk or cider.

1 CUP PLUS 2 TABLESPOONS SIFTED WHOLE WHEAT FLOUR

1 TEASPOON GROUND CINNAMON

¾ TEASPOON DOUBLE-ACTING BAKING POWDER

¼ TEASPOON BAKING SODA

¼ TEASPOON GROUND CLOVES

¼ TEASPOON FRESHLY GRATED NUTMEG

⅛ TEASPOON SALT

½ CUP VEGETABLE OIL

½ CUP PACKED DARK BROWN SUGAR

1 LARGE EGG, AT ROOM TEMPERATURE

2 TEASPOONS VANILLA EXTRACT

1 TEASPOON FINELY GRATED LEMON ZEST

1 CUP SHREDDED ZUCCHINI (ABOUT 1 SMALL ZUCCHINI)

⅓ CUP PLAIN LOW-FAT YOGURT (SPOONED INTO A MEASURING CUP AND LEVELED WITH THE EDGE OF A KNIFE)

¼ CUP PLUS 2 TABLESPOONS FINELY CHOPPED WALNUTS (EACH MEASUREMENT USED SEPARATELY)

2 TABLESPOONS CURRANTS

1   Put the flour, cinnamon, baking powder, baking soda, cloves, nutmeg, and salt in a 1½-quart bowl. Use a wire whisk and complete 12 to 15 strokes to ensure that the ingredients are thoroughly blended.

2   Using a hand-held electric mixer set at high speed, beat the oil, brown sugar, egg, vanilla extract and lemon zest in a 4-quart bowl until creamy and a light brown color. Stir in the zucchini and yogurt with a rubber spatula. Stir in ¼ cup of the walnuts and the currants. Add the flour mixture and stir until the batter is smooth. Let the batter stand for 5 minutes.

3   Line each cup of a 6-cup microwave-safe muffin pan with 2 paper baking cups. Fill the cups two-thirds full with batter. Microwave on HIGH (100 percent) power for 2 to 3½ minutes, rotating the pan, if you do not have a turntable, a half turn after 1 minute. Test for doneness after 2 minutes by inserting a wooden toothpick into the center of each muffin; it should come out clean. The tops of the muffins will no longer look wet. If not done, check the muffins at 10-second intervals.

4   Immediately remove the outer baking cup from each muffin. Set the muffins, still in the inner cups, on a wire rack to cool. While the muffins are still hot, sprinkle them with some of the remaining 2 tablespoons of chopped walnuts. Repeat the baking and cooling procedure twice more with the remaining muffin batter. Cook the last 2 muffins for 30 seconds to 1½ minutes, testing for doneness after 30 seconds. Serve the muffins warm or at room temperature. They may be stored for up to one day in an airtight container.

Lemon Blueberry Muffins

makes 12 muffins

preparation time: ABOUT 15 MINUTES PLUS 5 MINUTES STANDING

microwave time: 4 TO 7 MINUTES

If life were perfect, you would eat these muffins on a summer's morning, sitting on a sprawling farmhouse porch with a big pot of coffee at your elbow and the sunlight slanting over the cornfields as it rises in the azure sky. But although life is not like that (or only rarely) thank goodness we can always enjoy these light, lemony muffins, which taste as fresh as a summer morning.

¾ CUP SIFTED ALL-PURPOSE FLOUR

⅓ CUP SIFTED WHOLE WHEAT FLOUR

⅓ CUP GRANULATED SUGAR

1¼ TEASPOONS DOUBLE-ACTING BAKING POWDER

⅛ TEASPOON SALT

½ CUP LOW-FAT PLAIN YOGURT, AT ROOM TEMPERATURE (SPOONED INTO A MEASURING CUP AND LEVELED WITH THE EDGE OF A KNIFE)

⅓ CUP VEGETABLE OIL

1 LARGE EGG, AT ROOM TEMPERATURE

1 TEASPOON VANILLA EXTRACT

½ TEASPOON FINELY GRATED LEMON ZEST

⅔ CUP BLUEBERRIES

1 Put the flours, sugar, baking powder, and salt in a 2½-quart bowl. Use a wire whisk and complete 12 to 15 strokes to ensure that the ingredients are thoroughly blended.

2 Combine the yogurt, oil, egg, vanilla extract, and lemon zest in a 1-quart bowl. Whisk vigorously for 45 seconds, until the mixture is creamy.

3 Make a well in the center of the flour mixture and spoon the yogurt mixture and blueberries into it. Using a rubber spatula, mix the dry and wet ingredients together just until the batter is moistened. Let the batter stand for 5 minutes.

> **kitchen note:**
>
> *If the blueberries are especially large, cut them in half before adding them to the batter.*

4 Line each cup of a 6-cup microwave-safe muffin pan or cupcake pan with 2 paper baking cups. Fill the cups two-thirds full with batter. Microwave on HIGH (100 percent) power for 1¾ to 3½ minutes, rotating the pan, if you do not have a turntable, a half turn after 1 minute. Test for doneness after 1¾ minutes by inserting a wooden toothpick in the center of each muffin; it should come out clean. The tops of the muffins will no longer look wet. If not done, check the muffins at 10-second intervals.

5 Immediately remove the outside paper baking cup from each muffin and set the muffins on a wire rack to cool, leaving the inside paper baking cups in place.

6 Repeat the baking and cooling procedure with the remaining batter. Serve the muffins warm or at room temperature. You may store them for up to one day in an airtight container.

Chunky Apple Muffins

makes 12 muffins

preparation time: ABOUT 15 MINUTES PLUS 5 MINUTES STANDING

microwave time: 4 TO 7 MINUTES

These muffins pack the combined good flavor of applesauce and apples. They also require a long list of ingredients that should not dissuade you from making them because most are everyday spices you probably have in your cupboard. The moist, robust muffins make a good snack as well as a good morning muffin. Use your favorite apples in the recipe, the ones that taste best to you and are available when you plan to make the muffins. Firm, crisp apples such as McIntosh, Empire, Winesap, and Granny Smith are good choices.

½ CUP UNSWEETENED APPLESAUCE

¼ CUP PLUS 1 TABLESPOON CANOLA OR SAFFLOWER OIL

1 LARGE EGG WHITE, AT ROOM TEMPERATURE

2 TEASPOONS VANILLA EXTRACT

¾ CUP SIFTED ALL-PURPOSE FLOUR

½ CUP SIFTED WHOLE WHEAT FLOUR

1¼ TEASPOONS DOUBLE-ACTING BAKING POWDER

¾ TEASPOON GROUND CINNAMON

¼ TEASPOON BAKING SODA

¼ TEASPOON FRESHLY GRATED NUTMEG

⅛ TEASPOON SALT

⅛ TEASPOON GROUND CLOVES

⅓ CUP PACKED LIGHT BROWN SUGAR

1 CUP ¼-INCH-DICED APPLE (ABOUT 1 APPLE)

¼ CUP CURRANTS

CINNAMON SUGAR FOR GARNISH (OPTIONAL)

kitchen note:

Take care to cut the apples into ¼-inch pieces. Microwave muffins are small and won't work as well if the apple pieces are any larger.

1   Combine the applesauce, oil, egg white, and vanilla extract in a 1-cup microwave-safe glass measuring cup. Whisk vigorously for 45 seconds, until the mixture is smooth and light in color.

2   Put the flours, baking powder, cinnamon, baking soda, nutmeg, salt, and cloves in a 2½-quart bowl. Press the sugar through a coarse sieve over the flour mixture. Use a wire whisk and complete 12 to 15 strokes to ensure that the ingredients are thoroughly blended. With a rubber spatula, fold the diced apples and the currants into the dry ingredients.

3   Make a well in the center of the flour-fruit mixture and spoon the applesauce mixture into it. Using a rubber spatula,

mix the dry and wet ingredients together just until the batter is moistened. Let the batter stand for 5 minutes.

4   Line each cup of a 6-cup microwave-safe muffin pan or cupcake pan with 2 paper baking cups. Fill the cups three-fourths full of batter. Microwave on HIGH (100 percent) power for 2 to 3½ minutes, rotating the pan, if you do not have a turntable, a half turn after 1 minute. Test for doneness after 2 minutes by inserting a wooden toothpick in the center of each muffin; it should come out clean. The tops of the muffins will no longer look wet. If not done, check the muffins at 10-second intervals.

5   Immediately remove the outside paper baking cup from each muffin and set the muffins on a wire rack to cool, leaving the inside paper baking cups in place.

6   Repeat the baking and cooling procedure with the rest of the batter. When the muffins are still warm, sprinkle them with cinnamon sugar, if desired. Serve the muffins warm or at room temperature. You may store them for up to one day in an airtight container.

Coffee and Tea Cake Tips

*When making coffee and tea cake batters, the ingredients need to be at room temperature as they do for conventional batters.

*In recipes calling for room-temperature sour cream, yogurt, buttermilk, milk, or softened butter, we explain how to do it in the microwave.

*Eggs can be brought to room temperature by immersing them in a bowl of warm water for about 5 minutes. Dry the eggs before cracking them.

*Inaccurate measuring can affect the outcome of the recipe. For instance, too much flour results in a dry cake. We instruct you to sift the flour and then measure to ensure accuracy of measurement.

*Another way to ensure accuracy is to be sure to use the kind of measuring cup designed for dry ingredients—the kind that allow you to level the ingredients with the sweep of a knife thereby ensuring accuracy.

*We suggest using Jack Frost or Town House Fine Granulated sugar, which has finer grains than other brands. Other brands work well but should be sifted first. Do not use superfine sugar.

*To save time, measure the ingredients ahead of time (perhaps the night before or in the morning before work) and combine them just before baking. But please, do not mix them together any sooner. The liquid ingredients will activate the leavener (baking power and/or soda), something that should not happen until shortly before baking.

*Be sure to use the correct size pan for coffee and tea cakes. Batter rises more in the microwave because no protective crust forms in the oven and there is greater risk of overflow.

*It is important to oil or grease the pan thoroughly, as required in the recipe. In many cases, we give a measurement for the amount of shortening you will need to cover the pan completely. Do not substitute butter for shortening, as it may cause the cake to stick. If the recipe calls for chopped nuts or crumbs sprinkled in the pan, be sure you do so. Otherwise, the cake will stick to the pan.

*In some of the coffee cake recipes we instruct you to line the bottom of the baking dish or casserole with two circles of waxed paper. Lightly oil the bottom of the dish or casserole before lining it with the paper circles. To prevent sticking, be sure they cover the entire bottom of the dish or casserole. The circle closest to the bottom of the dish absorbs excess moisture from the batter and the one on top enables you to remove the baked cake from the dish or casserole easily.

To cut these circles, lay two sheets of waxed paper on the counter and set the dish or casserole on top of them. Using the point of a small, sharp knife, trace the outline of the circles and then cut both circles at once.

*For even baking, make sure to spread the coffee cake batter evenly in the pan.

*Elevate coffee and tea cakes on an inverted glass pie plate. This will allow microwaves to be more readily absorbed by the bottom of the cake and promote even cooking.

*When we bake coffee and tea cakes, we may regulate the microwave power, starting with the MEDIUM (50 percent) power and ending with HIGH (100 percent) power. This gives the batter time to expand and the crumb opportunity to develop.

*If you do not have a turntable, rotate the cake as instructed in the recipe, being sure you rotate it before increasing the power to HIGH.

*Be diligent about testing the coffee and tea cakes for doneness. After the first time check, test the cakes every 10 seconds. Otherwise, they could overcook. Overcooked cakes will be dry and tough.

*Because microwaves vary according to brand, wattage, model, and size, the visual doneness tests are crucial. Do not rely on time alone. A minute or two may not make much of a difference in a conventional oven, but in the microwave it can spell the difference between success and disaster.

*A paper towel loosely covering the coffee or tea cake as it cooks helps hold in just enough moisture to promote even cooking. It also prevents the batter from drying out. At the same time, the paper towel allows excess moisture to escape. Do not substitute plastic wrap, thinking it must be more efficient; it holds in too much moisture.

*Standing time completes the baking. If called for, be sure to allow the coffee cake to stand for as long as specified. Remember that any small wet patches will disappear well before it is time to unmold the coffee cake. Set the coffee cake on a flat heatproof surface rather than a wire rack for the most effective standing time. The heat trapped in the pan will complete the cooking.

*Before the coffee cake is turned out onto a rack or serving plate, we instruct you to sprinkle the top with graham cracker or cookie crumbs. The cake does not have a protective crust and this prevents it from sticking to the rack or plate.

*After the specified standing time, the paper towel should be replaced with a clean kitchen towel, which will protect the coffee or tea cake and keep it moist as it cools completely.

*Microwave coffee cakes will be just as crumbly as conventionally baked coffee cakes if cut into while still warm. All cakes slice more easily and neatly if allowed to cool completely.

*Round cake pans are a better shape than square or rectangular ones for microwave coffee and tea cakes. A Bundt pan is the most effective—the central tube allows for even baking.

*We developed the Walnut Fudge Brownies (page 245) in a 2-quart Pyrex Originals square glass cake dish with rounded corners. In recent years, Pyrex redesigned its square and oblong dishes with more rounded corners. This promoted more even baking. We recommend using these rather than older-style Pyrex dishes with ''squarer'' corners.

*Once cool, keep coffee and tea cakes under cake domes or large upturned bowls to hold in moisture. Remember, as with the muffins, these cakes have no protective crust.

Cinnamon Swirl Coffee Cake

serves 8

preparation time: ABOUT 25 MINUTES

microwave time: 11 MINUTES AND 15 SECONDS TO 15 MINUTES AND 45 SECONDS PLUS 20 MINUTES STANDING

A weekend breakfast is hardly complete without a sweet, moist cinnamon coffee cake. This one cooks in such record time that you can make it during the week, too. To save time in the morning, measure and mix the cinnamon swirl and the other dry ingredients the night before. Be very careful not to overbake the coffee cake, which would make it dry. The sugar in the swirl, which attracts microwaves, gets hot quickly and transmits heat to the batter.

Unbelievable Microwave Desserts

Cinnamon swirl:

¾ CUP FINELY CHOPPED WALNUTS

2 TABLESPOONS LIGHT BROWN SUGAR

2 TABLESPOONS UNSWEETENED COCOA
  POWDER

¾ TEASPOON GROUND CINNAMON

Coffee cake:

2 TABLESPOONS VEGETABLE
  SHORTENING

4 TABLESPOONS GRAHAM CRACKER
  CRUMBS (ABOUT 1½ CRACKERS)
  (USED IN TWO MEASUREMENTS)

¾ CUP PLUS 3 TABLESPOONS
  GRANULATED SUGAR (USED IN TWO
  MEASUREMENTS)

1¾ CUPS SIFTED ALL-PURPOSE FLOUR

2¾ TEASPOONS DOUBLE-ACTING BAKING
  POWDER

¼ TEASPOON SALT

¾ CUP SOUR CREAM

⅓ CUP MILK

8 TABLESPOONS UNSALTED BUTTER

2 LARGE EGGS, AT ROOM
  TEMPERATURE (LIGHTLY BEATEN)

2 TEASPOONS VANILLA EXTRACT

1 TEASPOON FINELY GRATED LEMON
  ZEST

1   To make the cinnamon swirl: Combine the walnuts, brown sugar, cocoa, and cinnamon in a 1-quart bowl. Stir until thoroughly blended.

2   To make the coffee cake: Using a pastry brush, thoroughly coat the bottom and sides of a 6-cup microwave-safe Bundt pan with vegetable shortening. Combine 3 tablespoons graham cracker crumbs and 1 tablespoon sugar in a small bowl until blended. Sprinkle the pan with the cracker mixture and turn it to coat evenly. Set aside.

3   Put the flour, baking powder, and salt in a 2½-quart bowl. Use a wire whisk and complete 12 to 15 strokes to ensure that the ingredients are thoroughly blended.

4   Combine the sour cream and milk in a 1-cup microwave-safe glass measuring cup and stir with a fork until blended. Microwave on MEDIUM-LOW (30 percent) power for 1 to 2 minutes, stirring every 20 seconds until the chill is off. Do not let the mixture get hot. Set aside.

5   Put the butter in a 4-quart microwave-safe bowl. Cover with waxed paper and microwave on HIGH (100 percent) power for 15 to 45 seconds, until the butter is slightly softened. Do not let the butter melt or become oily.

6   Using a hand-held electric mixer set at high speed, beat the butter for 30 seconds, until creamy. Add the sugar and continue to beat for 2 to 3 minutes,

(*CONTINUED*)

scraping down the sides of the bowl often until the mixture is nearly white and its texture is light.

7   While continuing to beat at medium speed, slowly add the egg. Beat until smooth. At low speed beat in the flour mixture, a third at a time, alternating with the sour cream mixture. Beat briefly, just until each addition is incorporated into the batter. Scrape down the sides of the bowl with a rubber spatula and beat a few seconds more.

8   Drop a third of the batter by spoonfuls evenly around the center tube of the prepared pan. Using the back of a spoon, spread the batter in an even layer. Sprinkle half of the cinnamon swirl mixture evenly over the batter. Drop half of the remaining batter by spoonfuls evenly around the center and spread it in an even layer. Sprinkle the remaining cinnamon swirl mixture evenly over the batter. Drop the remaining batter by spoonfuls evenly around the center and spread it evenly in the pan.

9   Swirl the batter by inserting a table knife, point downward, into the batter. Lift the knife up at a slight angle and gently fold the batter and cinnamon swirl together. Make sure to swirl the mixture throughout the batter to make a good pattern.

10   Insert the tip of the knife into the batter once more and draw it through the center of the batter, traveling all the way around the cake pan once. Smooth the batter with the back of a spoon.

11   Cover the top of the cake pan with a microwave-safe paper towel. Set the cake pan on an inverted 9-inch microwave-safe glass pie plate and microwave on MEDIUM (50 percent) power for 5 minutes, rotating the pan, if you do not have a turntable, a quarter turn every 2½ minutes.

12   Microwave on HIGH (100 percent) power for 2 to 5 minutes more, rotating the pan, if you do not have a turntable, a quarter turn every 60 seconds. Test for doneness after 2 minutes by inserting a wooden toothpick in the center of the cake; it should come out clean. The surface of the cake will appear dry. If not done, check the cake at 30-second intervals. Let the coffee cake stand, still covered with the paper towel, on a flat heatproof surface for 20 minutes.

13   Sprinkle the top of the cake with the remaining tablespoon of graham cracker crumbs. Run the tip of a knife around the center tube and around the edge of the cake pan to loosen the cake.

14   Cover the cake pan with a serving plate. Invert the cake pan and gently tap it to release the cake. If some of the graham cracker crumbs remain on the bottom of the pan and expose white patches on the cake, sprinkle the cake with more crumbs. Serve the coffee cake while it is still warm or at room temperature. Store any leftover coffee cake under a cake dome or large, upturned bowl for up to one day.

Blueberry Orange Tea Cake

serves 8

preparation time: ABOUT 25 MINUTES

microwave time: 11 MINUTES AND 45 SECONDS TO 15 MINUTES AND 45 SECONDS PLUS 20 MINUTES STANDING

*F*resh berries yield superior results, but this cake tastes very good when made with frozen blueberries or cranberries. Do not thaw the berries but lengthen the cooking time just a little. Let the cake cool before slicing it; as with cakes baked in conventional ovens, microwaved cakes are too crumbly to slice easily when still hot.

2 TABLESPOONS VEGETABLE SHORTENING

4 TABLESPOONS GRAHAM CRACKER CRUMBS (ABOUT 1½ CRACKERS) (USED IN TWO MEASUREMENTS)

¾ CUP PLUS 3 TABLESPOONS GRANULATED SUGAR (USED IN TWO MEASUREMENTS)

2 CUPS SIFTED CAKE FLOUR

2¾ TEASPOONS DOUBLE-ACTING BAKING POWDER

¼ TEASPOON SALT

¾ CUP PLUS 2 TABLESPOONS LOW-FAT PLAIN YOGURT

9 TABLESPOONS UNSALTED BUTTER

2 LARGE EGGS, AT ROOM TEMPERATURE (LIGHTLY BEATEN)

2 TEASPOONS VANILLA EXTRACT

¾ TEASPOON FINELY GRATED ORANGE ZEST

1 CUP SMALL BLUEBERRIES

CONFECTIONER'S SUGAR

1 Using a pastry brush, thoroughly coat the bottom and sides of a 6-cup microwave-safe Bundt pan with vegetable shortening. Combine 3 tablespoons graham cracker crumbs and 1 tablespoon sugar in a small bowl until blended. Sprinkle the pan with the cracker mixture and turn it to coat evenly. Set aside.

2 Put the flour, baking powder, and salt in a 2½-quart bowl. Use a wire whisk and complete 12 to 15 strokes to ensure that the ingredients are thoroughly blended.

3 Put the yogurt in a 1-cup microwave-safe glass measuring cup. Microwave uncovered on MEDIUM-LOW (30 percent) power for 1 to 2 minutes, stirring every 20 seconds until the chill is off. Do not let the yogurt get hot. Set aside.

4 Put the butter in a 4-quart microwave-safe bowl. Cover with waxed paper and microwave on HIGH (100 percent) power for 15 to 45 seconds, until the butter is slightly softened. Do not let the butter melt or become oily.

5   Using a hand-held electric mixer set at high speed, beat the butter for 30 seconds, until creamy. Add ¾ cup plus 2 tablespoons sugar and continue to beat for 2 to 3 minutes, scraping down the sides of the bowl often until the mixture is nearly white and its texture is light. Beat in the vanilla extract and orange zest.

6   While continuing to beat at medium speed, slowly add the egg. Beat until smooth. At low speed beat in the flour mixture, a third at a time, alternating with the yogurt. Beat briefly, just until each addition is incorporated into the batter. Scrape down the sides of the bowl with a rubber spatula and beat a few seconds more.

7   Drop a fourth of the batter by spoonfuls evenly around the center tube of the prepared pan. Using the back of a spoon, spread the batter in an even layer.

8   Fold the blueberries into the remaining batter. Drop the batter into the pan by spoonfuls and spread evenly.

9   Cover the top of the cake pan with a microwave-safe paper towel. Microwave the cake elevated on an inverted 9-inch glass pie plate on MEDIUM (50 percent) power for 5 minutes. If you do not have a turntable, rotate the pan a quarter turn every 2½ minutes.

10   Continue to microwave on HIGH (100 percent) power for 2 to 5 minutes, rotating the pan, if you do not have a turntable, a quarter turn every 60 seconds. Test the cake for doneness after 2 minutes by inserting a wooden toothpick in the center of the cake; it should come out clean. The surface of the cake will appear dry. If not done, check the cake at 30-second intervals. Let the coffee cake stand, still covered with the paper towel, on a flat heatproof surface for 20 minutes.

11   Remove the towel and sprinkle the top of the cake with the remaining tablespoon of graham cracker crumbs. Run the tip of a knife around the center tube and around the edge of the cake pan to loosen the cake.

12   Cover the cake pan with a serving plate. Invert the cake pan and gently tap it to release the cake. If some of the graham cracker crumbs remain on the bottom of the pan and expose white patches on the cake, sprinkle the cake with more crumbs. Serve the tea cake while it is still warm or at room temperature, lightly dusted with confectioner's sugar. Store any leftover tea cake under a cake dome or large upturned bowl for up to one day.

Cranberry Orange Tea Cake

Substitute 1 cup of coarsely chopped fresh or frozen cranberries for the blueberries. Toss the cranberries with 1 tablespoon of granulated sugar before folding them into the batter.

Pumpkin Ginger Tea Ring

serves 8

preparation time: ABOUT 20 MINUTES

microwave time: 7 TO 10 MINUTES PLUS 20 MINUTES STANDING

*W*hen Adrienne developed this recipe, she quickly decided it was one of her all-time favorites. ''I have a fondness for ginger,'' she admits. ''And this cake goes very nicely with a cup of afternoon tea.'' After a day of recipe development, Adrienne deserved that cup of tea and slice of cake. We use unsweetened pumpkin puree here because it produces such a moist cake and is so easy to find and use.

- 2 TABLESPOONS SOLID VEGETABLE SHORTENING
- 4 TABLESPOONS GRAHAM CRACKER CRUMBS (ABOUT 1½ CRACKERS) (USED IN TWO MEASUREMENTS)
- 1 CUP FINELY CHOPPED WALNUTS (USED IN TWO MEASUREMENTS)
- ½ CUP PLUS 1 TABLESPOON GRANULATED SUGAR (USED IN TWO MEASUREMENTS)
- 1⅓ CUPS SIFTED ALL-PURPOSE FLOUR
- 1 TEASPOON GROUND CINNAMON
- ¼ TEASPOON GROUND GINGER
- ¼ TEASPOON GROUND CLOVES
- ¼ TEASPOON FRESHLY GRATED NUTMEG
- 2 TEASPOONS DOUBLE-ACTING BAKING POWDER
- ½ TEASPOON BAKING SODA
- ½ TEASPOON SALT
- ¼ CUP CRYSTALLIZED GINGER
- ½ CUP PACKED LIGHT BROWN SUGAR
- ⅔ CUP VEGETABLE OIL
- 2 LARGE EGGS, AT ROOM TEMPERATURE
- 2 TEASPOONS VANILLA EXTRACT
- 1 CUP UNSWEETENED PUMPKIN PUREE
- ¾ CUP DARK RAISINS

1   Using a pastry brush, thoroughly coat the bottom and sides of a 6-cup microwave-safe Bundt pan with shortening. Combine 3 tablespoons graham cracker crumbs and 1 tablespoon sugar in a small bowl until blended. Sprinkle the pan with the walnut mixture and turn it to coat evenly. Set aside.

2   Combine the flour, cinnamon, ginger, cloves, nutmeg, baking powder, baking soda, and salt in a 1½-quart bowl. Use a wire whisk to complete 12 to 15 strokes to ensure that the ingredients are thoroughly blended.

3   Soak the crystallized ginger in warm tap water for a minute or two to remove the sugar coating. Rinse and drain well. Pat the ginger dry with a paper towel and then finely chop it.

4   In a 4-quart bowl, using a hand-held electric mixer set at high speed, beat the sugars, oil, eggs, and vanilla extract for 3 minutes, until creamy and a beige color. Reduce the speed to low and mix in the pumpkin puree until blended. Use a wire whisk to stir in the flour mixture until smooth. Using a rubber spatula, fold in the remaining ½ cup of walnuts, ginger, and raisins.

5   Scrape the batter into the prepared pan and spread it evenly with the back of a spoon.

6   Cover the pan with a microwave-safe paper towel and set it on an inverted 9-inch microwave-safe glass pie plate. Microwave on MEDIUM (50 percent) power for 6 minutes, rotating the pan, if you do not have a turntable, a quarter turn every 3 minutes.

7   Microwave on HIGH (100 percent) power for 3 to 6 minutes, rotating the pan, if you do not have a turntable, a quarter turn every 1½ minutes. Test for doneness after 3 minutes by inserting a wooden toothpick in the center of the cake; it should come out clean. The surface of the cake will appear dry. If not done, check the cake at 30-second intervals. Let the cake stand, still covered with the paper towel, on a flat heatproof surface for 20 minutes.

8   Sprinkle the top of the cake with the graham cracker or vanilla wafer cookie crumbs. Run the tip of a knife around the center tube and around the edge of the cake pan to loosen the cake. Invert the cake onto a plate to cool. Keep the cake covered with a clean kitchen towel until ready to serve or completely cool. Serve warm or at room temperature. Store the cake under a cake dome or a large, upturned bowl for up to four days.

Cranberry Streusel Coffee Cake

serves 8

preparation time: ABOUT 25 MINUTES

microwave time: 8 MINUTES AND 55 SECONDS TO 13 MINUTES AND 45 SECONDS PLUS 15 MINUTES STANDING

*B*ecause we like cranberries so much, we appreciate both the flavor and color they add to coffee cakes. What is more, they can often be used interchangeably with blueberries, which increases your options. This cake has a crumbly sweet streusel topping that will tempt early bird and sleepyhead alike. Provide a good cup of strong coffee, and we promise no complaints.

Streusel topping:

¼ CUP UNCOOKED QUICK-COOKING OATS

¼ CUP UNSIFTED ALL-PURPOSE FLOUR (LIGHTLY SPOONED INTO A MEASURING CUP AND LEVELED WITH THE EDGE OF A KNIFE)

4 TEASPOONS DARK BROWN SUGAR

¼ CUP PECAN HALVES

¼ TEASPOON GROUND CINNAMON

⅛ TEASPOON DOUBLE-ACTING BAKING POWDER

GENEROUS PINCH OF SALT

2 TABLESPOONS CHILLED, UNSALTED BUTTER, CUT INTO ½-INCH CUBES

Coffee cake:

1 CUP PLUS 2 TABLESPOONS SIFTED ALL-PURPOSE FLOUR

1½ TEASPOONS DOUBLE-ACTING BAKING POWDER

⅛ TEASPOON SALT

½ BUTTERMILK

6 TABLESPOONS UNSALTED BUTTER

½ CUP PLUS 1 TABLESPOON GRANULATED SUGAR (EACH MEASUREMENT USED SEPARATELY)

2 TEASPOONS VANILLA EXTRACT

¾ TEASPOON FINELY GRATED ORANGE ZEST

1 JUMBO EGG, AT ROOM TEMPERATURE (LIGHTLY BEATEN)

¾ CUP COARSELY CHOPPED CRANBERRIES

1   To MAKE STREUSEL TOPPING: Combine all the ingredients in a food processor fitted with the metal chopping blade. Process for 30 to 45 seconds until the mixture is crumbly. Set aside.

2   To MAKE THE COFFEE CAKE: Lightly oil the bottom of a high-sided 2-quart microwave-safe round glass casserole. Line the bottom of the casserole with 2 circles of waxed paper. Put an 8- to 10-ounce microwave-safe glass tumbler right side up in the center of the casserole.

3   Put the flour, baking powder, and salt in a 1-quart bowl. Use a wire whisk and complete 12 to 15 strokes to ensure that the ingredients are thoroughly blended.

4   Put the buttermilk in a 1-cup microwave-safe glass measuring cup. Microwave uncovered on MEDIUM-LOW (30 percent) power for 40 seconds to 2 minutes, stirring every 20 seconds until the chill is off. Do not let the buttermilk get hot. Set aside.

5   Put the butter in a 2½-quart microwave-safe bowl. Cover with waxed paper and microwave on HIGH (100 percent) power for 15 to 45 seconds, until the butter is slightly softened. Do not let the butter melt or become oily.

6   Using a hand-held electric mixer set at high speed, beat the butter for 30 seconds, until creamy. Add ½ cup sugar and continue to beat for 1 to 2 minutes, scraping down the sides of the bowl often until the mixture is nearly white and its texture is light. Beat in the vanilla extract and orange zest.

7   While continuing to beat at medium speed, slowly add the egg. Beat until smooth. At low speed beat in the flour mixture, a third at a time, alternating with the buttermilk. Beat briefly, just until each addition is incorporated into the batter. Scrape down the sides of the bowl with a rubber spatula and beat a few seconds more.

8   Drop one-third of the batter by spoonfuls evenly on the bottom of the prepared casserole. Using the back of a spoon, spread the batter in an even layer.

9   Put the cranberries in a 1-quart bowl and toss with the remaining tablespoon of granulated sugar. Fold the cranberry mixture into the remaining batter. Drop the batter by spoonfuls on top of the batter in the pan and spread evenly.

10   Cut an *X* in the center of a microwave-safe paper towel and press the towel over the glass so that it covers the top of the casserole.

11   Set the cake on an inverted 9-inch microwave-safe glass pie plate and microwave on MEDIUM (50 percent) power for 5 minutes, rotating the pan, if you do not have a turntable, a quarter turn every 2½ minutes. Gently sprinkle the streusel topping evenly over the cake batter.

12   Microwave, uncovered, on HIGH (100 percent) power for 3 to 6 minutes, rotating the pan, if you do not have a turntable, a quarter turn every 1½ minutes. Test for doneness after 3 minutes by inserting a wooden toothpick in the center of the cake; it should come out clean. If not done, check the cake at 30-second intervals. Let the coffee cake stand, uncovered, on a flat heatproof surface for 15 minutes.

13   Run the tip of a knife around the edge of the coffee cake to loosen it. Remove the glass tumbler from the center. Cover the coffee cake with a paper towel and invert onto a wire rack or plate. Remove the casserole and peel off the waxed paper. Cover the coffee cake with a serving plate and turn it right side up. Serve the coffee cake while it is still warm or at room temperature. Store any leftover coffee cake under a cake dome or an upturned bowl.

variation

Blueberry Streusel Coffeecake

Substitute ¾ cup of small blueberries for the cranberries. Do not toss the blueberries in granulated sugar.

Walnut Fudge Brownies

makes 16 brownies

preparation time: ABOUT 15 MINUTES PLUS CHILLING

microwave time: 7 MINUTES 20 SECONDS TO 11 MINUTES 45 SECONDS PLUS STANDING

A *friend of ours said these brownies were "almost too good." We know what he meant but are afraid we cannot agree. How can anything this dark, moist, and fudgy be other than fantastic? Shall we say it again? It is hard to believe they were baked in a microwave oven. For a more cakelike brownie, leave out the water in the recipe or top the cooled brownies with Fudgy Chocolate Frosting (page 297) instead of the melted semisweet chocolate chips.*

1 CUP SIFTED ALL-PURPOSE FLOUR

½ CUP SIFTED UNSWEETENED ALKALIZED COCOA POWDER SUCH AS HERSHEY'S EUROPEAN STYLE OR DROSTE

½ TEASPOON DOUBLE-ACTING BAKING POWDER

¼ TEASPOON SALT

8 TABLESPOONS UNSALTED BUTTER

¾ CUP GRANULATED SUGAR

¼ CUP LIGHT CORN SYRUP

2 LARGE EGGS

2 TEASPOONS WATER

2 TEASPOONS VANILLA EXTRACT

½ CUP PLUS 2 TABLESPOONS COARSELY CHOPPED WALNUTS (EACH MEASUREMENT USED SEPARATELY)

1⅓ CUPS SEMISWEET CHOCOLATE CHIPS

kitchen note:

Chilling the brownies after they are baked enhances their moist, fudgy texture and enables you to cut them sooner. For best results use unsweetened alkalized (Dutch-processed) cocoa such as Hershey's European style or Droste. The strips of aluminum foil over the corners of the pan keep them from overbaking. Be sure the foil is facing shiny side up. The paper towel holds in moisture.

1   Lightly oil the bottom of a 2-quart microwave-safe square glass cake dish with rounded corners (This dish shape promotes more even baking than the older ones which have more angular corners).

2   Put the flour, cocoa, baking powder, and salt in a 1½-quart bowl. Complete 12 to 15 strokes with a wire whisk to ensure that the ingredients are thoroughly blended.

3   Put the butter in a 4-quart microwave-safe glass bowl. Cover with waxed paper and microwave on HIGH (100 percent) power for 20 to 45 seconds, until the butter is slightly softened. Do not let the butter melt or become oily.

4   Add the sugar and corn syrup to the butter. Using a hand-held electric mixer set at high speed, beat for 45 seconds, until creamy. Add the eggs one at a time, beating well after each addition. Beat in the water and vanilla extract. Reduce the speed to low and beat in the flour-cocoa mixture just until combined. Do not overmix. Using a rubber spatula, stir in ½ cup of walnuts and ⅓ cup of chocolate chips. Scrape the batter into the prepared baking dish and spread evenly with the back of a spoon.

5   Wrap the top 4 corners of the dish with 2-inch-wide aluminum foil strips, shiny sides facing up. Cover the top of the dish with a microwave-safe paper towel. Set the dish on a 9-inch microwave-safe glass pie plate and microwave on MEDIUM (50 percent) power for 5 minutes, rotating the pan, if you do not have a turntable, a quarter turn every 2½ minutes.

6   Continue to microwave on HIGH (100 percent) power for 2 to 5 minutes. Test for doneness after 2 minutes by inserting a wooden toothpick in the center of the brownie; it should come out with a few moist crumbs clinging to it. If not

done, continue microwaving and test the brownies every 30 seconds until done. Any moist spots on the surface of the brownie will dry while standing.

7   Put the brownie dish on a flat heatproof surface. Remove the foil strips and paper towel. Sprinkle the remaining 1 cup of chocolate chips evenly over the surface of the brownie. Cover with the paper towel again and let it stand for 15 minutes.

8   Remove the paper towel. Using a small metal cake spatula or the back of the spoon, gently spread the melted chocolate chips evenly over the brownie. Sprinkle the remaining 2 tablespoons of walnuts on top.

9   Refrigerate the brownie, uncovered, for 45 minutes to 1 hour. Using a hot knife, cut the brownie into 16 squares, rinsing the knife blade in hot water and wiping it dry before making each cut. Store the brownies in an airtight container in the refrigerator for up to three days. Serve the brownies chilled or at room temperature.

CHAPTER NINE

Candies and Chocolates

Almond-Dusted Chocolate-Coated Strawberries

Chocolate Walnut Fudge

Cashew Brittle

Toffee-Coated Popcorn

Chocolate Raspberry Truffles

Peanut Butter Crunchies

Glazed Fruit

Tiger Butter

Chocolate Almond Bark

White Chocolate Apricot Pecan Squares

Milk Chocolate Raisin and Nut Clusters

You may never have seriously considered making candies and chocolates at home, envisioning cake, pie, or ice cream when you thought of dessert. But please consider candies and chocolates as delicious endings to any meal or additions to the afternoon tea table. After your next Saturday night dinner party, serve an elegant plate of Chocolate Raspberry Truffles, Almond-Dusted Chocolate-Coated Strawberries, and colorful Glazed Fruit to eat while sipping deep, rich coffee.

Or make Toffee-Coated Popcorn (a snap in the microwave) or Cashew Brittle for the family the next time you get together to watch slides of your last vacation or a video. If you are invited for a weekend in the country or at the seashore, bring along a tin of Chocolate Almond Bark or Chocolate Walnut Fudge as a gift. And invalids and shut-ins will surely appreciate tissue-paper-lined boxes or tins of Milk Chocolate Raisin and Nut Clusters, White Chocolate Apricot Pecan Squares, or any other sweet in this chapter.

Using the microwave oven for sugar syrups and melting and tempering chocolate makes candy-making easy. Yet there are some methods and procedures to follow carefully when attempting these recipes. Read the tips thoroughly and refer to them before beginning any recipe. Although some of our chocolate candies are best when the chocolate is tempered, we have provided variations, when appropriate, for making them without tempering. But you needn't be daunted by tempering, particularly since Adrienne has adapted a quick method for the microwave oven.

These delightful creations are delicious and often stunning. We hope this chapter will introduce anyone who has not made homemade candies and chocolates to the pleasures of doing so and will give the more experienced candy maker new challenges and ideas.

Candy-Making Tips

*Many of our recipes require the use of a microwave-safe candy thermometer to cook sugar syrup; a conventional candy thermometer will not do.

*A candy thermometer that is inaccurate, even by a degree or two, can affect the outcome of a recipe, especially when making sugar-based syrups for candy recipes such as fudge. To test a thermometer for accuracy, fill a 2-cup microwave-safe glass measuring cup with 1 cup of water. Attach the thermometer to the side of the cup, making sure the bulb of the thermometer is submerged in the water. Microwave on HIGH (100 percent) power for 2 to 4 minutes, or until the water comes to a rapid boil. If the thermometer registers above or below 212°F., adjust the recipe accordingly. For example, if the thermometer reads 210°F. subtract 2 degrees from the recipe temperature(s). If it reads 214°F., add 2 degrees to the recipe temperature(s).

*After taking a microwave-safe candy thermometer from a hot sugar mixture, put it in a measuring cup of hot water. Do not try to rinse the thermometer under cold water because it will crack.

*Soak casseroles and other containers coated with sticky toffee or other candy mixtures in hot tap water for a few minutes to dissolve the sugary coating. When it is dissolved, wash the dish.

*For a successful sugar syrup, the sugar crystals must dissolve completely before the syrup reaches a boil. To facilitate this process, cover the measuring cup holding the syrup with waxed paper. The loose cover holds in moisture that accumulates on the sides of the cup and washes down clinging crystals. For this same reason it is crucial that you stir the syrup with a wooden spoon.

*Sugar syrup cooks quickly in the microwave oven. Watch it carefully; if the temperature climbs higher than required by the recipe, add about a tablespoon of water to the syrup. Stir it very gently with a wooden spoon and microwave again to the desired temperature.

*Use an accurate, easy-to-read thermometer when quick-tempering or making handmade chocolates. We recommend a digital instant-read thermometer with 1-degree increments (see page 18 for more detailed information). Do not use a candy thermometer because the temperature gauge does not register low enough. Check the thermometer for accuracy as explained above.

*When tempering, we save time by using chocolate chips. They melt quickly and at an even rate, too. A bar of chocolate works just as well but must be chopped first.

*Temper chocolate chips in a clean, dry bowl; use a dry rubber spatula to stir the melted chocolate. The slightest amount of moisture will cause the chocolate to seize.

*During quick tempering, as the chocolate chips melt, they "seed" the already melted chocolate with stable cocoa butter crystals, which allow the chocolate to reharden with a fine-grained texture and shiny appearance. It is a simple procedure and gets easier each time you do it, but you must watch the temperature of the chocolate closely.

*During the seeding stage of tempering, the temperature should never exceed 91°F. for dark chocolate and 88°F. for white and milk chocolate.

*For an accurate temperature reading, the thermometer must be immersed in at least 2 inches of melted chocolate. If the chocolate is not deep enough, insert the stem of the thermometer at an angle. Do not let the tip of the thermometer touch the bottom or sides of the bowl because this can give a false reading.

*Be sure to stir the tempered chocolate for at least 45 seconds before reading the thermometer. The temperature of the melted chocolate will continue to rise even after it has been removed from the microwave.

*Chocolate that has been quick tempered is shiny, has good "snap," and can be stored at room temperature, the ideal temperature for storing chocolate.

Almond-Dusted Chocolate-Coated Strawberries

makes 20

preparation time: ABOUT 10 MINUTES

microwave time: 1½ TO 3 MINUTES PLUS 10 TO 20 MINUTES CHILLING

The second best way to eat plump, juicy strawberries is dipped in chocolate (the best way to eat them is straight from the berry patch, with the early summer sun on your back). These take only minutes to prepare and are as delicious in midwinter as in June—perhaps more so because they are so welcome. Use them to garnish a dessert table, to accent a plate of homemade or store-bought truffles, or to set on top of a glazed cake. Or serve them on their own.

20 MEDIUM, WELL-FORMED FRESH
    STAWBERRIES (ABOUT 1 PINT), WITH
    HULLS AND PRETTY GREEN STEMS
3 TABLESPOONS CARAMELIZED ALMONDS
    (PAGE 309) OR TOASTED SLICED
    ALMONDS (PAGE 25)

3 OUNCES SEMISWEET CHOCOLATE,
    COARSELY CHOPPED

---

kitchen note:

*Semisweet chocolate
does not melt
completely in the
microwave without
stirring.*

---

1 Wash and carefully dry the strawberries. Put the dry berries on a baking sheet lined with waxed paper.

2 Put the almonds in a sealable plastic bag and crush them by rolling over the bag with a rolling pin. When they are coarsely crushed, transfer them to a 6-ounce custard cup.

3 Put the chocolate in another 6-ounce microwave-safe custard cup. Microwave, uncovered, on MEDIUM (50 percent) power for 2 to 4 minutes, stirring every 60 seconds, until the chocolate is melted and smooth.

4 Holding it at the stem end, dip a strawberry into the chocolate so that two-thirds of the berry is coated. Dip the tip of the coated strawberry in the crushed almonds. Return the strawberry to the waxed-paper-lined baking sheet. Continue this procedure with all the strawberries. Refrigerate them for 10 to 20 minutes, until the chocolate is set. Store the strawberries in an airtight container for up to twenty-four hours.

Chocolate Walnut Fudge

makes 36 squares

preparation time: ABOUT 20 MINUTES PLUS 30 TO 60 MINUTES CHILLING

microwave time: 10 TO 17 MINUTES

We combined semisweet chocolate with fluffy, sweet marshmallow cream and came up with a truly delicious candy that will satisfy any and all cravings for thick, smooth, rich fudge. The marshmallow cream allows you to skip the traditional cooling and beating process.

Although if you freeze it, you can cut the fudge soon after it is made, it will taste even better if you let it mellow overnight in an airtight container. Line the pan with foil to make it easy to remove the fudge before cutting it into neat squares. If you make it without walnuts, use an 8-inch rather than a 9-inch pan.

12 OUNCES (2 CUPS) SEMISWEET
 CHOCOLATE CHIPS
 2 OUNCES UNSWEETENED CHOCOLATE,
 FINELY CHOPPED
 1 CUP MARSHMALLOW CREAM
 (SPOONED INTO A MEASURING CUP
 AND LEVELED WITH THE EDGE OF A
 KNIFE)

1¼ CUPS SIFTED GRANULATED SUGAR
 1 CUP HEAVY CREAM
 ¼ CUP LIGHT CORN SYRUP
 ⅛ TEASPOON SALT
 1 CUP COARSELY CHOPPED WALNUTS
 2 TEASPOONS VANILLA EXTRACT

1 Line a 9-inch square metal baking pan with aluminum foil so that the foil extends 2 inches beyond two opposite sides of the pan. Do not oil the pan or foil.

2 Combine the chocolates and the marshmallow cream in a heatproof 2½-quart bowl.

3 Combine the sugar, cream, corn syrup, and salt in a 2-quart microwave-safe glass measuring cup. Cover with waxed paper and microwave on HIGH (100 percent) power for 3 to 5 minutes, until steaming hot. Do not let the mixture boil. Stir with a wooden spoon until the sugar is almost completely dissolved.

4 Cover the cup again and microwave on HIGH (100 percent) power for 2 to 4 minutes, until the syrup comes to a rapid boil.

5 Attach a microwave-safe candy thermometer to the side of the measuring cup, making sure that the bulb is submerged in the syrup. Microwave, uncovered, on HIGH (100 percent) power for 5 to 8 minutes, until the syrup registers 234°F., soft-ball stage, on the thermometer.

6 Pour the hot syrup over the chocolate-marshmallow mixture. Stir the mixture with a clean wooden spoon, completing only 3 to 6 strokes to blend the chocolate and syrup evenly. Let the mixture stand for 1 minute. Add the walnuts and vanilla extract, and stir gently just until the chocolate is completely melted and the fudge is smooth. Do not overmix.

(*CONTINUED*)

kitchen note:

Be sure to sift the sugar so that the crystals will dissolve easily and completely. The fudge will be grainy if any undissolved crystals remain in the syrup after it has boiled.

Fudge must be cooked to precisely 234°F., or the texture will be unpleasant. If undercooked, the fudge will be too soft; if overcooked, it will be dry and crumbly. This temperature is the low end of the soft-ball stage range (234°F. to 240°F.). Be sure to check the microwave candy thermometer for accuracy (see the tips at the beginning of the chapter).

7   Quickly scrape the fudge into the foil-lined pan and spread it evenly with the back of a spoon. Refrigerate or freeze the fudge, uncovered, for 30 to 60 minutes, until firm enough to cut.

8   Cover the top of the fudge with a cutting board and invert. Carefully peel off the aluminum foil. Invert the fudge again onto a smooth cutting surface so that it is right side up. Using a large knife, score the fudge into thirty 1¼-inch squares. Cut the fudge with a hot knife, rinsing the knife with hot water and wiping it dry between cuts. Store the fudge between layers of waxed paper in an airtight container at room temperature for up to five days.

Cashew Brittle

makes about ¾ pound of candy

preparation time: ABOUT 15 MINUTES PLUS 30 MINUTES COOLING

microwave time: 7½ TO 15 MINUTES

In this recipe we have combined lightly salted, roasted cashews with buttery, slightly caramelized sugar syrup to make a sweet, crunchy candy that is perfect for serving at home or packing in pretty tins to give away as gifts. Although you can eat the brittle while it is still warm, it tastes best when allowed to age overnight in an airtight container.

1 CUP SIFTED GRANULATED SUGAR	¾ CUP COARSELY CHOPPED, LIGHTLY
¼ CUP LIGHT CORN SYRUP	SALTED, ROASTED CASHEWS
¼ CUP WATER	1 TEASPOON BAKING SODA
2 TABLESPOONS UNSALTED BUTTER	1 TEASPOON VANILLA EXTRACT

1   Rinse a large, heavy baking sheet under very hot tap water and wipe it dry. Thoroughly oil the baking sheet and the blade of a large offset (crooked) metal cake spatula. Set aside in a draft-free spot on a flat heatproof surface.

2   Put the sugar, corn syrup, and water in a 1-quart microwave-safe glass measuring cup. Cover with waxed paper and microwave on HIGH (100 percent) power for 2 to 4 minutes, until steaming hot. Stir with a wooden spoon until the sugar crystals are almost completely dissolved.

3   Cover the cup again and microwave on HIGH (100 percent) power for 1½ to 3 minutes, until the mixture comes to a rapid boil. Remove the waxed paper and attach a microwave-safe candy thermometer to the side of the measuring cup, making sure that the bulb is submerged in the syrup. Microwave, uncovered, on HIGH (100 percent) power for 4 to 7 minutes without stirring, until the mixture registers 290°F., soft-crack stage.

4   Stir in the butter with a clean wooden spoon until it melts. Stir in the chopped nuts. Continue to microwave, covered, on HIGH (100 percent) power for 2 to 5 minutes more, without stirring, until the mixture is golden and registers 311°F., very hard-crack stage.

5   Quickly combine the baking soda and vanilla extract in a small custard cup and immediately add it to the hot brittle. Stir with a clean wooden spoon until foamy and thoroughly blended.

6   Scrape the mixture onto the prepared baking sheet and, working quickly, spread it with the oiled spatula into a 10-by-8-inch rectangle about ⅜ inch thick. Let the brittle cool for 3 to 8 minutes, until the surface feels warm to your fingers. Slide the blade of the oiled spatula under the brittle to release it from the baking sheet and flip up over. With your fingers, stretch the warm brittle as thin as possible, about ⅛ inch, and let it cool completely.

7   Using your fingers, break the brittle into pieces and store them between layers of waxed paper in an airtight container at room temperature in a dry place for up to two weeks.

kitchen note:

Sifted granulated sugar will dissolve faster and more easily. Be sure all crystals are completely dissolved before bringing the syrup to a boil.

It is important to cook the brittle to 311°F., very hard-crack stage. If the brittle does not reach this high temperature, it will be sticky and unpleasant to eat.

To stretch the candy, pour the brittle onto a warm and well-oiled, large, heavy baking sheet. The edges of the candy will not set too quickly if the sheet is warm, and the brittle will not stick if the sheet is thoroughly oiled. To warm the baking sheet, run hot water over it and dry it well before oiling. Watch the candy carefully during the last stage of cooking so that it does not overcook and turn to caramel.

Finally, do not attempt to make brittle in humid weather.

Toffee-Coated Popcorn

makes about 12 cups or 3 quarts

preparation time: ABOUT 15 MINUTES PLUS TIME TO POP THE POPCORN AND 10 TO 15 MINUTES COOLING

microwave time: 12 TO 18 MINUTES

This mixture of toffee-coated popcorn and nuts is the sort of snack you cannot stop eating. The thin, crisp sheath of toffee provides a sweet butteriness that goes well with the popcorn and lightly salted nuts, and literally melts in your mouth. Make this the next time you rent a video for home viewing or when your child deserves a special treat. (The toffee gets very hot, so this is not really a good choice to make with a young child.) You can use any sort of popped popcorn as long as it is unflavored, but we suggest microwave popcorn.

kitchen note:

The toffee will not harden if you make this on a humid day. Be sure the sugar is sifted so that the crystals will dissolve completely.

Use a microwave-safe candy thermometer and cook the syrup to 311°F., very hard-crack stage. If the sugar syrup does not reach this stage, the toffee will be sticky, and the popcorn will be unpleasant to eat. Watch the syrup carefully during the last stage of cooking so that it does not overcook and turn to caramel.

10 CUPS POPPED POPCORN
1½ CUPS LIGHTLY SALTED ROASTED PEANUTS OR MIXED NUTS
1⅓ CUPS SIFTED GRANULATED SUGAR
⅓ CUP PACKED LIGHT BROWN SUGAR

14 TABLESPOONS UNSALTED BUTTER (1 STICK PLUS 6 TABLESPOONS), CUT INTO TABLESPOONS
⅓ CUP WATER
⅛ TEASPOON SALT

1 Put the popcorn and nuts in a 6-quart bowl and stir together. Oil the blade of a metal pancake spatula and the bowl of a wooden spoon.

2 Combine the sugars, butter, water, and salt in a 2-quart microwave-safe glass measuring cup. Cover with waxed paper and microwave on HIGH (100 percent) power for 2 to 4 minutes, until steaming hot and the butter has melted. Stir with an unoiled wooden spoon until the sugar crystals are almost completely dissolved.

3 Cover again and microwave on HIGH (100 percent) power for 2 to 4 minutes, until the mixture comes to a rapid boil.

4 Remove the waxed paper and attach a microwave-safe candy thermometer to the side of the casserole, making sure the bulb is submerged in the toffee mixture. Microwave, uncovered, on HIGH (100 percent) power for 8 to 10 minutes, until the thermometer registers 311°F., very hard-crack stage.

5 Immediately pour the hot toffee mixture over the bowl of popcorn and nuts. Stir with the oiled wooden spoon until evenly coated. Scrape the toffee-coated popcorn and nuts onto a marble slab or two large baking sheets. Using the oiled pancake spatula, flatten the popcorn into a single layer. Cool for 10 to 15 minutes, or until firm.

6 Using your fingers, break the candied popcorn into bite-size pieces. Store in an airtight container at room temperature for up to 2 weeks.

Chocolate Raspberry Truffles

makes about 24 truffles

preparation time: ABOUT 1 HOUR PLUS 1 TO 2 HOURS FREEZING

microwave time: 3½ TO 6 MINUTES 50 SECONDS

For those of us who have followed Adrienne's career, it comes as no surprise that she wanted to include a truffle recipe in the book. When she worked at Bloomingdale's in the early 1980s, New York Magazine *dubbed Adrienne's truffles the best in the city. She has turned this skill to making truffles in the microwave—the perfect environment for cooking the rich, dark centers and then for melting the chocolate for coating them. Make these for guests, as a hostess present, or anytime you want to indulge in pure chocolate ecstasy.*

Truffle centers:

6 OUNCES SEMISWEET CHOCOLATE, COARSELY CHOPPED

¼ CUP HEAVY CREAM

2 TEASPOONS UNSALTED BUTTER

FEW GRAINS OF SALT

¼ CUP SEEDLESS RASPBERRY PRESERVES

1 TEASPOON FRAMBOISE (CLEAR, UNSWEETENED RASPBERRY BRANDY) OR COGNAC (OPTIONAL)

1 TEASPOON VANILLA EXTRACT

CONFECTIONER'S SUGAR FOR DUSTING

(INGREDIENTS CONTINUED)

Coating:

3 CUPS UNSWEETENED ALKALIZED
(DUTCH-PROCESSED) COCOA

12 OUNCES SEMISWEET CHOCOLATE,
COARSELY CHOPPED

2 TABLESPOONS VEGETABLE OIL

1   To MAKE THE TRUFFLE CENTERS: Combine the chocolate, cream, butter, and salt in a 1½-quart microwave-safe glass bowl. Cover with waxed paper and microwave on MEDIUM-HIGH (70 percent) power for 1½ to 3½ minutes, until the mixture is steaming hot. Do not let the mixture boil. Let it stand for 1 minute.

2   Put the raspberry preserves in a 6-ounce microwave-safe custard cup and microwave on MEDIUM (50 percent) power for 15 seconds at a time, until warm. Add the warm preserves, liqueur, and vanilla extract to the chocolate mixture and whisk until smooth.

3   Cover the surface of the truffle mixture with plastic wrap and freeze for 1 to 2 hours, until stiff. Using a melon-baller or 2 teaspoons, scoop the mixture into 1-inch mounds and drop them into two 9-inch round metal cake pans or square baking pans. Freeze for 30 minutes to 1½ hours, until firm enough to roll.

4   Sift a light dusting of confectioner's sugar over the mounds and roll them into irregularly shaped 1-inch balls. Return the truffle centers to the pans. Cover tightly with plastic wrap and freeze for 30 minutes to 1½ hours, until firm. The centers may be prepared up to one day in advance.

5   To MAKE THE COATING: Sift the cocoa into a 2-quart oval baking dish.

6   Put the chocolate in a 1-quart microwave-safe glass bowl. Microwave, uncovered, on MEDIUM (50 percent) power for 2 to 4 minutes, stirring every 60 seconds, until the chocolate is melted and smooth. Stir in the oil until blended. Set the bowl of chocolate over a slightly smaller bowl of warm, 90°F., water so that the bottom of the bowl of chocolate touches the water.

7   Remove one of the pans from the freezer. If you are right-handed, arrange the work area so that the bowl of melted chocolate is in the center with the pan of truffle centers to the left and the dish of cocoa on the right. Reverse this order if you are left-handed.

8   Turn the dish of cocoa so that one of its long sides is closest to you. Using the tip of a finger, make 1-inch-wide troughs running the length of the dish. With your left hand, pick up a truffle center and drop it gently onto the surface of the melted chocolate. Using the forefinger and middle finger of the right hand, dip the center in the chocolate. If you are left-handed, use the opposite hands for this procedure.

9 Roll the center gently between your fingers on the surface of the chocolate to get an even coating. Lift up the coated center above the surface and move your fingers in a modified scissorlike motion to release any drips. Scrape the excess chocolate from your fingertips onto the edge of the bowl.

10 Place the coated truffle in the upper end of a cocoa trough, withdrawing your second finger with a twisting motion. Using your other hand, cover the truffle with some of the cocoa.

11 When all the truffles from the first cake pan have been coated, transfer them to a large sieve and gently shake to remove the excess cocoa. Transfer the truffles to a plate and refrigerate.

12 Coat the remaining pan of truffle centers in the same manner. If the chocolate begins to stiffen, reheat it slightly in the microwave on LOW (10 percent) power for 10-second intervals. Replace the water in the bowl with more warm water.

13 Put the truffles in small paper candy cups and store in an airtight container for up to five days in the refrigerator. Let the truffles stand at room temperature for 10 minutes before serving. If desired, the truffles may be frozen for up to a month. Thaw the frozen truffles overnight in the refrigerator.

Peanut Butter Crunchies

makes about 36 chocolates

preparation time: ABOUT 1½ HOURS PLUS 30 TO 60 MINUTES FREEZING

microwave time: 4½ TO 8½ MINUTES

S*ince so many people (including us) love the combination of peanut butter and chocolate, we could not resist including these pretty little round chocolates. The centers are a dreamy combination of white chocolate and smooth peanut butter, with crunch provided by a handful of crispy rice cereal.*

The chocolate coating, studded with rice cereal and chopped peanuts, is even crunchier. Use either semisweet or milk chocolate for the coating, as you prefer.

The method for coating the centers is identical to that used in making Chocolate Raspberry Truffles, so if you have mastered that, these will be easy. In any event, once you have successfully coated two or three centers, you will get the hang of it.

Filling:

3 OUNCES WHITE BAKING CHOCOLATE

1 TABLESPOON UNSALTED BUTTER

⅔ CUP CREAMY PEANUT BUTTER

¾ CUP PLUS 2 TABLESPOONS SIFTED CONFECTIONER'S SUGAR (EACH MEASUREMENT USED SEPARATELY)

1 TABLESPOON VANILLA EXTRACT

¾ CUP CRISPED RICE CEREAL, LIGHTLY CRUSHED WITH THE PALM OF YOUR HAND

Coating:

12 OUNCES SEMISWEET OR MILK CHOCOLATE CHIPS

2 TABLESPOONS VEGETABLE OIL

⅔ CUP CRISPED RICE CEREAL, LIGHTLY CRUSHED WITH THE PALM OF YOUR HAND

⅔ CUP FINELY CHOPPED, UNSALTED, ROASTED PEANUTS

1 TO MAKE THE FILLING: Put the white chocolate in a 2½-quart microwave-safe bowl. Microwave, uncovered, on MEDIUM (50 percent) power for 2 to 4 minutes, stirring every 60 seconds, until the chocolate is melted and smooth. Set aside.

2   Put the butter in a 6-ounce microwave-safe custard cup. Cover with waxed paper and microwave on HIGH (100 percent) power for 15 to 25 seconds, until softened. Do not let the butter melt or become oily.

3   Add the peanut butter and softened butter to the bowl of melted chocolate. Using a hand-held electric mixer set at high speed, beat for 30 to 60 seconds, until the mixture is smooth and creamy. Reduce the speed to low and beat in the ¾ cup of confectioner's sugar. Beat in the vanilla extract. At this point the mixture will be quite stiff.

4   With your hands, knead the rice cereal into the mixture. If necessary, add as much of the remaining 2 tablespoons of confectioner's sugar as needed to make a firm but not sticky mixture. Form the filling into a ball.

5   Pinch off about a teaspoon of filling and roll it into a smooth 1-inch ball. Repeat with the remaining filling to make the centers for the chocolates. Divide the centers evenly between two 9-inch round metal cake pans. Cover tightly with plastic wrap and freeze for 30 to 60 minutes, until firm. The centers may be prepared up to one day in advance.

6   TO MAKE THE COATING: Put the semisweet or milk chocolate chips in a 1-quart microwave-safe glass bowl. Microwave, uncovered, on MEDIUM (50 percent) power for 3 to 5 minutes, stirring every 60 seconds, until the chocolate is melted and smooth. Stir in the oil until blended. Add the rice cereal and chopped nuts, and stir until well blended. Set the bowl over a slightly smaller bowl of warm, 90°F., water so that the bottom of the bowl of chocolate touches the water.

7   Line 2 baking sheets with waxed paper. Remove one of the pans from the freezer. If you are right-handed, arrange the work area so that the bowl of melted chocolate is in the middle with the pan of centers to the left and the paper-lined baking sheet on the right. Reverse this order if you are left-handed.

8   With your left hand, pick up a center and drop it gently onto the surface of the melted chocolate. Using the forefinger and middle finger of the right hand, dip the center in the chocolate. If you are left-handed, use the opposite hands for this procedure.

9   Roll the center gently between your fingers on the surface of the chocolate to get an even coating. Lift up the coated center above the surface and move your fingers in a modified scissorlike motion to release any drips. Scrape the excess chocolate from your fingertips onto the edge of the bowl.

10   Gently place the coated center on the paper-lined baking sheet, withdrawing your second finger with a twisting motion. When all the centers from the first cake pan are coated, put the baking sheet in the refrigerator.

11   Coat the remaining pan of truffle centers in the same manner. If the chocolate begins to stiffen, reheat it slightly in the microwave on LOW (10 percent) power for 10-second intervals. Replace the water in the bowl with more warm water.

12 Put the coated chocolates in small paper candy cups and store in an airtight container for up to two weeks in the refrigerator. Let the chocolates stand at room temperature for 10 minutes before serving. If desired, the chocolates may be frozen for up to a month. Thaw the frozen Peanut Butter Crunchies overnight in the refrigerator.

Glazed Fruit

makes about 50 pieces

preparation time: 35 MINUTES PLUS 20 MINUTES SETTING

microwave time: 13 TO 18 MINUTES

These colorful pieces of sugar-coated fruit would make a pleasing surprise at your next dinner party. Serve them with coffee for that little "something sweet" everyone craves at evening's end. The microwave oven is a good place to cook the simple sugar syrup to a temperature hot enough to coat the dry fruit with a shiny, crackling thin sheath. The coated fruit keeps for about three hours.

kitchen notes:

Do not attempt the glazed fruit on a humid day. Humidity will quickly make the sugar coating sticky. Even in dry weather, the glaze will last for only two or three hours, so plan to serve the fruit within that time.

1 PINT MEDIUM STRAWBERRIES, WITH HULLS AND PRETTY GREEN STEMS, IF POSSIBLE

½ POUND LARGE RED AND GREEN GRAPES, WITH STEMS

2 CUPS GRANULATED SUGAR

¾ CUP WATER

½ TEASPOON LEMON JUICE

1 Line a baking sheet with paper towels. Wash the fruit and drain it well. Pat the strawberries dry with paper towels and put them on the lined baking sheet. Using scissors, snip the grapes, leaving some stem attached to each one. Pat the grapes dry and lay them on the baking sheet.

2   Oil a large baking sheet.

3   Put the sugar, water, and lemon juice in a 1-quart microwave-safe glass measuring cup. Cover with waxed paper and microwave on HIGH (100 percent) power for 3 minutes. Stir with a wooden spoon until the sugar is almost completely dissolved.

4   Cover the cup again and microwave on HIGH (100 percent) power for 2 to 4 minutes, until the syrup starts to boil.

5   Remove the waxed paper and attach a microwave-safe candy thermometer to the side of the measuring cup, making sure the bulb is submerged. Microwave, uncovered, on HIGH (100 percent) power for 8 to 11 minutes, until the thermometer registers 311°F., very hard-crack stage.

6   Remove the thermometer and put it into hot water. Pour the hot syrup into a 2-cup microwave-safe measuring cup to stop the cooking process.

7   As soon as the syrup stops bubbling, begin dipping the fruit. Holding on to the stems, quickly dip each piece of fruit in the syrup. Let the excess syrup drip back into the measuring cup. Place the coated fruit on the oiled baking sheet. Allow the sugar coating to set for 20 minutes. Do not refrigerate. Serve within two to three hours.

Before glazing, the fruit must be completely dry. Use a microwave-safe candy thermometer and be sure to cook the syrup to 311°F., very hard-crack stage. If the syrup does not reach this temperature, the coating will be sticky. Watch the sugar syrup carefully during the last few minutes of cooking. If overcooked, it will caramelize.

Finally, be very careful when dipping the fruit in the extremely hot syrup. Do not leave it within reach of children. If the syrup cools before you finish dipping, microwave it on MEDIUM (50 percent) power for 20-second intervals. Do not stir the syrup, or it will crystallize.

Tiger Butter

makes 36 squares

preparation time: ABOUT 20 MINUTES PLUS 10 TO 20 MINUTES CHILLING

microwave time: 5½ TO 10 MINUTES

As the food editor for Chocolatier *magazine, Adrienne received a recipe for tiger butter submitted by Vita Hall, from California. Intrigued by the idea, she asked Associate Editor Cathy Garvey to adapt it for the magazine. A few months later a food editor from Florida wrote inquiring about tiger butter although she had not seen the recipe in the magazine. She had heard of the confection from several of her readers and decided she, too, needed a recipe. Luckily, Adrienne could help her. From this activity it seems that, from California to Florida, the candy is growing in popularity. Now you can make it regardless of where you live. We have updated the recipe for the microwave oven—the ideal place to melt chocolate, we think.*

---

kitchen note:

White chocolate sometimes turns lumpy and gritty when it is melted, but this usually has more to do with storage than melting technique. If poorly stored white chocolate absorbs moisture, the milk proteins clump together. This same clumping can result from overheating. If your melted white chocolate is either lumpy or gritty, strain it through a fine-meshed sieve.

White chocolate that is more than six months old

---

18 OUNCES WHITE CHOCOLATE BAKING BARS, COARSELY CHOPPED

½ CUP CREAMY PEANUT BUTTER

1 TABLESPOON PLUS ¾ TEASPOON VEGETABLE OIL (USED IN TWO MEASUREMENTS)

1½ OUNCES SEMISWEET CHOCOLATE

1   Line a 9-inch square baking pan with aluminum foil so that the foil extends 2 inches beyond two opposite sides of the pan. Do not oil the pan or foil.

2   Put the white chocolate and peanut butter in a 1½-quart microwave-safe bowl. Microwave on MEDIUM-LOW (30 percent) power for 4 to 7 minutes, stirring every 60 seconds, until smooth. Stir in 1 tablespoon of oil until blended. Scrape the white chocolate–peanut butter mix-

ture into the prepared pan and spread evenly with the back of a spoon.

3   Put the semisweet chocolate in the 1½-quart microwave-safe glass bowl. It is not necessary to wash the bowl. Microwave on MEDIUM (50 percent) power for 1 to 3 minutes, stirring every 60 seconds, until the chocolate is melted and smooth. Stir in the remaining ¾ teaspoon oil, until blended.

4   Using a spoon and a back-and-forth motion, drizzle the melted semisweet chocolate across the top of the white chocolate–peanut butter mixture. Insert the tip of a knife into an upper corner of the mixture and draw it up and down several times to create tiger stripes. Freeze the tiger butter for 10 to 20 minutes, until firm enough to cut but not completely hardened.

may have an unpleasant, bitter, soapy flavor and a dry, lumpy texture when melted.

The solution is to buy white chocolate in a store that sells a lot of it, and do not let it linger in your pantry. Line the square pan with foil to make it easy to unmold the tiger butter so that it can be cut into neat squares.

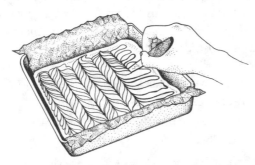

5   Cover the pan with a cutting board and invert the tiger butter onto it. Carefully peel off the foil. Invert the tiger butter onto a smooth cutting surface so that it is facing right side up. Using a large knife, score the butter into thirty-six 1¼-inch squares. Cut the candy, rinsing the knife in hot water and wiping it dry between each cut. Store the tiger butter between layers of waxed paper in an airtight container in the refrigerator for up to ten days. Let the tiger butter soften for 10 minutes at room temperature before serving. Do not let the tiger butter sit out longer than 20 minutes—it will become grainy.

Chocolate Almond Bark

makes 35 squares

preparation time: ABOUT 20 MINUTES PLUS COOLING AND 10 TO 15 MINUTES CHILLING

microwave time: 8½ TO 13 MINUTES

Chocolate bark is one of the easiest and best homemade chocolate candies we know. You simply mix melted chocolate with nuts, spread it on a baking sheet, let it chill, and cut it into bite-size pieces before it hardens completely. Eat it yourself or pack the bark between layers of tissue paper in pretty tins to give away as gifts.

This recipe explains how to ''quick temper'' chocolate. Tempered chocolate maintains its shine and breaks with a reassuring ''snap.'' Be sure to read the tips explaining quick tempering in the beginning of the chapter before attempting this recipe. If you are short of time, we have explained how to make the bark without tempering the chocolate. It will taste just as delicious but will not look as pretty and glossy. This same technique is applied to White Chocolate Apricot Pecan Squares (page 270) and Milk Chocolate Raisin and Nut Clusters (page 272).

1 CUP WHOLE UNBLANCHED ALMONDS

12 OUNCES SEMISWEET CHOCOLATE CHIPS (USED IN TWO MEASUREMENTS) (2 CUPS)

kitchen note:

Try the bark with other roasted nuts and other kinds of chocolate for variety. For instance, roasted cashews, hazelnuts, macadamias, peanuts, and pecans are delicious with chocolate. Or try a combination of nuts. Substitute milk or white chocolate for the semisweet for a different flavor and texture.

1   Put the almonds in a 9-inch microwave-safe glass pie plate and spread into a single layer. Microwave on HIGH (100 percent) power for 2 minutes. Stir with a wooden spoon.

2   Continue to microwave on HIGH (100 percent) power for 4 to 7 minutes, stirring every 60 seconds, until the nuts are fragrant. Test for doneness by cutting an almond in half. The inside of the nut should have turned from white to tan. Transfer the almonds to a plate and cool completely.

3   Line a baking sheet with waxed paper.

4   Put 1 cup of the chocolate chips in a 1½-quart microwave-safe bowl. Microwave on MEDIUM (50 percent) power for 2 to 4 minutes, stirring every 60 seconds, until smooth. Add the remaining cup of chocolate chips and stir for 1 minute, until half melted.

5   Scrape the chocolate into another 1½-quart microwave-safe glass bowl. This will help lower the temperature of the chocolate. Continue to stir the chocolate. If many chips are still unmelted after 1 minute, microwave on MEDIUM-LOW (30 percent) power for 10-second intervals, stirring until only a few unmelted chips remain. Be careful not to overheat the chocolate.

6   Continue to stir for about 1 minute, until the chocolate is completely smooth. Check the temperature of the chocolate with an instant-read thermometer. It should register between 84°F. and 88°F. for milk chocolate or between 86°F. and 91°F. for dark chocolate. If the chocolate has become hotter than required, it will not harden unless refrigerated, nor will it have a glossy appearance. If the chocolate is cooler than required, microwave on LOW (10 percent) power for 5 seconds, stir for at least 45 seconds, and then check the temperature again. Microwave on LOW (10 percent) power for 5-second intervals until the chocolate reaches the correct temperature.

7   As soon as the chocolate reaches the correct temperature, add the toasted almonds. Stir with a rubber spatula until blended. Scrape the mixture onto the prepared baking sheet and spread it into a 10½-by-7½-inch rectangle. Refrigerate for 5 to 15 minutes, until the chocolate is no longer wet but not completely hardened. The time will depend on the temperature of the refrigerator.

8   Peel off the waxed paper and transfer the chocolate to a cutting surface. Using a large knife, score the rectangle into thirty-six 1½-inch squares. Cut into squares, wiping the knife clean between each cut. Store the almond bark between layers of waxed paper in an airtight container at room temperature for up to two weeks.

variation

Chocolate Almond Bark with Untempered Chocolate

Put the entire 12 ounces of chocolate chips in 1½-quart microwave-safe glass bowl in step 4. Microwave on MEDIUM (50 percent) power for 3 to 5 minutes, stirring every 60 seconds, until smooth. Add the toasted almonds to the melted chocolate and proceed as instructed. Store the almond bark between layers of waxed paper in an airtight container in the refrigerator for up to two weeks.

White Chocolate Apricot Pecan Squares

makes 36 squares

preparation time: ABOUT 20 MINUTES PLUS COOKING AND 10 TO 15 MINUTES CHILLING

microwave time: 7½ TO 12 MINUTES

Slightly tart California dried apricots perfectly accent the sweet, creamy white chocolate and toasted pecans in this simple candy. If you like white chocolate or know someone who does, try these quick squares. Feel free to substitute Turkish apricots.

1 CUP PECAN HALVES	**¾** CUP COARSELY CHOPPED
18 OUNCES (3 CUPS) WHITE	DRIED CALIFORNIA OR
CHOCOLATE CHIPS	TURKISH APRICOTS

1   Put the pecans in a 9-inch microwave-safe glass pie plate and spread into a single layer. Microwave on HIGH (100 percent) power for 2 minutes. Stir with a wooden spoon.

2   Continue to microwave on HIGH (100 percent) power for 3 to 6 minutes, stirring every 60 seconds, until the pecans are fragrant. Transfer to a plate to cool completely.

3   Line a 9-inch square baking pan with aluminum foil so that it extends 2 inches beyond two opposite sides of the pan. Do not oil the pan or foil.

4   Put 1½ cups of the chocolate chips in a 1½-quart microwave-safe glass bowl. Microwave on MEDIUM (50 percent) power for 2 to 4 minutes, stirring every 60 seconds, until smooth. Add the remaining 1½ cups of chocolate chips and stir for 1 minute, until half melted.

5   Scrape the chocolate into another 1½-quart microwave-safe glass bowl. This will help bring down the temperature of the chocolate. Continue to stir the chocolate. If many of the chips are still unmelted after 1 minute, microwave on MEDIUM-LOW (30 percent) power for

kitchen note:

This recipe can be made with tempered or untempered white chocolate (instructions for making it without tempering follow the recipe). Before proceeding, please read the notes on quick tempering at the beginning of the chapter. While tempered white chocolate does not shine with the gleam of dark chocolate, its texture is much improved by tempering, and it breaks with a reassuring snap.

Lining the pan with aluminum foil makes it easy to remove the white chocolate mixture so that it can be cut into neat squares. Remember that untempered chocolate must be kept in the refrigerator in an airtight container.

10-second intervals, stirring until only a few unmelted chips remain. Be careful not to overheat the chocolate.

6 Continue to stir for about 1 minute, until the chocolate is completely smooth. Check the temperature of the chocolate with an instant-read thermometer. It should register between 84°F. and 88°F. If the chocolate has become hotter than required, it will not harden unless refrigerated, nor will it have a glossy appearance. If the chocolate is cooler than required, microwave on LOW (10 percent) power for 10-second intervals. Stir for at least 45 seconds and then check the temperature again. Microwave on LOW (10 percent) power for 5-second intervals until the chocolate reaches the correct temperature.

7 As soon as the chocolate reaches the correct temperature, add the pecans and apricots to the bowl of tempered chocolate and stir with a rubber spatula until blended. Scrape the mixture into the foil-lined pan and spread evenly with the back of a spoon. Refrigerate for 10 to 15 minutes, until the chocolate is no longer wet but not completely hardened.

8 Cover the top of the pan with a cutting board and invert the chocolate square onto it. Carefully peel off the aluminum foil and invert the square again onto a smooth cutting surface. Using a large knife, score the chocolate into thirty-six 1¼-inch squares. Cut the squares, wiping the knife clean between each cut. Store the squares at room temperature for up to two weeks.

variation

White Chocolate Apricot Pecan Squares with Untempered Chocolate

Put the entire 18 ounces of white chocolate chips in a 1½-quart microwave-safe bowl in step 4. Microwave on MEDIUM (50 percent) power for 3 to 5 minutes, stirring every 60 seconds, until smooth. Add the pecans and apricots to the bowl and proceed as instructed. Refrigerate the mixture for 15 to 25 minutes, until the chocolate is no longer wet but not completely hardened, in step 7. Store the squares between layers of waxed paper in an airtight container in the refrigerator for up to two weeks.

Milk Chocolate Raisin and Nut Clusters

makes 24 clusters

preparation time: ABOUT 15 MINUTES PLUS 10 TO 20 MINUTES CHILLING

microwave time: 2½ TO 4 MINUTES

These chunky little chocolates look pretty in miniature pleated paper cups or simply set on a plate or in a candy dish. They are surprisingly easy to make, and everyone loves the seductive combination of milk chocolate, sweet raisins, and crunchy, lightly salted nuts.

12 OUNCES MILK CHOCOLATE CHIPS (2 CUPS) (USED IN TWO MEASUREMENTS)

¾ CUP DARK OR GOLDEN RAISINS

¾ CUP LIGHTLY SALTED, ROASTED CASHEW PIECES OR PEANUTS

¾ CUP CRISPED RICE CEREAL

1   Line twenty-four mini muffin cups with 1¾-inch midget paper liners or line a baking sheet with waxed paper.

2   Put 1 cup of the chocolate chips in a 1½-quart microwave-safe glass bowl. Microwave on MEDIUM (50 percent) power for 2 to 4 minutes, stirring every 60 seconds, until smooth. Add the remaining chocolate chips and stir for 1 minute, until half melted.

3   Scrape the chocolate into another 1½ quart microwave-safe glass bowl. This will help bring down the temperature of the chocolate. Continue to stir the chocolate. If many of the chips are still unmelted after 1 minute, microwave on MEDIUM-LOW (30 percent) power for 10-second intervals, stirring until only a few unmelted chips remain. Be careful not to overheat the chocolate.

4   Continue to stir for about 1 minute, until the chocolate is completely smooth. Check the temperature of the chocolate with an instant-read thermometer. It should register between 84°F. and 88°F. If the chocolate has become hotter than required, it will not harden unless refrigerated, nor will it have a glossy appearance. If the chocolate is cooler than required, microwave on LOW (10 percent) power for 5-second intervals. Stir for at least 45 seconds and then check the temperature again.

Microwave on LOW (10 percent) power for 5-second intervals, until the chocolate reaches the correct temperature.

5   As soon as the chocolate reaches the correct temperature, add the raisins, nuts, and rice cereal, and stir with a rubber spatula until evenly coated. Working quickly, spoon about 1 tablespoon of the mixture into each paper cup or spoon it into mounds on the waxed-paper baking sheet.

6   Refrigerate the clusters for 10 to 20 minutes, until the chocolate is set. Store the clusters in an airtight container at room temperature for up to two weeks.

variation

Milk Chocolate Raisin and Nut Clusters with Untempered Chocolate

Put the entire 12 ounces of chocolate chips in a 1½-quart microwave-safe glass bowl in step 2. Microwave on MEDIUM (50 percent) power for 3 to 5 minutes, stirring every 60 seconds, until smooth. Proceed as instructed. Store the clusters in an airtight container in the refrigerator for up to two weeks.

CHAPTER TEN

Sauces, Toppings, Frostings, and Fillings

Raspberry Sauce

Blueberry Sauce

Strawberry Sauce

Melba Sauce

Plum Sauce

Butterscotch Sauce

Vanilla Custard Sauce

Rum Raisin Cider Sauce

Satiny Chocolate Sauce

Quick Hot Fudge Sauce

Bittersweet Chocolate Sauce

Caramel Rum Sauce

Fresh Fruit Medley

Blueberry Topping

Shiny Chocolate Glaze

White Chocolate Sour Cream Frosting

Fudgy Chocolate Frosting

Cream Cheese Frosting

Chocolate Raspberry Frosting

Vanilla Buttercream Frosting

Chocolate Buttercream Frosting

Chocolate Chantilly

Quick Chocolate Frosting

Vanilla Pastry Cream

Lime Pastry Cream

Caramelized Almonds

The expression "the frosting on the cake" certainly can extend to "the sauce on the sundae" or "the glaze on the cupcake." In this chapter you will find all the delectable extras that make desserts irresistible. Fruit, berry, chocolate, and butterscotch sauces . . . chunky fruit toppings . . . vanilla and chocolate frostings . . . a shiny chocolate glaze . . . a rich custard sauce . . . and smooth pastry creams all enrich our recipes with their own seductive accent and character.

The microwave oven is the perfect place to create these enhancements. The recipes are fast, easy, efficient, and delicious—everything you could ask for. We have used these sauces, toppings, frostings, glazes, and fillings throughout the book. However, because it would make the text cumbersome, we have not cross-referenced them here in this chapter, although we occasionally refer to the recipes for which they were developed.

Turn the following pages slowly and savor the ingredients and flavor combinations. You will quickly discern ways to use them with our desserts and with many of your family favorites. Experiment freely and become well acquainted with these delicious embellishments, each one of which was designed to transform an ordinary dessert into one deserving rich praise.

Sauce, Topping, Frosting, and Filling Tips

Some sauces are thickened with arrowroot, which gives them a lovely, translucent sheen that holds up after refrigeration. Cornstarch, another good thickener, tends to get cloudy in the refrigerator, but we use cornstarch in the Rum Raisin Cider Sauce because it works better than arrowroot in apple juice–based recipes.

Do not use semisweet chocolate chips unless specified. Semisweet block chocolate gives the best results.

*Chopped baking chocolate and chocolate chips do not melt to a liquid pool in the microwave. Avoid overheating by microwaving the chocolate on MEDIUM (50 percent) power just until it is shiny, then stir it until it is smooth.

Use only unsalted butter. Salted butter is too salty and often is not as fresh-tasting as unsalted.

*Measure sour cream and yogurt in metal measuring cups designed for dry ingredients. Spoon the sour cream into the cup and then level it with a knife to ensure accuracy.

*Butter and cream cheese soften at different rates and must be softened separately.

*A sturdy, standing mixer works best when beating buttercreams, although you can use a hand-held electric mixer, too.

*Be sure to whisk chilled pastry cream vigorously until creamy before using it to fill a tart shell.

*To facilitate reheating, store leftover chocolate or butterscotch sauce in microwave-safe containers. Microwave them, uncovered, at MEDIUM (50 percent) power for 1 to 3 minutes, stirring every 30 seconds until warm or hot.

*Store leftover buttercream or fudge frosting in a microwave-safe glass bowl so that you can easily soften it in the microwave before using. Microwave it, uncovered, at MEDIUM-LOW (30 percent) power for 10-second intervals, until soft. Use an electric mixer to whip buttercream frostings briefly until light and creamy.

Raspberry Sauce

makes about 2 cups

preparation time: ABOUT 10 MINUTES PLUS 1 TO 2 HOURS CHILLING

microwave time: 4½ TO 6½ MINUTES

*W*e *make this chunky sauce, redolent of fruit, with frozen raspberries, which are readily available in supermarkets and less expensive and fragile than fresh. Using arrowroot instead of cornstarch gives the sauce a beautiful, translucent sheen.*

2 10-OUNCE PACKAGES FROZEN RED
   RASPBERRIES IN LIGHT SYRUP (ABOUT 4
   CUPS)
4 TEASPOONS ARROWROOT

1 TABLESPOON ORANGE-FLAVORED
   LIQUEUR SUCH AS GRAND MARNIER,
   COINTREAU, OR TRIPLE SEC

1   Cut a 1-inch slit in the bags of frozen raspberries. Put the bags, slit side up, side by side in a 10-inch microwave-safe pie plate. Microwave on HIGH (100 percent) power for 2½ to 3½ minutes, until the juices start to thaw but the berries are still partially frozen.

2   Empty the berries into a strainer set over a 2½-quart bowl. Let the raspberries drain briefly. Reserve 1 cup of the juice in a 2-cup microwave-safe glass measuring cup. Put the drained raspberries in a 2½-quart bowl.

3   Put the arrowroot in a small cup. Slowly stir in 1 tablespoon of the raspberry juice until the mixture is completely smooth. Pour the mixture back into the measuring cup of raspberry juice and stir until blended.

4   Cover the top of the measuring cup with plastic wrap, turning back a fold over the pouring spout. Microwave on HIGH (100 percent) power for 2 to 3 minutes, whisking every 60 seconds, until the sauce is translucent and comes to a full boil. Do not boil for longer than 30 seconds, or the sauce will become watery. Stir in the liqueur.

5   Pour the sauce over the raspberries in the bowl. Shake the bowl to distribute the sauce; do not stir, or the raspberries will break up. Cover the sauce and refrigerate for 1 to 2 hours or up to two days. Serve chilled.

Blueberry Sauce

makes about 1½ cups

preparation time: ABOUT 5 MINUTES PLUS COOLING

microwave time: 7 TO 9 MINUTES

This smooth sauce is best if the blueberries are a little tart. If the sauce is a touch bland for your taste, add a squeeze or two of lemon or lime juice.

3 CUPS FRESH BLUEBERRIES

⅓ CUP GRANULATED SUGAR

FRESH LEMON OR LIME JUICE TO TASTE

1   Combine the blueberries and sugar in a 2-quart microwave-safe glass measuring cup. Stir with a wooden spoon until mixed. Cover with waxed paper and microwave on HIGH (100 percent) power for 3 minutes. Stir to dissolve any remaining sugar crystals.

2   Cover the cup again and microwave on HIGH (100 percent) power for 3 to 5 minutes, until the mixture comes to a rapid boil. Remove the waxed paper and continue to microwave on HIGH (100 percent) power for 1 minute more.

3   Press the mixture through a fine-meshed sieve into a noncorrosive bowl. Cool the sauce to room temperature. Stir in lemon or lime juice to taste. Cover and refrigerate for up to five days.

Strawberry Sauce

makes about 1½ cups

preparation time: ABOUT 10 MINUTES PLUS COOLING

microwave time: 13½ TO 18½ MINUTES

*F*rozen, whole, unsweetened strawberries combine with sugar and orange-flavored liqueur to make a wonderfully fresh-tasting and especially pretty sauce. Spoon it over everything from cake to ice cream to chopped fresh fruit.

1 20-OUNCE BAG FROZEN UNSWEETENED
  STRAWBERRIES (ABOUT 4 CUPS)
½ CUP GRANULATED SUGAR
4 TEASPOONS ARROWROOT

4 TEASPOONS ORANGE-FLAVORED
  LIQUEUR SUCH AS GRAND MARNIER,
  COINTREAU, OR TRIPLE SEC
FRESH LEMON JUICE TO TASTE

1   Combine the frozen strawberries and sugar in a 2-quart microwave-safe glass measuring cup. Stir with a wooden spoon until mixed. Cover the cup with waxed paper and microwave on HIGH (100 percent) power for 6 minutes. Stir to dissolve any remaining sugar crystals.

2   Cover the cup again and microwave on HIGH (100 percent) power for 4 to 7 minutes more, until the mixture is steaming hot and the berries are very soft. Do not let the mixture boil.

3   Press the strawberry mixture through a fine-meshed sieve into a 1-quart measuring cup, reserving 1½ cups of the juice. Discard the pulp and seeds. Return the strawberry juice to the 2-quart microwave-safe glass measuring cup.

4   Put the arrowroot in a small cup. Slowly stir in 2 tablespoons of the strawberry juice until the mixture is completely smooth. Pour the mixture back into the large measuring cup of strawberry juice and stir until blended.

5   Cover the top of the measuring cup with waxed paper. Microwave on HIGH (100 percent) power for 1½ minutes. Whisk until smooth.

6   Cover the measuring cup again and continue to microwave on HIGH (100 percent) power for 2 to 4 minutes more, whisking every 60 seconds, until the sauce is translucent and comes to a rapid boil. Do not boil for longer than 30 seconds, or the sauce will become watery.

7   Cool the sauce to room temperature. Stir in the liqueur and lemon juice to taste. Cover and refrigerate until chilled. The sauce may be prepared up to two days in advance.

Melba Sauce

makes about 1 cup

preparation time: ABOUT 10 MINUTES PLUS CHILLING

microwave time: 8½ TO 13½ MINUTES

*T*his seedless raspberry sauce, which has a beautiful translucent sheen, was named after Nellie Melba, a famous opera singer who had a passion for good food and all things sweet. See the note for Peach Melba Ice Cream Sundae on page 205 for more information on Dame Melba and the creations named for her.

1 12-OUNCE BAG FROZEN UNSWEETENED RASPBERRIES (ABOUT 3 CUPS)
¾ CUP GRANULATED SUGAR
2 TEASPOONS ARROWROOT

2 TABLESPOONS KIRSCH, DARK RUM, OR ORANGE-FLAVORED LIQUEUR SUCH AS GRAND MARNIER, COINTREAU, OR TRIPLE SEC

1 Combine the frozen raspberries and sugar in a 2-quart microwave-safe glass measuring cup. Stir with a wooden spoon until blended. Cover the measuring cup with waxed paper and microwave on HIGH (100 percent) power for 4 minutes. Stir to dissolve any remaining sugar crystals.

2 Cover the measuring cup again and microwave on HIGH (100 percent) power for 2½ to 5 minutes more, until the mixture is steaming hot and the berries are soft. Do not let the mixture boil.

3 Press the raspberry mixture through a fine-meshed sieve into a 1-quart microwave-safe glass measuring cup, reserving 1 cup of raspberry puree. Discard the seeds.

4 Put the arrowroot in a small cup. Slowly stir in 2 tablespoons of the raspberry puree until completely smooth. Pour the mixture back into the large measuring cup of raspberry puree and stir until blended.

5 Cover the measuring cup with waxed paper. Microwave on HIGH (100 percent) power for 2 to 4 minutes, whisking every 60 seconds, until the sauce is translucent and comes to a rapid boil. Do not boil for more than 30 seconds, or the sauce will become watery.

6 Stir in the liqueur. Cover and refrigerate until chilled. The sauce may be prepared up to two days in advance.

Plum Sauce

makes 2¾ cups

preparation time: ABOUT 15 MINUTES PLUS COOLING

microwave time: 19 TO 25 MINUTES

*S*erve our chunky plum sauce over ice cream or with biscuits, muffins, pancakes, or waffles. Try it as a filling for crepes or an old-fashioned jam cake. Plums get more flavorful as they cook, and the chopped kernels from the pits add subtle almond flavor. Purple or black skins provide rich color. Add a little lemon juice if the sauce tastes flat or too sweet.

1 SMALL ORANGE	¾ CUP GRANULATED SUGAR
1½ POUNDS FIRM, RIPE PURPLE OR BLACK PLUMS (ABOUT 5 LARGE PLUMS)	FRESH LEMON JUICE TO TASTE

1 Peel off eight ¾-by-2½-inch strips of orange zest using a swivel vegetable peeler. Be careful not to include any of the bitter white pith beneath the orange skin. Use a large, sharp knife and finely chop the zest to make 4 teaspoons.
2 Cut the plums into quarters and remove the pits. Reserve 3 pits and discard the others. With a large, sharp knife, crack the 3 pits in half and remove the kernels. Finely chop the kernels and set aside. Cut each plum into 8 pieces.
3 In a 2-quart microwave-safe glass measuring cup, combine the plums, sugar, chopped plum kernels, and zest. Cover with waxed paper and microwave on HIGH (100 percent) power for 7 to 10 minutes, stirring once after 4 minutes, until the mixture starts to boil.
4 Remove the waxed paper and continue to microwave on HIGH (100 percent) power for 12 to 15 minutes more, stirring once after 6 or 7 minutes, until the chunks of fruit are translucent and the mixture reduces to about 2¾ cups. Let the sauce cool for 10 minutes. Taste the sauce and add the lemon juice if needed. Stir and taste again. Serve the sauce at room temperature or chilled. Store any leftover sauce in an airtight container in the refrigerator for up to two weeks.

Butterscotch Sauce

makes 2 cups

preparation time: ABOUT 15 MINUTES PLUS COOLING

microwave time: 11 TO 16 MINUTES

T*his old-fashioned butterscotch sauce gets its buttery, caramelized flavor by cooking it to the hard-ball stage (250°F.), easily done in the microwave. The sauce keeps for up to three weeks in an airtight, lidded jar in the refrigerator, so it makes a great gift. Be sure to enclose reheating instructions when giving it as a present.*

1 CUP PACKED LIGHT BROWN SUGAR
1 CUP HEAVY CREAM (USED IN TWO
    MEASUREMENTS)
½ CUP LIGHT CORN SYRUP
PINCH OF SALT

5 TABLESPOONS UNSALTED BUTTER, CUT
    INTO 5 PIECES
PINCH OF BAKING SODA
2 TEASPOONS VANILLA EXTRACT

kitchen note:

Be sure to use a microwave-safe candy thermometer. The pinch of baking soda neutralizes the acid in the brown sugar and cream, and prevents curdling.

1   In a 2-quart microwave-safe glass measuring cup, combine the sugar, ½ cup of cream, corn syrup, and salt. Stir with a wooden spoon until the lumps of brown sugar are completely broken up. Add the butter. Cover with waxed paper and microwave on HIGH (100 percent) power for 3 minutes. Stir until the butter is completely melted and the mixture is smooth.

2   Cover the cup again with waxed paper and microwave on HIGH (100 percent) power for 1 to 3 minutes more, until the mixture comes to a full boil. Add the baking soda. Use a long-handled wooden spoon to stir the mixture until blended. Keep in mind that it may froth up a bit.

3   Attach a microwave-safe candy thermometer to the side of the cup, making sure that the bulb is submerged in the mixture. Microwave, uncovered, on HIGH (100 percent) power for 7 to 10 minutes, until the thermometer registers 250°F., hard-ball stage.

4   Using a long-handled wooden spoon, slowly stir the remaining ½ cup cream into the sauce. Let the sauce cool for 10 minutes. Stir in the vanilla extract.

5   Serve the sauce warm over ice cream or cake. Store leftover sauce in an airtight jar in the refrigerator for up to 2 weeks. Reheat in a loosely covered microwave-safe container on MEDIUM (50 percent) power for 1 to 3 minutes, stirring every 30 seconds until hot.

Vanilla Custard Sauce

makes about 2 cups

preparation time: ABOUT 15 MINUTES PLUS 5 TO 10 MINUTES COOLING TIME

microwave time: 5 TO 8 MINUTES

Custard sauces are easily prepared in the microwave oven. Use them to add smooth, comforting sweetness to bread puddings, gingerbread, fruit crumbles, upside-down cakes, and so on. Although the eggs are thoroughly cooked in this custard, do not leave it at room temperature for longer than necessary. Refrigerate it for up to a day in an airtight container.

2 LARGE EGGS PLUS 2 LARGE EGG YOLKS
1/3 CUP PLUS 1 TABLESPOON GRANULATED
   SUGAR
1/8 TEASPOON SALT

1 CUP HEAVY CREAM
2/3 CUP MILK
1 TABLESPOON VANILLA EXTRACT

1 In a 1-quart microwave-safe glass measuring cup, combine the eggs and egg yolks, sugar, and salt. Using a small wire whisk, stir vigorously until thoroughly blended. Stir in the cream and milk.

2 Microwave, uncovered, on MEDIUM-HIGH (70 percent) power for 2 minutes. Whisk vigorously.

3 Continue to microwave, uncovered, on MEDIUM-HIGH (70 percent) power for 3 to 6 minutes, whisking every 60 seconds until the sauce thickens slightly. Do not let it become so hot that it curdles. Test for doneness by coating the back of a metal spoon with some of the sauce; it's done when you can run your finger

SAUCES, TOPPINGS, FROSTINGS, and FILLINGS   285

down the back of the coated spoon and the path remains in the custard. It will register 175°F. on an instant-read thermometer.

4   Strain the sauce into a noncorrosive metal bowl. Set the bowl over a larger bowl containing ice and ice water, and stir the sauce for 5 to 10 minutes, until completely cool. Remove the bowl from the larger one holding ice water. Stir in the vanilla extract.

5   Serve immediately or pour the sauce into an airtight container and refrigerate for up to one day.

variations

Lemon Custard Sauce

Add 1 teaspoon of finely grated lemon zest to the eggs, egg yolks, sugar, and salt in step 1. Use only 1 teaspoon of vanilla extract in step 4.

Orange Custard Sauce

Add ½ teaspoon of finely grated orange zest to the eggs, egg yolks, sugar, and salt in step 1. Use only 1 teaspoon of vanilla extract in step 4, and stir 1 tablespoon of orange-flavored liqueur such as Grand Marnier, Cointreau, or Triple Sec into the cooled sauce with the vanilla extract.

Mocha Custard Sauce

At the end of step 3 stir 2 teaspoons of instant coffee granules into the hot custard until dissolved.

Rum Raisin Cider Sauce

makes about 2 cups

preparation time: ABOUT 10 MINUTES

microwave time: 5 TO 7 MINUTES

*M*ake this sauce in the fall when cider is fresh and sweet, and serve it warm with *Apple and Pear Crumble (page 149), French Apple Cake (page 108), or Pumpkin Gingerbread (page 118).*

2 CUPS FRESH APPLE CIDER
3 TABLESPOONS DARK RAISINS
3 TABLESPOONS LIGHT BROWN SUGAR
2 TABLESPOONS CORNSTARCH

2 TABLESPOONS DARK RUM
1½ TEASPOONS VANILLA EXTRACT
FRESH LEMON JUICE TO TASTE

kitchen note:

In this instance cornstarch is a better thickener than arrowroot because it produces a better consistency and because the sauce is not refrigerated.

1   Combine the cider, raisins, and sugar in a 1-quart microwave-safe glass measuring cup.

2   Put the cornstarch in a small cup. Slowly stir in 2 tablespoons of the cider mixture until completely smooth. Pour the mixture into the measuring cup and stir until blended.

3   Cover the measuring cup with waxed paper. Microwave on HIGH (100 percent) power for 2 minutes. Whisk until blended.

4   Cover the measuring cup again and continue to microwave on HIGH (100 percent) power for 3 to 6 minutes, whisking every 60 seconds, until the sauce is translucent and comes to a rapid boil. Do not boil for longer than 30 seconds, or the sauce will become watery.

5   Stir in the rum and vanilla extract. Add lemon juice to taste. Serve the sauce warm.

Satiny Chocolate Sauce

makes about 2 cups

preparation time: ABOUT 5 MINUTES

microwave time: 2½ TO 4½ MINUTES PLUS 30 SECONDS STANDING

*T*his is one of our favorite and most versatile sauces. Smooth and chocolaty, it may be flavored with any one of several spirits. (If you prefer, leave out the alcohol altogether and increase the cream by 2 tablespoons.) It also works beautifully as a fondue sauce, served with chunks of pound cake or ripe, fresh fruit. Leftover sauce may be refrigerated for as long as five days and reheated as instructed in the recipe.

8 OUNCES SEMISWEET CHOCOLATE, COARSELY CHOPPED

¾ CUP PLUS 2 TABLESPOONS HEAVY CREAM

FEW GRAINS OF SALT

3 TABLESPOONS LIGHT CORN SYRUP

2 TABLESPOONS DARK RUM; COGNAC; COFFEE-FLAVORED LIQUEUR SUCH AS KAHLÚA OR TÍA MARIA; CRÈME DE MENTHE; OR ORANGE-FLAVORED LIQUEUR SUCH AS GRAND MARNIER, COINTREAU, OR TRIPLE SEC; OR FRAMBOISE (CLEAR RASPBERRY BRANDY) OR CHAMBORD (BLACK-RASPBERRY LIQUEUR)

2 TEASPOONS VANILLA EXTRACT

1 Put the chocolate in a 1-quart bowl.

2 Combine the cream, salt, and corn syrup in a 2-cup microwave-safe measuring cup. Cover with waxed paper and microwave on HIGH (100 percent) power for 2½ to 4½ minutes, until the mixture comes to a full boil.

3 Pour the hot cream mixture over the chocolate and let the mixture stand for 30 seconds. Whisk gently until smooth. Stir in the liqueur and vanilla extract.

4 Serve the sauce while it is still warm or at room temperature. Any leftover sauce may be stored in an airtight container in the refrigerator for up to five days. To reheat, cover the sauce with waxed paper and microwave on MEDIUM (50 percent) power for 1 to 3 minutes, stirring every 30 seconds, until warm.

Quick Hot Fudge Sauce

makes 1 cup

preparation time: ABOUT 5 MINUTES

microwave time: 1½ TO 3 MINUTES

*Y*ou will find countless uses for this warm, thick, fudgy sauce. For starters, imagine it over vanilla or strawberry ice cream. We offer all sorts of variations so that you can flavor it to suit your personal preferences. Leftover sauce can be stored in an airtight container in the refrigerator for up to five days.

6 OUNCES SEMISWEET CHOCOLATE, COARSELY CHOPPED

¼ CUP LIGHT CORN SYRUP

3 TABLESPOONS HEAVY CREAM

2 TEASPOONS UNSALTED BUTTER

FEW GRAINS OF SALT

2 TEASPOONS VANILLA EXTRACT

1   Combine the chocolate, corn syrup, cream, butter, and salt in a 1-quart microwave-safe glass measuring cup. Stir with a wooden spoon until blended.

2   Cover the cup with waxed paper. Microwave on HIGH (100 percent) power for 1½ to 3 minutes, until the mixture comes to a boil. Whisk until smooth. Stir in the vanilla extract. Serve the sauce warm.

3   Store the sauce in a microwave-safe airtight container in the refrigerator for up to five days. Reheat it, uncovered, by microwaving it on MEDIUM (50 percent) power for 1 to 3 minutes, stirring every 30 seconds, until hot.

variations

Quick Mocha Hot Fudge Sauce

Increase the amount of semisweet chocolate to 7 ounces and add ½ teaspoon of instant coffee granules to the ingredients in step 1. Stir 2 tablespoons of coffee-flavored liqueur such as Kahlúa or Tía Maria into the sauce when adding the vanilla extract in step 2.

Quick Orange Hot Fudge Sauce

Increase the amount of semisweet chocolate to 7 ounces. Stir 2 tablespoons of orange-

(CONTINUED)

flavored liqueur such as Grand Marnier, Cointreau, or Triple Sec and ¼ teaspoon of finely grated orange zest into the sauce when adding the vanilla extract in step 2.

Quick Mint Hot Fudge Sauce

Increase the amount of semisweet chocolate to 7 ounces. Stir 2 tablespoons of crème de menthe liqueur and ⅛ teaspoon of peppermint extract into the sauce when adding the vanilla extract in step 2.

Quick Rum, Cognac, or Brandy Hot Fudge Sauce

Increase the amount of semisweet chocolate to 7 ounces. Stir 2 tablespoons of dark rum, cognac, or brandy into the sauce when adding the vanilla extract in step 2.

Bittersweet Chocolate Sauce

makes 1½ cups

preparation time: ABOUT 5 MINUTES

microwave time: 2½ TO 4 MINUTES

Bittersweet chocolate lovers—and we count ourselves among them—will find this sauce delicious. Spoon it generously over ice cream, cake, or whatever strikes your fancy. Try the variations, too.

6 OUNCES SEMISWEET CHOCOLATE, COARSELY CHOPPED

1 OUNCE UNSWEETENED CHOCOLATE, COARSELY CHOPPED

⅓ CUP PLUS 2 TABLESPOONS LIGHT CORN SYRUP

⅓ CUP HEAVY CREAM

1 TABLESPOON UNSALTED BUTTER

FEW GRAINS OF SALT

1 TABLESPOON VANILLA EXTRACT

1   Combine the chocolates, corn syrup, cream, butter, and salt in a 1-quart microwave-safe glass measuring cup. Stir with a wooden spoon until blended.

2   Cover the cup with waxed paper. Microwave on HIGH (100 percent) power for 2½ to 4 minutes, until the mixture comes to a boil. Whisk until smooth. Stir in the vanilla extract. Serve the sauce warm.

3   Store the sauce in an airtight microwave-safe container in the refrigerator for up to five days. Reheat it, uncovered, by microwaving it on MEDIUM (50 percent) power for 1 to 3 minutes, stirring every 30 seconds, until hot.

variations

Mocha Bittersweet Chocolate Sauce

Increase the amount of semisweet chocolate to 7 ounces and add ¾ teaspoon of instant coffee granules to the ingredients in step 1. Stir 2 tablespoons of coffee-flavored liqueur such as Kahlua or Tía Maria into the sauce when adding the vanilla extract in step 2.

Orange Bittersweet Chocolate Sauce

Increase the amount of semisweet chocolate to 7 ounces. Stir 2 tablespoons of orange-flavored liqueur such as Grand Marnier, Cointreau, or Triple Sec and ¼ teaspoon of finely grated orange zest into the sauce when adding the vanilla extract in step 2.

Mint Bittersweet Chocolate Sauce

Increase the amount of semisweet chocolate to 7 ounces. Stir 2 tablespoons of crème de menthe liqueur and ⅛ teaspoon of peppermint extract into the sauce when adding the vanilla extract in step 2.

Rum, Cognac, or Brandy Bittersweet Chocolate Sauce

Increase the amount of semisweet chocolate to 7 ounces. Stir 2 tablespoons of dark rum, cognac, or brandy into the sauce when adding the vanilla extract in step 2.

Caramel Rum Sauce

makes about 1½ cups

preparation time: ABOUT 15 MINUTES

microwave time: 7 TO 9 MINUTES

Here is an ultra-rich and creamy caramel sauce that does not require a candy thermometer. It is a snap to make and tastes especially good served warm or at room temperature with Apple and Pear Crumble (page 149), French Apple Cake (page 108), or Ginger Pecan Ice Cream (page 200).

1 CUP GRANULATED SUGAR

3 TABLESPOONS WATER

2 TABLESPOONS LIGHT CORN SYRUP

¼ TEASPOON LEMON JUICE

⅔ CUP HEAVY CREAM

5 TABLESPOONS UNSALTED BUTTER, CUT INTO ½-INCH CUBES

1 TABLESPOON DARK RUM

1 TEASPOON VANILLA EXTRACT

1   Combine the sugar, water, corn syrup, and lemon juice in a high-sided 1½-quart microwave-safe glass ceramic casserole. Cover with waxed paper and microwave on HIGH (100 percent) power for 2 minutes until steaming hot. Stir with a wooden spoon until the sugar crystals are completely dissolved. Cover the casserole again and continue to microwave on HIGH (100 percent) power for 2 minutes, until the syrup comes to a rapid boil.

2   Remove the waxed paper and continue to miocrowave on HIGH (100 percent) power for 3 to 5 minutes, without stirring, until the syrup turns to a dark amber caramel. Watch the syrup closely. When the syrup starts to turn color, swirl the casserole 2 or 3 times during the cooking process so that the caramel will brown evenly. Do not let the caramel become too dark or it will burn.

3   Put the casserole on a flat, heatproof work surface. Slowly pour the heavy cream into the hot caramel, being very careful it does not splash. Stir with a long-handled wooden spoon until blended. Stir in the butter until melted. Stir in the rum and vanilla. Serve the sauce while it is still warm or at room temperature. Store any leftover sauce in an airtight jar in the refrigerator for up to 2 weeks. Reheat in a loosely covered microwave-safe container on MEDIUM (50 percent) power for 1 to 3 minutes, stirring every 20 seconds until warm.

Fresh Fruit Medley

makes about 2½ cups

preparation time: ABOUT 15 MINUTES

microwave time: 2 TO 4 MINUTES

Serve this refreshing medley with the White Chocolate Orange Mousse Quenelles on page 82. It is also wonderful with vanilla ice cream, pound cake, vanilla yogurt, an assortment of sorbets, Vanilla Bean Pudding (page 34), and Lemon-Poached Pears (page 141).

⅓ CUP WATER

⅓ CUP GRANULATED SUGAR

3 MEDIUM ORANGES

2 KIWI FRUIT

1 CUP WHOLE STRAWBERRIES

1 TABLESPOON ORANGE-FLAVORED LIQUEUR SUCH AS GRAND MARNIER, COINTREAU, OR TRIPLE SEC

1 Combine the water and sugar in a 1-cup microwave-safe glass measuring cup. Cover with waxed paper and microwave for 1 minute. Stir with a wooden spoon to dissolve any remaining sugar crystals.

2 Cover again and microwave on HIGH (100 percent) power for 1 to 3 minutes, until the syrup comes to a boil. Let the syrup cool while preparing the fruit.

3 Slice off the top and bottom ends of the oranges with a serrated knife. Stand the oranges upright on a cutting board and, using the same knife, remove the rinds and membranes.

4 Holding the oranges over a 1½-quart bowl, slice between the orange sections, letting the sections and juice fall into the bowl. Remove any pits that fall into the bowl and squeeze the remaining juice from the leftover membrane into the bowl.

5 Remove the skin from the kiwi fruit with a small, sharp knife. Slice the fruit crosswise into ⅛-inch-thick rounds. Cut the rounds into quarters and add them to the bowl containing the oranges.

6 Hull the strawberries and cut them lengthwise into ⅛-inch-thick slices. Cut the slices in half lengthwise and add them to the bowl of fruit.

7 Stir the orange-flavored liqueur into the cooled sugar syrup. Pour the syrup over the fruit and stir it gently to combine. Serve immediately or cover and refrigerate for no longer than two hours before serving.

SAUCES, TOPPINGS, FROSTINGS, and FILLINGS

Blueberry Topping

makes about 2½ cups

preparation time: ABOUT 10 MINUTES PLUS COOLING

microwave time: 7 TO 13 MINUTES

This full-flavored, textural topping falls into a category between a sauce and a compote. Spoon it over cheesecake, ice cream sundaes, pound cake, biscuits, pancakes, and waffles. For the best results use slightly tart, flavorful summer berries.

1 MEDIUM ORANGE

4 CUPS FRESH BLUEBERRIES

⅓ CUP GRANULATED SUGAR

1 CINNAMON STICK, ABOUT 3½ INCHES

FRESH LEMON JUICE TO TASTE

1   Using a swivel vegetable peeler, peel six ¾-by-2½-inch strips of zest from the orange, being careful not to include any bitter white pith. Use a large, sharp knife and finely chop the zest to make 2 teaspoons.

2   Put the orange zest, 2 cups of blueberries, sugar, and cinnamon stick in a 2-quart microwave-safe measuring cup. Stir with a wooden spoon until blended. Cover with waxed paper and microwave on HIGH (100 percent) power for 2 minutes. Stir to dissolve any remaining sugar crystals.

3   Cover the cup again and microwave on HIGH (100 percent) power for 2 to 4 minutes, until the mixture comes to a full boil. Remove the waxed paper and continue to microwave on HIGH (100 percent) power at the boil for 3 to 7 minutes, until the mixture is reduced to 1½ cups.

4   Stir in the remaining 2 cups of blueberries. Cool the topping to room temperature. Remove the cinnamon stick and stir in lemon juice to taste. Refrigerate in an airtight container for up to three days.

Shiny Chocolate Glaze

makes about ¾ cup

preparation time: ABOUT 5 MINUTES

microwave time: 1½ TO 2½ MINUTES PLUS 30 SECONDS STANDING

*W*e use this glaze on cupcakes in Chapter 4, but you also might choose to pour it over *your favorite chocolate or vanilla cake. It's made with chocolate chips, something almost everyone has on hand, which makes it fast and convenient. When glazing a cake, set it on a rack positioned over a shallow pan to catch the dripping glaze.*

¾ CUP SEMISWEET CHOCOLATE CHIPS

⅓ CUP HEAVY CREAM

1 TABLESPOON LIGHT CORN SYRUP

FEW GRAINS OF SALT

1 TEASPOON VANILLA EXTRACT

1   Put the chocolate chips in a 1-quart bowl.

2   Combine the cream, corn syrup, and salt in a 2-cup microwave-safe glass measuring cup. Cover the cup with waxed paper and microwave on HIGH for 1½ to 3 minutes, until the mixture boils.

3   Pour the hot cream over the chocolate chips and let the mixture stand for 30 seconds. Whisk gently until the glaze is smooth, then stir in the vanilla extract. Use the glaze while it is still warm.

White Chocolate Sour Cream Frosting

makes about 1 cup

preparation time: ABOUT 10 MINUTES PLUS 1 TO 2 HOURS CHILLING

microwave time: 1½ TO 3 MINUTES PLUS 30 SECONDS STANDING

This wonderfully versatile frosting has a slight tang of sour cream, which makes it ideal for carrot and spice cakes. Remember that it must be chilled for an hour or so before its final whipping.

1 CUP WHITE CHOCOLATE CHIPS

⅓ CUP SOUR CREAM (SPOONED INTO A
    MEASURING CUP AND LEVELED WITH
    THE EDGE OF A KNIFE)

2 TEASPOONS VANILLA EXTRACT

1   Put the white chocolate chips and the sour cream in a 2½-quart microwave-safe glass bowl. Stir them together until the chips are evenly coated.

2   Cover the bowl with waxed paper. Microwave on MEDIUM-HIGH (70 percent) power for 1½ to 2½ minutes, until the mixture is steaming hot. Do not let the mixture boil, or the sour cream will curdle and the chips may turn grainy. Let the mixture stand for 30 seconds, then whisk gently until smooth. If the chips are not fully melted after whisking, cover again and microwave on MEDIUM-HIGH (70 percent) power for 30 seconds more. Stir in the vanilla extract.

3   Cover the surface of the frosting with plastic wrap and refrigerate for 1 to 2 hours, until the frosting thickens to the consistency of pudding.

4   Using a hand-held electric mixer set at high speed, beat the frosting for 1 to 2 minutes, until soft peaks form. Do not overbeat. Use the frosting immediately.

variation

White Chocolate Sour Cream Frosting with Orange or Lemon Zest

Add ¼ teaspoon of finely grated orange zest or ¾ teaspoon of finely grated lemon zest to the hot mixture when stirring in the vanilla extract at the end of step 2.

Fudgy Chocolate Frosting

makes about 1 cup

preparation time: ABOUT 10 MINUTES PLUS 10 TO 20 MINUTES CHILLING

microwave time: 1 MINUTE AND 45 SECONDS TO 3 MINUTES AND 45 SECONDS

*W*hen *you want a thick and buttery fudge frosting, try this one. We have several easy variations for it, too.*

1 TABLESPOONS UNSALTED BUTTER

6 OUNCES SEMISWEET CHOCOLATE, COARSELY CHOPPED

¼ CUP HEAVY CREAM

3 TABLESPOONS LIGHT CORN SYRUP

FEW GRAINS OF SALT

2 TEASPOONS VANILLA EXTRACT

1 Put the butter in a 6-ounce microwave-safe custard cup. Cover with waxed paper and microwave on HIGH (100 percent) power for 15 to 45 seconds, until the butter is soft. Set aside.

2 Put the chocolate in a food processor fitted with the metal chopping blade. Process for 20 to 30 seconds, until finely ground.

3 Combine the cream, corn syrup, and salt in a 2-cup microwave-safe glass measuring cup. Cover with waxed paper and microwave on HIGH (100 percent) power for 1½ to 3 minutes, until the mixture starts to boil. Whisk until smooth.

4 With the food processor running, pour the hot cream mixture through the feed tube. Process for 15 to 30 seconds, until the chocolate is melted and the mixture is smooth. Scrape down the sides of the work bowl. Add the softened butter and the vanilla extract. Process for 5 to 10 seconds, until creamy.

5 Transfer the frosting to a 1-quart bowl. Cover the surface with plastic wrap and refrigerate for 10 to 20 minutes, until thick enough to spread. If the frosting becomes too stiff, microwave, uncovered, on MEDIUM-LOW (30 percent) power for 10-second intervals until softened.

variations

Mocha Fudge Frosting

Add ¾ teaspoon of instant coffee granules to the chocolate in step 2.

(CONTINUED)

Orange Fudge Frosting

Add ¼ teaspoon of finely grated orange zest when you add the butter in step 4.

Fudgy Mint Frosting

Add ⅛ teaspoon of peppermint extract when you add the butter in step 4.

Cream Cheese Frosting

makes about 1 cup

preparation time: ABOUT 5 MINUTES

microwave time: 30 SECONDS TO 1½ MINUTES

This fluffy frosting is so simple to make, you will find yourself relying on it time and again. For a special taste treat, try the ginger variation. Because butter and cream cheese soften at different rates, they must be softened in the microwave oven separately.

4 TABLESPOONS UNSALTED BUTTER

3 OUNCES CREAM CHEESE

1⅔ CUPS CONFECTIONER'S SUGAR
(LIGHTLY SPOONED INTO A
MEASURING CUP AND LEVELED WITH
THE EDGE OF A KNIFE)

1 TEASPOON VANILLA EXTRACT

1 Put the butter in a 6-ounce custard cup. Cover with waxed paper and microwave on HIGH (100 percent) power for 15 to 60 seconds, until the butter is slightly softened.

2 Put the cream cheese in a 4-quart microwave-safe bowl. Cover with waxed paper and microwave on HIGH (100 percent) power for 15 to 60 seconds, until slightly softened.

3 Add the softened butter to the bowl of cream cheese. Using a hand-held electric mixer set at high speed, beat the cream cheese and butter until blended.

Gradually beat in the sugar. Continue beating for 45 to 60 seconds, until the frosting is very light and creamy. Beat in the vanilla extract.

variations

Cream Cheese Frosting with Orange or Lemon Zest

Add ¼ teaspoon of finely grated orange zest or ¾ teaspoon of finely grated lemon zest when beating the cream cheese and butter in step 3.

Cream Cheese Frosting with Fresh Ginger

Add 2 teaspoons of finely grated fresh ginger when beating the cream cheese and butter in step 3.

Chocolate Raspberry Frosting

makes about 1 cup

preparation time: ABOUT 10 MINUTES PLUS 10 TO 20 MINUTES CHILLING

microwave time: 2 MINUTES AND 5 SECONDS TO 4½ MINUTES

This frosting really exploits the glorious flavor combination of chocolate and raspberry. The combination of preserves and raspberry-flavored liqueur emphasizes the unmistakably remarkable flavor of the berry. Spread it between layers of chocolate cake or use it to frost a single layer cake or cupcakes. It's absolutely delicious.

1 TABLESPOON UNSALTED BUTTER
6 OUNCES SEMISWEET CHOCOLATE, COARSELY CHOPPED
¼ CUP HEAVY CREAM
FEW GRAINS OF SALT

¼ CUP SEEDLESS RASPBERRY PRESERVES
1 TEASPOON FRAMBOISE (CLEAR RASPBERRY BRANDY) (OPTIONAL)
1 TEASPOON VANILLA EXTRACT

1   Put the butter in a 6-ounce microwave-safe custard cup. Cover with waxed

paper and microwave on HIGH (100 percent) power for 15 to 45 seconds, until slightly softened.

2   Put the chocolate in a food processor fitted with the metal chopping blade. Process for 20 to 30 seconds, until finely ground.

3   Combine the cream and salt in a 2-cup microwave-safe glass measuring cup. Cover with waxed paper and microwave on HIGH (100 percent) power for 1½ to 3 minutes, until the mixture comes to a rapid boil.

4   With the food processor running, quickly pour the hot cream mixture through the feed tube. Process for 15 to 30 seconds, until the chocolate is almost completely melted and the mixture is smooth. Scrape down the sides of the work bowl.

5   Put the raspberry preserves in a 6-ounce microwave-safe custard cup. Microwave, uncovered, on MEDIUM (50 percent) power for 15 to 45 seconds, until hot. Add the hot preserves, butter, raspberry brandy, and vanilla extract to the chocolate mixture. Process for 10 to 20 seconds, until the mixture is smooth and creamy. Scrape the frosting into a 1-quart bowl. Cover the surface with plastic wrap and refrigerate for 10 to 20 minutes, until thick enough to spread. If the frosting becomes too stiff, microwave, uncovered, on MEDIUM-LOW (30 percent) power for 20-second intervals, until softened.

Vanilla Buttercream Frosting

makes about 1½ cups

preparation time: ABOUT 10 MINUTES

microwave time: 30 TO 60 SECONDS

*S*mooth, creamy buttercream frostings are the staple of cake bakers and the passion of cake lovers. In addition to their incomparable flavor, they are relatively stable and hold up well when the cake has to sit out for an hour or so.

This recipe makes enough buttercream for a dozen or so cupcakes. It is also an ample amount to frost a single-layer 8-inch cake. The lemon, orange, and coffee variations make it perfect for nearly any flavor cake.

10 TABLESPOONS UNSALTED	1½ CUPS SIFTED CONFECTIONER'S
BUTTER	SUGAR
PINCH OF SALT	1 TABLESPOON VANILLA EXTRACT

1   Put the butter in a 2½-quart microwave-safe bowl. Cover with waxed paper and microwave on HIGH (100 percent) power for 30 to 60 seconds, until the butter is slightly softened. Do not let the butter melt or become oily.

2   Using a hand-held electric mixer or standing mixer with a paddle attachment set at high speed, beat the butter for 30 seconds, until creamy. Add the salt and gradually beat in the sugar. Continue beating for 5 to 7 minutes, until the buttercream is very light in texture and almost white. Add the vanilla extract and beat until smooth.

variations

Lemon Buttercream Frosting

Before adding the sugar in step 2, beat in 1 teaspoon of finely grated lemon zest. Use 2 teaspoons of vanilla extract. If desired, beat in lemon juice to taste.

Orange Buttercream Frosting

Before adding the sugar in step 2, beat in ½ teaspoon of finely grated orange zest. Use 2 teaspoons of vanilla extract. If desired, beat in 1 tablespoon of Grand Marnier.

Coffee Rum Buttercream Frosting

Put the vanilla extract in a 6-ounce microwave-safe custard cup. Add 1½ teaspoons of instant coffee granules and microwave, uncovered, on HIGH (100 percent) power for 10 to 30 seconds, until warm. Stir until the coffee is dissolved. Set aside to cool. At the end of step 2, add this vanilla-coffee mixture and beat until smooth. Beat in 2 tablespoons of dark rum.

kitchen note:

Although buttercream needs a little salt to lift its flavor, do not use salted butter. It is too salty and very often is not as fresh as it could be. As in nearly all our recipes, we suggest using a hand-held electric mixer, although in this case a standing mixer with a paddle attachment works even better. The buttercream will still require 5 to 7 minutes of beating for a light, creamy texture. Buttercream can be made a day or two ahead of time and kept in the refrigerator—just bring it to room temperature and whip again before using. Or better yet, soften the chilled buttercream in the microwave set at MEDIUM-LOW (30 percent) power for 10-second intervals and then whip the buttercream.

Chocolate Buttercream Frosting

makes 1½ cups

preparation time: ABOUT 15 MINUTES

microwave time: 3 TO 5 MINUTES

*A*dding *chocolate to a buttercream frosting almost seems like overkill, but it is a delicious indulgence. As with Vanilla Buttercream Frosting on page 300, we suggest using a standing mixer with a paddle attachment if you have one. With either a hand-held mixer or a standing one, you will have to beat the frosting for 5 to 8 minutes to achieve the characteristic light, creamy texture associated with buttercreams. This recipe makes enough for 12 to 14 cupcakes or a single-layer 8-inch cake.*

2 OUNCES UNSWEETENED CHOCOLATE, COARSELY CHOPPED	1⅓ CUPS SIFTED CONFECTIONER'S SUGAR
10 TABLESPOOONS UNSALTED BUTTER	2 TEASPOONS VANILLA EXTRACT
PINCH OF SALT	

kitchen note:

Although buttercream needs a little salt to lift its flavor, do not use salted butter. It is too salty and very often is not as fresh as it could be.

1   Put the chocolate in a 6-ounce microwave-safe custard cup. Microwave on MEDIUM (50 percent) power for 2½ to 5 minutes, until the chocolate is shiny. Stir until smooth. Let the chocolate cool for 5 to 10 minutes, until tepid.

2   Meanwhile, put the butter in a 4-quart microwave-safe bowl and cover with waxed paper. Microwave on HIGH (100 percent) power for 30 to 60 seconds, until the butter is slightly softened. Do not let the butter melt or become oily.

3   Using a hand-held electric mixer or a standing mixer with a paddle attachment set at high speed, beat the butter for 30 seconds, until creamy. Reduce the speed to low and add the salt. Gradually beat in the sugar.

4   Increase the speed to high and continue beating for 5 to 8 minutes, frequently scraping down the sides of the bowl, until the buttercream is very light in texture and almost white in color. Beat in the cooled, melted chocolate and vanilla extract. Beat until smooth.

Chocolate Chantilly

makes about 1½ cups

preparation time: ABOUT 10 MINUTES PLUS 30 TO 40 MINUTES CHILLING

microwave time: 1 MINUTE 30 SECONDS TO 3 MINUTES

*W*e developed this recipe to use with Walnut Brownie Cake on page 104. You will find plenty of other uses for it as well. It's extremely easy to make and even easier to eat.

3 OUNCES SEMISWEET CHOCOLATE	1 TEASPOON GRANULATED SUGAR
¾ CUP HEAVY CREAM (USED IN TWO MEASUREMENTS)	1 TEASPOON DARK RUM
	½ TEASPOON VANILLA EXTRACT

1 Combine the chocolate, ¼ cup of the cream, and the sugar in a 2½-quart microwave-safe glass bowl. Cover with waxed paper and microwave on MEDIUM-HIGH (70 percent) power for 1½ to 3 minutes, until steaming hot. Do not boil.

2 Let the mixture stand 30 seconds to melt the chocolate. Whisk until smooth. Stir in the rum and vanilla extract. Cover the surface with plastic wrap and refrigerate for 30 to 40 minutes, until the mixture is cold and thick. Do not let the mixture become stiff.

3 Gently stir ½ cup cream into the chilled mixture. Using a hand-held electric mixer set at medium speed, beat for 1 to 2 minutes, until stiff peaks start to form. Do not overbeat or the chantilly will become grainy. Use the chocolate chantilly immediately.

Quick Chocolate Frosting

makes about 1½ cups

preparation time: ABOUT 10 MINUTES

microwave time: 3 MINUTES 15 SECONDS TO 5 MINUTES 45 SECONDS

W*e developed this rich, luscious chocolate frosting for the Walnut Brownie Cake (page 104).*

3 TABLESPOONS UNSALTED BUTTER
8 OUNCES SEMISWEET CHOCOLATE
½ CUP EVAPORATED MILK

3 TABLESPOONS LIGHT CORN SYRUP
2 TEASPOONS VANILLA EXTRACT

1   Put the butter in a 6-ounce microwave-safe custard cup. Cover with waxed paper and microwave on HIGH (100 percent) power for 15 to 45 seconds, until the butter is slightly softened. Do not let the butter melt. Set aside.

2   Put the chocolate in a 1-quart microwave-safe glass bowl. Microwave uncovered on MEDIUM (50 percent) power for 3 to 5 minutes, stirring every 60 seconds, until melted.

3   Combine the milk, corn syrup, and vanilla extract in an electric blender. Add the butter and melted chocolate. Cover and blend at low speed for 20 to 45 seconds, until the frosting is thick and creamy. Use immediately.

Vanilla Pastry Cream

makes about 2¼ cups

preparation time: ABOUT 10 MINUTES PLUS CHILLING

microwave time: 6½ TO 10½ MINUTES

This is a classic vanilla pastry cream, the sort found in tarts nestled under colorful and enticing rows of precision-sliced fruit. We use it for our tarts in Chapter 6, and you will find lots of other uses for it. If you make it ahead of time and refrigerate it, whisk it vigorously before using.

¼ CUP CORNSTARCH (LIGHTLY SPOONED INTO A MEASURING CUP AND LEVELED WITH THE EDGE OF A KNIFE)

2 CUPS MILK (USED IN TWO MEASUREMENTS)

2 LARGE EGG YOLKS

½ CUP GRANULATED SUGAR

PINCH OF SALT

1 TABLESPOON UNSALTED BUTTER, CUT INTO ½-INCH CUBES

2 TEASPOONS VANILLA EXTRACT

1　Put the cornstarch in a 1-quart microwave-safe measuring cup. Gradually stir in ¼ cup of milk and whisk until smooth. Whisk in the egg yolks, sugar, and salt until blended. Stir in the remaining 1¾ cups of milk.

2　Cover the cup with plastic wrap, turning back a fold over the pouring spout. Microwave on HIGH (100 percent) power for 4 minutes. Whisk until smooth.

3　Cover the cup again, turning back a fold over the pouring spout, and microwave on HIGH (100 percent) power for 2 to 5 minutes, whisking every 60 seconds, until the mixture starts to thicken and bubble around the edges. Whisk until smooth.

4　Cover the cup again, turning back a fold over the pouring spout, and microwave on HIGH (100 percent) power for 30 seconds to 1½ minutes, until the pastry cream comes to a full boil. Note that the pastry cream will be very thick at first; after it boils its consistency will thin a little.

5　Add the butter and whisk until smooth.

6　Strain the pastry cream through a fine-meshed sieve into a noncorrosive metal 2½-quart bowl. Push the pastry cream through the sieve with a rubber spatula.

7　Set the bowl over a larger bowl containing ice and ice water for 5 to 10 minutes, stirring frequently, until the pastry cream is cold and starts to thicken. Remove the bowl of pastry cream from the larger bowl holding the ice water. Whisk in the vanilla extract.

8   Use the party cream immediately or transfer it to a smaller bowl, cover, and refrigerate. Pastry cream can be stored in the refrigerator for up to two days. Before using the chilled pastry cream, whisk it vigorously until creamy.

variations

Chocolate Pastry Cream

At the end of step 4, add 4 ounces of finely chopped semisweet chocolate. Let the mixture stand for 30 seconds and then whisk until smooth.

Coffee Rum Pastry Cream

At the end of step 4, add 2 teaspoons of instant coffee granules and whisk until dissolved. In step 5, whisk in 1 tablespoon of dark rum with the vanilla extract.

Lime Pastry Cream

makes about 2⅓ cups

preparation time: ABOUT 10 MINUTES PLUS CHILLING

microwave time: 6½ TO 10½ MINUTES

Similar in composition to Vanilla Pastry Cream, this has a subtle tang that makes it just right for our Blueberry Tart on page 168. If you make it ahead of time and refrigerate it, whip it vigorously before using.

¼ CUP CORNSTARCH (LIGHTLY SPOONED INTO A MEASURING CUP AND LEVELED WITH THE EDGE OF A KNIFE)

2 CUPS MILK (USED IN TWO MEASUREMENTS)

2 LARGE EGG YOLKS

½ CUP GRANULATED SUGAR

1¼ TEASPOONS FINELY GRATED LIME ZEST (USED IN TWO MEASUREMENTS)

⅛ TEASPOON SALT

1 TABLESPOON UNSALTED BUTTER, CUT INTO ½-INCH CUBES

2 TABLESPOONS FRESH LIME JUICE

1 TEASPOON VANILLA EXTRACT

1 Put the cornstarch in a 1-quart microwave-safe measuring cup. Gradually stir in ¼ cup of milk and whisk until smooth. Whisk in the egg yolks, sugar, 1 teaspoon of zest, and salt until blended. Stir in the remaining 1¾ cups of milk.

2 Cover the cup with plastic wrap, turning back a fold over the pouring spout. Microwave on HIGH (100 percent) power for 4 minutes. Whisk until smooth.

3 Cover the cup again, turning back a fold over the pouring spout, and microwave on HIGH (100 percent) power for 2 to 5 minutes, whisking every 60 seconds, until the mixture starts to thicken and bubble around the edges. Whisk until smooth.

4 Cover the cup again, turning back a fold over the pouring spout, and microwave on HIGH (100 percent) power for 30 seconds to 1½ minutes, until the pastry cream comes to a full boil. Note that the pastry cream will be very thick at first; after it boils its consistency will thin a little.

5 Add the butter and whisk until smooth. Stir in the lime juice.

6 Strain the pastry cream through a fine-meshed sieve into a noncorrosive metal 2½-quart bowl. Push the pastry cream through the sieve with a rubber spatula.

7   Set the bowl over a larger bowl containing ice and ice water for 5 to 10 minutes, stirring frequently, until the pastry cream is cold and starts to thicken. Remove the bowl of pastry cream from the larger bowl holding the ice water. Whisk in the vanilla extract and the remaining lime zest.

8   Use the pastry cream immediately or transfer it to a smaller bowl, cover, and refrigerate. Pastry cream can be stored in the refrigerator for up to two days. Before using the chilled pastry cream, whisk it vigorously until creamy.

variations

Lemon Pastry Cream

Substitute lemon zest and lemon juice for the lime zest and juice.

Orange Pastry Cream

Substitute ½ teaspoon of finely grated orange zest for the lime zest in step 1. Do not add more orange zest in step 5. Instead, whisk in 1 tablespoon of orange-flavored liqueur such as Grand Marnier, Cointreau, or Triple Sec with the vanilla extract.

Caramelized Almonds

makes about 1⅓ cups

preparation time: ABOUT 5 MINUTES PLUS 10 MINUTES COOLING

microwave time: 8 TO 10 MINUTES

These sugary almonds are great for decorating cakes and make a delightfully crunchy topping for ice cream sundaes. When serving fondue, use them to garnish chocolate-drenched pound cake and fruit.

1 CUP NATURAL OR BLANCHED SLICED ALMONDS

1 TABLESPOON EGG WHITE, BEATEN UNTIL FROTHY

2 TABLESPOONS SIFTED GRANULATED SUGAR

1   Using your hands, mix the almonds with the egg whites in a 10-inch microwave-safe glass pie plate until the mixture is moist. Add the sugar and mix until the almonds are evenly coated. Spread the almond mixture in a single layer in the pie plate.

2   Microwave, uncovered, on HIGH (100 percent) power for 2 minutes. Stir the almonds with a wooden spoon.

3   Continue to microwave, uncovered, on HIGH (100 percent) power for 6 to 8 minutes, stirring every 60 seconds, until the sugar is caramelized and the almonds are golden. Let the almonds cool in the pie plate on a flat heatproof surface for 10 minutes. The almonds will continue to toast slightly after they have been removed from the microwave. Cool completely and store at room temperature in an airtight container for up to two weeks.

Index

Metric Conversion Chart

LIQUID AND DRY MEASURE EQUIVALENCIES

Customary	Metric
¼ teaspoon	1.25 milliliters
½ teaspoon	2.5 milliliters
1 teaspoon	5 milliliters
1 tablespoon	15 milliliters
1 fluid ounce	30 milliliters
¼ cup	60 milliliters
⅓ cup	80 milliliters
½ cup	120 milliliters
1 cup	240 milliliters
1 pint (2 cups)	480 milliliters
1 quart (4 cups, 32 ounces)	960 milliliters (.96 liter)
1 gallon (4 quarts)	3.84 liters
1 ounce (by weight)	28 grams
¼ pound (4 ounces)	114 grams
1 pound (16 ounces)	454 grams
2.2 pounds	1 kilogram (1000 grams)

OVEN TEMPERATURE EQUIVALENCIES

Description	°Fahrenheit	°Celsius
Cool	200	90
Very slow	250	120
Slow	300–325	150–160
Moderately slow	325–350	160–180
Moderate	350–375	180–190
Moderately hot	375–400	190–200
Hot	400–450	200–230
Very hot	450–500	230–260

About the Authors

Adrienne Welch is the food editor of *Chocolatier* magazine. She is the author of *Sweet Seduction: Chocolate Truffles* (Harper & Row, 1984) and currently is working on a book on handmade chocolates. Ms. Welch studied with Madeleine Kamman and Albert Kumin and at École Le Nôtre in France and the Richemont School in Switzerland. She currently lives in Philadelphia.

Mary Goodbody is a senior editor of *Chocolatier* magazine and a freelance food writer and editor. She is the coauthor of *Pretty Cakes* (Harper & Row, 1986) and *Glorious Chocolate: The Ultimate Chocolate Cookbook* (Simon & Schuster, 1989). She has collaborated on a number of cookbooks and written for numerous national publications. She lives in Fairfield, Connecticut.